PERSPECTIVES 2

Daniel **BARBER**

Lewis **LANSFORD**

Amanda **JEFFRIES**

NATIONAL GEOGRAPHIC LEARNING

Australia · Brazil · Canada · Mexico · Singapore · United Kingdom · United States

NATIONAL GEOGRAPHIC LEARNING

Perspectives 2
Daniel Barber, Lewis Lansford, Amanda Jeffries

Publisher: Sherrise Roehr
Executive Editor: Sarah Kenney
Publishing Consultant: Karen Spiller
Managing Editor: Claudienma Mimó
Senior Development Editor: Brenden Layte
Development Editor: Lewis Thompson
Director of Global Marketing: Ian Martin
Product Marketing Manager: Anders Bylund
Director of Content and Media Production: Michael Burggren
Production Manager: Daisy Sosa
Media Researcher: Leila Hishmeh
Manufacturing Customer Account Manager: Mary Beth Hennebury
Art Director: Brenda Carmichael
Production Management and Composition: 3CD
Cover Image: This image, created by TED Prize winner JR, was on the cover of The New York Times Magazine's "Walking New York" issue. ©JR-art.net

WCN: 01-100-393

Student Edition: Level 2
ISBN: 978-1-337-27713-6

National Geographic Learning
5191 Natorp Boulevard
Mason, OH 45040
USA

Locate your local office at **international.cengage.com/region**

Visit National Geographic Learning online at **ELTNGL.com**
Visit our corporate website at **www.cengage.com**

Photography Credits **4** (tl1) Denis Allard/REA/Redux, (tl2) © Christoph Otto, (cl) © Joey Schusler, (bl1) © Srdjan Stepanovic, (bl2) © Veronika K Ko, **5** (tl1) © Marla Aufmuth/TED, (tl2) © Wolfram Scheible/TED, (cl) © James Duncan Davidson/TED, (bl1) © James Duncan Davidson/TED, (bl2) © Mark Tioxon/TED, **6** (tl1) K H Fung/Science Source, (t12) © Prasad Ambati, (cl) © almalki abdulrahman/500px Prime, (bl1) © Murdo Macleod, (bl2) Randy Olson/National Geographic Creative, **7** (tl1) (tl2) (cl) (bl1) © TED, (bl2) © Ryan Lash/TED, **8-9** Denis Allard/REA/Redux, **10-11** Dinodia Photo/Passage/Getty Images, **12-13** (t) National Geographic Creative, **14** Boomer Jerritt/All Canada Photos/Getty Images, **15** DJTaylor/Shutterstock.com, **16-17** (t) © Marla Aufmuth/TED, **16** (cr) jsnyderdesign/DigitalVision Vectors/Getty Images, **18-19** imagebroker/Alamy Stock Photo, **20-21** © Christoph Otto, **22-23** Gary Conner/Photolibrary/Getty Images, **24-25** Bradley Garrett/eyevine/Redux, **26** Christopher Groenhout/Lonely Planet Images/Getty Images, **27** piola666/E+/Getty Images, **28-29** © Wolfram Scheible/TED, **31** Panther Media GmbH/Alamy Stock Photo, **32-33** © Joey Schusler, **34-35** Zuma Press, Inc./Alamy Stock Photo, **36-37** © Thomas Mukoya/Reuters, **38** Foto Arena LTDA/Alamy Stock Photo, **39** Ian Walton/Getty Images Sport/Getty Images, **40-41** © James Duncan Davidson/TED, **43** asiseeit/E+/Getty Images, **44-45** © Srdjan Stepanovic, **46-47** Wolfgang Rattay/Reuters, **48** Tom Cockrem/Lonely Planet Images/Getty Images, **50** UniversalImagesGroup/Getty Images, **51** Charoenkrung.Studio99/Shutterstock.com, **52-53** © James Duncan Davidson/TED, **54-55** Design pics Inc/National Geographic Creative, **56-57** © Veronika K Ko, **58-59** Bloomberg/Getty Images, **61** Vasin Lee/Shutterstock.com, **62** Past Pix/SSPL/Getty Images, **63** Buyenlarge/Archive Photos/Getty Images, **64-65** © Mark Tioxon/TED, **66-67** deimagine/E+/Getty Images, **68-69** K H Fung/Science Source, **70-71** Aaron Huey/National Geographic Creative, **73** Aurora Photos/Alamy Stock Photo, **74** Shaun Curry/AFP/Getty Images, **75** Huw Jones/Lonely Planet Images/Getty Images, **76-77** © TED, **78** Ammit/Alamy Stock Photo, **79** Pete Maclaine/Alamy Stock Photo, **80-81** © Prasad Ambati, **82-83** © Vasie Papadopoulos, **85** Toshiyuki Shirai/EyeEm/Getty Images, **86** © Mapping specialists Ltd, **87** Tobias Gerber/laif/Redux, **88-89** © TED, **90-91** RosalreneBetancourt 11/Alamy Stock Photo, **92-93** © Almalki abdulrahman/500px Prime, **94-95** NASA, **97** © Crossing Borders Education, **98** martin-dm/E+/Getty Images, **100-101** © TED, **102-103** Richard Newstead/Moment/Getty Images, **104-105** © Murdo Macleod, **106-107** © Johannes Stötter, **108** © Artez, **110** © Jason Larkin/Panos, **111** John Blanding/The Boston Globe/Getty Images, **112-113** © TED, **114-115** Lucas Vallecillos/Alamy Stock Photo, **116-117** Randy Olson/National Geographic Creative, **118** (bl) John Rensten/Stone/Getty Images, (br) Jim Richardson/National Geographic Creative, **119** (tr) Bettmann/Getty Images, (bl) Design Pics Inc/National Geographic Creative, (br) Alison Wright/National Geographic Creative, **121** Steve Vidler/Alamy Stock Photo, **122** Terry Williams/The Image Bank/Getty Images, **123** STR/AFP/Getty Images, **124-125** © Ryan Lash/TED, **126** Ableimages/David Harrigan/Getty Images, **151** (br)(bc) cTermit/Shutterstock.com, (bl) AFP/Getty Images, **152** (tr1) iStock.com/RapidEye, (tr2) Pavel_D/Shutterstock.com.

Text Credits **26** Text about "freeganism in Sydney" by Becky Khalil., **94** Text about "Getting your message out" there by Chris Hadfield.

Printed at CLDPC, USA, 06-24

ACKNOWLEDGMENTS

Paulo Rogerio RoPaulo Rogerio Rodrigues
Escola Móbile, São Paulo, Brazil

Claudia Colla de Amorim
Escola Móbile, São Paulo, Brazil

Antonio Oliveira
Escola Móbile, São Paulo, Brazil

Rory Ruddock
Atlantic International Language Center, Hanoi, Vietnam

Carmen Virginia Pérez Cervantes
La Salle, Mexico City, Mexico

Rossana Patricia Zuleta
CIPRODE, Guatemala City, Guatemala

Gloria Stella Quintero Riveros
Universidad Católica de Colombia, Bogotá, Colombia

Mónica Rodriguez Salvo
MAR English Services, Buenos Aires, Argentina

Itana de Almeida Lins
Grupo Educacional Anchieta, Salvador, Brazil

Alma Loya
Colegio de Chihuahua, Chihuahua, Mexico

María Trapero Dávila
Colegio Teresiano, Ciudad Obregon, Mexico

Silvia Kosaruk
Modern School, Lanús, Argentina

Florencia Adami
Dámaso Centeno, Caba, Argentina

Natan Galed Gomez Cartagena
Global English Teaching, Rionegro, Colombia

James Ubriaco
Colégio Santo Agostinho, Belo Horizonte, Brazil

Ryan Manley
The Chinese University of Hong Kong, Shenzhen, China

Silvia Teles
Colégio Cândido Portinari, Salvador, Brazil

María Camila Azuero Gutiérrez
Fundación Centro Electrónico de Idiomas, Bogotá, Colombia

Martha Ramirez
Colegio San Mateo Apostol, Bogotá, Colombia

Beata Polit
XXIII LO Warszawa, Poland

Beata Tomaszewska
V LO Toruń, Poland

Michał Szkudlarek
I LO Brzeg, Poland

Anna Buchowska
I LO Białystok, Poland

Natalia Maćkowiak
one2one, Kosakowo, Poland

Agnieszka Dończyk
one2one, Kosakowo, Poland

The author and publishers would like to thank the following for their help: Artez; Sophie-chan; Emma Gore-Lloyd; Becky Khalil; Nick Robinson.

Perspectives teaches learners to think critically and to develop the language skills they need to find their own voice in English. The carefully guided language lessons, real-world stories, and TED Talks motivate learners to think creatively and communicate effectively.

In *Perspectives*, learners develop:

• AN OPEN MIND

Every unit explores one idea from different perspectives, giving learners opportunities for practicing language as they look at the world in new ways.

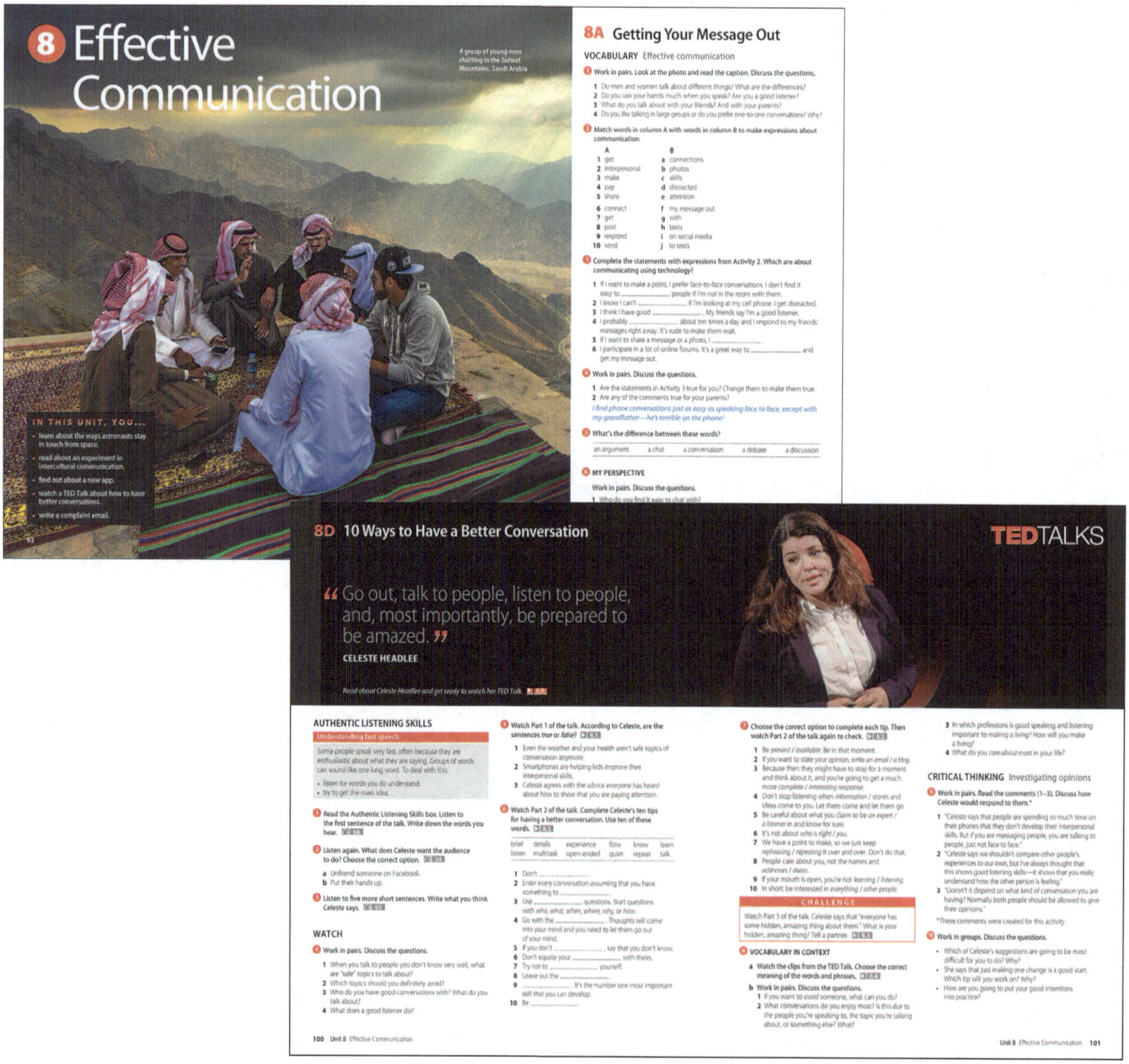

• A CRITICAL EYE

Students learn the critical thinking skills and strategies they need to evaluate new information and develop their own opinions and ideas to share.

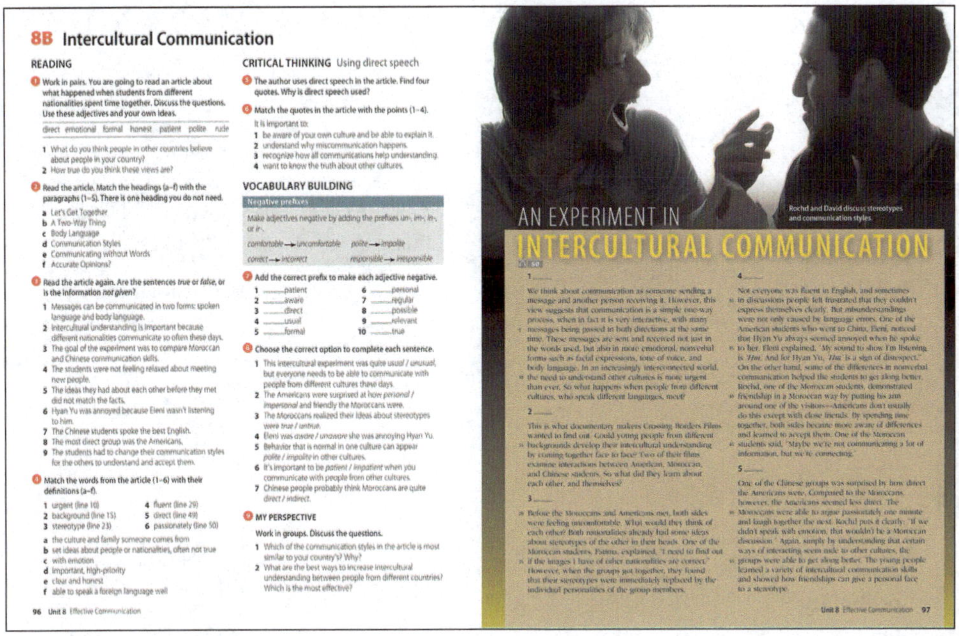

• A CLEAR VOICE

Students respond to the unit theme and express their own ideas confidently in English.

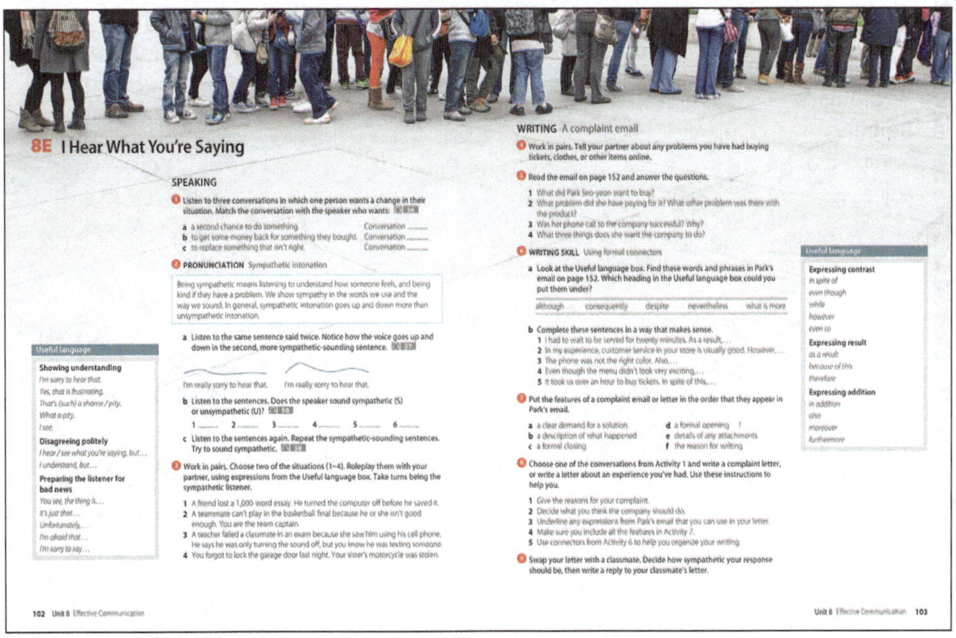

CONTENTS

GRAMMAR	TEDTALKS		SPEAKING	WRITING
Talking about the present	 This app knows how you feel—from the look on your face.	**RANA EL KALIOUBY** Rana el Kaliouby's idea worth spreading is that by teaching computers how to understand emotions on the faces of users, we can make more personal connections with the devices we use. **Authentic Listening Skills** Content words	Asking follow-up questions	A review **Writing Skill** Emphasis
Narrative forms **Pronunciation** *Used to*	 Happy maps	**DANIELE QUERCIA** Daniele Quercia's idea worth spreading is that the fastest route may be efficient, but there are times when taking a different route can be more interesting and memorable. **Authentic Listening Skills** Understanding accents	Asking for and giving directions	A story **Writing Skill** *just*
Present perfect and present perfect continuous **Pronunciation** *For*	 How I swam the North Pole	**LEWIS PUGH** Lewis Pugh's idea worth spreading is that sometimes we have to do extraordinary things to make people pay attention to important issues. **Authentic Listening Skills** Signposts	Agreeing and disagreeing	An opinion essay **Writing Skill** Giving your opinion
Making predictions **Pronunciation** Sentence stress with the future continuous and future perfect	 Why I'm a weekday vegetarian	**GRAHAM HILL** Graham Hill's idea worth spreading is that cutting meat from our diet—even just part of the time—can have a powerful impact on the planet. **Authentic Listening Skills** Pausing **Critical Thinking** Persuading	Talking about hopes and goals	A social media update **Writing Skill** Interesting language
Present and past modals	 Why the best hire might not have the perfect résumé	**REGINA HARTLEY** Regina Hartley's idea worth spreading is that our résumés tell employers about our experiences, determination, and ability to deal with life's challenges. **Authentic Listening Skills** Understanding contrasts	Job interviews **Pronunciation** *quite*	A cover letter **Writing Skill** Hedging

CONTENTS

GRAMMAR	TEDTALKS		SPEAKING	WRITING
Second conditional **Pronunciation** *I wish* and *If only*	 Deep sea diving… in a wheelchair	**SUE AUSTIN** Sue Austin's idea worth spreading is that a wheelchair doesn't have to mean "disability," it can be an exhilarating new way to see and experience the world. **Authentic Listening Skills** Following the argument	Describing photos	An informal email describing people **Writing Skill** Informal language
have / get something done **Pronunciation** Sentence stress	 Grow your own clothes	**SUZANNE LEE** Suzanne Lee's idea worth spreading is that we can use bacteria to produce materials that we can turn into clothes, as sustainable and biodegradable alternatives to leather, cotton, and plastics. **Authentic Listening Skills** Reformulating	Shopping for clothes	An announcement **Writing Skill** Relevant information
Reported speech: verb patterns with reporting verbs **Pronunciation** Contrastive stress	 10 ways to have a better conversation	**CELESTE HEADLEE** Celeste Headlee's idea worth spreading is that when we talk and listen with genuine interest in the other person, we will learn amazing things. **Authentic Listening Skills** Understanding fast speech **Critical Thinking** Investigating opinions	Responding sympathetically **Pronunciation** Sympathetic intonation	A complaint email **Writing Skill** Using formal connectors
Defining and non-defining relative clauses **Pronunciation** Relative clauses	 The world's most boring television …and why it's hilariously addictive	**THOMAS HELLUM** Thomas Hellum's idea worth spreading is that Slow TV provides real-time, surprisingly popular entertainment which viewers can relate to. **Authentic Listening Skills** Collaborative listening **Critical Thinking** Supporting your argument	Asking for and making recommendations	An email describing a place and its culture **Writing Skill** Paragraphing
Modals: past speculation, deduction, and regret **Pronunciation** Weak forms: *have*	 Inside the mind of a master procrastinator	**TIM URBAN** Tim Urban's idea worth spreading is that procrastination can keep us from chasing our dreams, and we're all affected by it. **Authentic Listening Skills** Guessing the meaning of new words	Explaining causes and reasons	A pro and con essay **Writing Skill** Using discourse markers

1 In Touch with Your Feelings

Hundreds of anonymous black and white photos make up a giant collage on the floor of the Pantheon in Paris, created by the French artist, JR.

IN THIS UNIT, YOU...

- talk about emotions.
- read about smiles.
- learn about the benefits of being outdoors.
- watch a TED Talk about an app that can "read" your facial expressions.
- write a review.

1A Show Your Emotions

VOCABULARY Describing emotions

1 Look at the photo and read the caption. What message do you think the artist is trying to communicate in this project?

2 **MY PERSPECTIVE**

Complete the sentence so it's true for you.

Happiness is *diving under the water on a sunny day*.

3 Match the sentences (1–9) with the follow-up comments (a–i).

1 I sometimes get **scared** when I'm on my own.
2 You must be **delighted**—that's great news!
3 I'm feeling more **relaxed** now that it's Saturday.
4 I got a little **confused** at the beginning of the movie.
5 My brother isn't normally this **nervous**.
6 Traveling to school on your own can be very **lonely**.
7 My parents started to dance. I was so **embarrassed**!
8 I'm feeling very **stressed** right now.
9 Please don't be **angry** with me.

a But it was great to see them having fun.
b It's been a very busy week, so it's nice to have some time off.
c I have so much work to do.
d I was only trying to help.
e I don't even like being at home without anyone else, really.
f He's doing a presentation in class this afternoon.
g I understood most of it, though.
h Sometimes I like having quiet time before a busy day, though.
i When did they tell you you're on the team?

4 Complete the questions with an adjective in bold from Activity 3.

1 Are you __________ of anything, like spiders, for example?
2 Have you ever been really __________ with your test results?
3 Do you get __________ if you cry in public?
4 Is it possible to feel __________ when you are with lots of people?
5 Do you get __________ before going to the dentist or speaking in class?
6 When you're feeling __________, what do you do to relax?
7 Are you __________ about the meaning of any new words today?
8 If someone is late, do you feel __________?
9 Does reading make you feel __________?

5 **PRONUNCIATION** *-ed* adjectives

1 Listen and repeat. How many syllables does each word have? 1
2 Listen again. Do the adjectives end in /t/, /d/, or /ɪd/? 1

6 Work in pairs. Ask and answer the questions in Activity 4.

LISTENING

7 **Work in pairs. Look at the photo and answer the questions.**

1 What do you know about tigers?
2 Can photographers take photos like this safely? How?
3 How would you feel if you came face to face with a tiger in the wild?

8 **Listen to descriptions of three National Geographic explorers' work. What emotions are the speakers describing? Why?** 2

anger	excitement	fear
nervousness	unhappiness	worry

1 Matthew Luskin ________ , ________
2 William Allard ________ , ________ , ________
3 Chris Bashinelli ________

9 **Listen again. Which explorer (Matthew, William, or Chris):** 2

1 described an event with a happy ending for someone who wasn't the speaker?
2 did something he had never done before?
3 wasn't talking about his emotions?
4 was trying to solve a problem in his work?
5 was probably very tired?
6 was surprised at how he felt?

GRAMMAR Subject / object questions

10 **Work in pairs. Can you remember the answers to these questions? Listen to William's story again and check your answers.** 3

1 What does William Allard do?
2 Who killed Eduardo's sheep?
3 Who collected money for Eduardo's family?
4 How much did they collect?

Tigers live in Bangladesh, Bhutan, India, Indonesia, Malaysia, Nepal, Russia, and Thailand.

Subject / object questions

a *Who collected money for Eduardo's family?* National Geographic *readers collected money for him.*

b *How much did they collect? They collected* over $7,000.

Check page 128 for more information and practice.

11 Read the questions in the Grammar box. Then choose the correct option to complete the sentences.

1. The question word in question *a / b* asks about the subject of the answer (subject question).
2. The question word in question *a / b* asks about the object of the answer (object question).
3. To make *a subject / an object* question in the simple present and simple past we need an auxiliary verb, e.g., *do, does, did*.
4. *Subject / Object* questions in the simple present and simple past do not need the auxiliary verb *do* or *did*.

12 Use the prompts to write questions about Chris Bashinelli and Matthew Luskin's stories.

1. whose story / happen / in Mongolia?
2. what / the men / invite / Chris / to do?
3. what / Chris / say / about the experience?
4. what / Matthew / studying?
5. how many people / tigers / kill / before the expedition?
6. how many people / hide / in the tree?

13 Work in pairs. Discuss the answers to the questions in Activity 12.

14 Complete the questions about emotions.

1. How often ______________________________?
   I laugh every time I'm with my friends.
2. What TV shows ______________________________?
   Singing competitions on TV make me angry.
3. Who ______________________________?
   My little sister cries the most in my family, definitely!
4. Which horror movies you've seen ______________________________?
   Don't Breathe and *Krampus* were both scary, but *Don't Breathe* scared me the most!
5. When you feel confused about homework, what ______________________________?
   I call a friend!
6. Who ______________________________ you recently?
   My mom embarrassed me an hour ago!

15 Work in pairs. Ask and answer the questions in Activity 14.

16 Write five more questions about emotions to ask your classmates.

What makes you most excited about the future?

17 Work in groups. Ask and answer your questions.

1B Fake It until You Feel It

Why do people smile?

4 "Say cheese!" In English-speaking countries, this is what you say to people to make them smile before you take their photo. "Service with a smile" is a common message for store assistants and receptionists. Workers in call centers are even told to smile so they sound friendly when they speak to customers on the phone! The idea is that callers will notice if the phone operators aren't smiling. But why should we want people to smile?

We've always known that smiling can express enjoyment, affection, or friendliness, but we're learning more and more about facial expressions, and realizing that their effect on our relationships is more powerful than that. We know that smiling helps us connect with other people in social situations and get out of arguments and embarrassing situations. We know from studies that smiling regularly may even increase the chances of living longer. In fact, it's such an important part of being human that we start it very young. You probably started smiling to show your happiness when you were just a few weeks old, but you've known how to smile for even longer. Unborn babies get used to moving their facial muscles by smiling, in the same way they practice kicking using their leg muscles. And we aren't the only animals that

VOCABULARY BUILDING

Suffixes

We can make nouns from adjectives by adding suffixes.

adjective	suffix	noun
embarrass~~ed~~	+ *ment*	embarrassment
friendl~~y~~	+ *ness*	friendliness
depress~~ed~~	+ *ion*	depression

1 Write nouns using *-ment*, *-ness*, or *-ion*. Use a dictionary if necessary.

1 nervous
2 sad
3 excited
4 disappointed
5 happy
6 exhausted
7 confused
8 lonely

2 Complete the sentences with a noun or an adjective from Activity 1.

1 Many people say that money can't buy __________, but I think it helps.
2 I felt very __________ at summer camp. It was my first time away from home and I didn't know anyone.
3 I had to sing on my own in the show. I felt so __________ that I couldn't sleep.
4 Emin studied hard for his tests. He didn't want to be a __________ to his parents.
5 There was a lot of __________ in the class. The teacher said the school trip was on Wednesday but the email said Thursday.

READING

3 Work in pairs. Try to make your partner smile. How easy is it? Then discuss the questions.

1 Look at the pairs of photos (a–c). Which smiles do you think are genuine (real)? Which smiles do you think are fake (not real)?
2 Why would you pretend to smile?
3 Are you good at recognizing genuine and fake smiles?

4 Make a list of things that make you smile. Compare your list with a partner.

when my team wins a game, chocolate,...

5 Read the article quickly. Choose the best subtitle.

1 How our bodies affect our emotions
2 The secret power of smiling
3 Smiling expresses many emotions

6 Read the article again. Are these sentences *true* or *false*, or is the information *not given*?

1 Some employees are taught to smile when they speak to people who can't see them.
2 You could stop a disagreement by smiling.
3 People who don't smile are more likely to get sick.
4 Other animals smile for the same reasons as humans.
5 Eating chocolate has a more powerful effect on our emotions than smiling.

smile to communicate happiness—chimpanzees do it, too, suggesting that smiling existed before we did!

Have you ever been in this situation: you are angry with a friend but you can't stay angry because they're smiling at you? This is because smiles pass from person to person, and it's hard not to smile back. We actually lose some control of our own facial muscles when we look at someone smiling at us. When this happens, we automatically copy their expression, and smiling like them may actually help us understand their emotions better.

Being happy makes us smile, of course. But smiling also makes us happy. Scientists can take pictures of the brain to see what happens when a person is happy. They see the same effect when the person smiles, whether they're really happy or not. So a smile isn't just a sign to others; it is also a message to our brain telling it to feel happy. One study showed that a smile can have the same positive effect on the brain as eating 2,000 bars of chocolate! So, even if you're feeling depressed, a fake smile can make all the difference. If you know someone who's always smiling, perhaps they're using it to control their emotions. Why not control your emotions the same way? If you sometimes feel sad, worried, or angry, try smiling. You might feel better.

7 **Summarize the article in no more than twenty words.**

Smiling…

8 **MY PERSPECTIVE**

Work in groups. Discuss the questions.

1 Do you think smiling really is a good way to feel better?
2 What do you do if you aren't feeling very happy?
3 Who do you think smiles more, younger or older people, women or men? Why?
4 Do you know anyone who smiles too much / doesn't smile enough?

CRITICAL THINKING Rhetorical questions

9 **Work in pairs. Read the Critical Thinking box and discuss the questions (1–4).**

> Rhetorical questions are used to make a point, but a reply is not expected. They are often used to:
>
> - tell readers what information they can expect to read.
> - emphasize a point.
> - make a suggestion or persuade.
> - help readers relate the text to their own experience.

1 Look at the title of the article and list all the reasons that people smile.
2 Why is it a good idea to have a question as a title?
3 There are three more questions in the article. Underline them. Match the questions with three of the functions in the Critical Thinking box.
4 Write a question to include in the article for one of the other two functions.

10 **Read about the "Pan Am smile." Then look at the photos again. Can you find the fake smiles more easily?**

The "Pan Am smile" is named after the flight attendants of this old American airline. They were famous for their friendly customer service and for always smiling at the passengers. Everyone knew that these smiles weren't genuine but they were an expression of friendliness and had a positive effect on the passengers.

We all use Pan Am smiles because there are many situations where showing unhappiness would be rude. Smiling has the important social function of keeping people happy.

But how can you tell the difference between a genuine smile and a fake smile? In the nineteenth century, French scientist Guillaume Duchenne noticed that we use two sets of facial muscles to smile: around the mouth and around the eyes. Pan Am smiles only use the mouth, so the secret is to look at the eyes.

1C A Breath of Fresh Air

GRAMMAR Talking about the present

1 Read the sentences in the Grammar box. Underline examples of the simple present, present continuous, and present perfect.

Talking about the present

a *We've always known that smiling can express enjoyment, affection, or friendliness.*
b *We're learning more and more about facial expressions.*
c *We know from studies that smiling may even increase the chances of living longer.*
d *We aren't the only animals that smile to communicate happiness—chimpanzees do it, too.*
e *You're angry with a friend but you can't stay angry because they're smiling at you.*
f *If you know someone who's always smiling,…*
g *If you sometimes feel sad, worried, or angry, try smiling.*

Check page 128 for more information and practice.

2 Complete the rules by writing *simple present*, *present perfect*, or *present continuous*. Then match each rule with an example from the Grammar box.

1 The ______________ is used:
- to talk about things that are always or generally true, e.g., scientific facts.
- to describe habits and routines (often with words like *sometimes* and *never*).
- with stative verbs, e.g., *enjoy*, *agree*, *think*.

2 The ______________ is used:
- to talk about actions happening at or around the present time, or at the time of speaking/writing.
- to talk about changing situations.
- with *always* to describe actions that happen often. They may cause an emotional response in the speaker.

3 The ______________ is used:
- to describe actions that started in the past and continue to the present.

3 Choose the correct options to complete the paragraph.

(1) *Are you feeling / Have you felt* stressed right now? Perhaps it's because you (2) *are always sitting / have always sat* in front of a computer screen these days. So what should you do? You could be the type of person who (3) *is usually reading / usually reads* a book, for instance, or (4) *plays / has played* video games for relaxation. Or perhaps you (5) *are believing / believe* that the answer to everyday stress is more time outside, surrounded by nature. (6) *Are you enjoying / Do you enjoy* getting away from cities, cars, and computers and heading into the mountains? It's true that we (7) *need / are needing* time off work to relax, though it (8) *becomes / is becoming* more and more difficult to get away. But people (9) *enjoy / have enjoyed* forests, parks, lakes, and rivers for thousands of years, so if life (10) *gets / has gotten* to be too much to cope with recently, think about taking a break out in the woods or a walk in the park, even if it's just for an hour or two.

4 Read about the effect nature can have on our brains. Complete the text with the best form of the verbs: simple present, present continuous, or present perfect.

A group of 22 students (1) __________ (take) a break from their everyday lives at the University of Utah. Normally, they (2) __________ (sit) in front of their computer screens studying psychology, but this week they (3) __________ (camp) with Professor David Streyer in the mountains of Utah. Streyer (4) __________ (spend) many years studying the effect of nature on our brains.

We (5) __________ (know) about the benefits of nature on the body for many years, but now we can see what nature (6) __________ (do) to the brain. Our stress levels (7) __________ (drop) just by looking at photos of nature. Many people (8) __________ (think) that little by little technology (9) __________ (destroy) our lives, but Streyer (10) __________ (believe) that after just two or three days away from modern life, we can start to think differently and in a healthier way.

5 **Read about healing forests in South Korea. Correct the verbs that are wrong. Not all items have an error.**

1. Nature is being very important in Korean culture for hundreds of years.
2. But most South Koreans live "digital lives" in large cities nowadays.
3. Their lives become more digital and more stressful every year.
4. Koreans work very long hours, and stress levels among workers and students go up in recent years.
5. The government has believed that the answer can be found in "healing forests."
6. These are places of natural beauty where people go to relax, to reconnect with nature, and to rest.
7. We now know that spending time outside reduces stress chemicals in the body and helps it to fight disease.
8. Currently there have been 37 healing forests in Korea, and they are becoming very popular.
9. Many of them are close to big cities like Seoul, where people can get to them easily.
10. People are often going there to walk, learn about plants, do yoga, or just relax under the trees.

6 **Use the prompts to write questions using the best tense: simple present, present continuous, or present perfect.**

1. you / go / out to the woods much recently?
2. where / you / usually / go / to spend time outdoors?
3. what / you / like / doing outdoors?
4. your parents / always / make / you do activities that you don't enjoy?
5. you / normally / feel / relaxed when you get home?
6. you / always / check / your cell phone, or can you leave it at home?
7. if / you / live / in a town or city, / you / be / happy?
8. you / plan / to go out in nature any time soon?

7 **Work in pairs. Ask and answer the questions you wrote in Activity 6.**

8 **Work in groups. Discuss the questions.**

1. Are young people spending as much time outside now as in the past? Why?
2. What are the advantages of doing outdoor activities?
3. What kinds of activities do you and your friends like doing outdoors?
4. What outdoor activities are popular with young people these days?

9 **Design an ad for an outdoor activity center in your country. Answer these questions about the ad.**

1. What type of activity center will it be—more like a healing forest or an adventure park?
2. What will get a lot of people interested? What will be good for young people's health and happiness?
3. How will you attract people to your center?
4. What photos or other images will you include?

10 **CHOOSE**

Choose one of the following activities.

1. On your own, write a radio ad for the activity center. Read it to the class.
2. In pairs, record or act out a TV ad promoting the activity center.
3. In groups, make a brochure (text and images) for your activity center.

1D This app knows how you feel—from the look on your face.

“I want to bring emotions back into our digital experiences.”

RANA EL KALIOUBY

Read about Rana el Kaliouby and get ready to watch her TED Talk. ▶ 1.0

AUTHENTIC LISTENING SKILLS

Content words

It is difficult to listen for every word a speaker says. When we listen, it is easier to understand the important content words, because these are usually stressed. Content words usually give enough information for us to understand the meaning of a sentence.

1 **Read and listen to the first sentence in the TED Talk. Notice how many of the content words are stressed.** 5

Our emotions influence every aspect of our lives, from our health and how we learn, to how we do business and make decisions, big ones and small.

2 **Look at the types of words that are usually stressed. Read this excerpt from the talk and underline the words you think will be stressed. Then listen and check.** 6

Stressed	Not stressed	
adjectives	articles	pronouns
nouns	conjunctions	auxiliary verbs
main verbs	prepositions	
adverbs		

Our emotions also influence how we connect with one another. We've evolved to live in a world like this, but instead, we're living more and more of our lives like this… So I'm on a mission to change that. I want to bring emotions back into our digital experiences.

WATCH

3 **Look at the emojis. Then discuss the questions in pairs.**

1 What emotions do these emojis express?

2 Do you ever use emojis? Which ones? Where do you use them: email, text messages, social media?
3 Is it sometimes difficult to find the right emoji to express how you are feeling? Why?
4 What other ways can you use to express your feelings online?

4 **Watch Part 1 of the talk. Are the sentences *true* or *false* according to Rana?** ▶ 1.1

1 It's difficult to connect emotionally with others in text messages, emails, etc.
2 Rana was with her husband in Cambridge.
3 The human face can show 45 emotions.
4 It's hard to teach a computer the difference between a smile and a smirk.
5 The computer studied lots of similar faces.

5 **Watch Part 2 of the talk. Which emotions does Cloe demonstrate?** ▶ 1.2

1 a little bit happy
2 angry
3 confused
4 disgusted
5 nervous
6 no emotion (“poker face”)
7 sad
8 scared
9 surprised
10 very happy

6 Watch Part 3 of the talk. Choose the correct option to complete each sentence. ▶ 1.3

1 Women in the *UK* / *US* are more expressive than men.
2 The most expressive age group is people *older* / *younger* than 50.
3 People with autism could *use their phones* / *wear special glasses* to help them understand other people's emotions.
4 Rana *can* / *can't* think of many other ways her technology could be used.

7 Work in pairs. Watch Part 3 of the talk again. What use of the technology that Rana mentions is your favorite? Why? ▶ 1.3

8 **VOCABULARY IN CONTEXT**

a Watch the clips from the TED Talk. Choose the correct meaning of the words and phrases. ▶ 1.4

b Work in pairs. Complete the sentences in your own words. Then compare your sentences with your partner.

1 I felt *homesick* once when I...
2 I get a sense of *curiosity* when...
3 The person in my family with the most *wrinkles* is...
4 The *characteristics* of a good friend are...
5 *Joy* for me is...

9 Work in groups. Think of different ways Rana's software could be used. Think about:

- advertising or social media
- entertainment (TV, movies, concerts, theater, etc.)
- health and medicine
- people with physical problems and learning difficulties
- shopping and fashion

10 Think about your ideas. Which ones could:

1 make tons of money?
2 help people with problems?
3 be a lot of fun?

CHALLENGE

Put comments a–d in order (1–4). The comment you agree with most is 1; the comment you agree with least is 4.*

a "This technology is fun, but I don't think it's necessary anymore. These days, we communicate more with webcams and video. We don't need the computer to read faces for us. We can read them ourselves."

b "We don't need to read faces when we communicate by phone. Why do we need it now?"

c "I think Rana's technology is amazing, but I worry that companies will only use it to sell more products to us."

d "I don't like the idea of my computer reading my emotions. It's a scary idea!"

*These comments were created for this activity.

Work in pairs. Compare your ideas. How do you think Rana would respond to the comments?

1E The Feel-Good Factor

SPEAKING

1 Work in pairs. Read about India's longest-running movie. Discuss the questions.

The Bollywood movie *Dilwale Dulhania Le Jayenge* is one of India's most successful movies. It was still showing at one cinema in Mumbai more than twenty years after it came out. It is a classic feel-good love story with a happy ending.

1 What does "the feel-good factor" mean?
2 Are there feel-good movies that people in your country watch more than once?
3 What are your favorite feel-good movies?

2 Check that you know the meaning of the words in bold in these sentences.

1 I don't think anyone could survive in space for that long, but the **special effects** were amazing!
2 The first movie was so scary, there's no way I'm going to watch the **sequel**.
3 It has a great **soundtrack** but some of the actors can't sing very well.
4 It's an emotional story about a group of soldiers during the Second World War. The **cast** is amazing—Tom Hanks and Matt Damon are in it.
5 The **plot** was really exciting. The **ending** was a complete surprise!
6 One **scene** made me laugh so hard that I cried!

3 Match the types of movie (a–f) with the sentences (1–6) in Activity 2.

a a comedy
b a drama
c a horror movie
d a musical
e a sci-fi movie
f a thriller

4 Listen to two friends talking about a movie. Choose the correct options. 7

Name of movie: *The Way We Were / The Way Way Back*
Starring: *Steve Carell / Collette*
Release date: *2003 / 2013*
Type of movie: *animation / comedy*
Set in: *a hotel / a water park*
Plot: An unhappy *teenager / father* goes on vacation with his family and makes new friends.
Recommended? *Yes / No*

5 Listen again. Which follow-up questions in the Useful language box do you hear? 7

Useful language

Asking follow-up questions

Who's in it?
What else has he / she been in?
What's the acting like?
When did it come out?
So what's it about?
What sort of movie is it?
Who directed it?
Where is it set?
Would you recommend it?

Using Emphasis

The special effects were really disappointing.
I couldn't put it down!
The sequel was even better!

Outdoor movie theater in the castle courtyard, Esslingen am Neckar, Germany

6 Match the questions you heard in Activity 5 with these answers about a different movie. Do you know the movie?

1 It's a sci-fi movie. It's the first in a series of four.
2 It was released in 2012.
3 She played one of the main characters in *X-Men: Apocalypse*.
4 It tells the story of a young woman who fights for her life in a competition.
5 In a country of the future called Panem.
6 It stars Jennifer Lawrence.

7 Work in pairs.

Student A: Tell Student B about a movie you've seen.
Student B: Ask follow-up questions to find out more.

A *I watched a great movie last night… Have you seen it?*

WRITING A review

8 Are the expressions in the Useful language box used to talk about books, movies, or both?

9 Read the review on page 149. How many stars does the writer give the novel?

☆ ☆ ☆ ☆ ☆

10 Read the review again. List the book's good points and the reviewer's criticisms.

11 **WRITING SKILL** Emphasis

a Which sentence emphasizes more the way the person feels about the plot?

1 I really loved the plot. **2** What I really loved was the plot.

b Find three more sentences in the review that add emphasis.

c Complete these sentences so that they are true for the movie you talked about in Activity 7.

1 One thing that I loved about the movie was…
2 What I found disappointing was…
3 What made me really think was…

12 Choose a movie or a book you know. Write a review that includes:

- introductory sentences that give basic information about the book or movie.
- a short description of the plot.
- the good and bad things about it.
- your opinion and emotional response to it.
- a sentence that tells the reader to read or watch it (or not).

13 Read other students' reviews. Which books or movies would you like to read / see?

Useful language

Talking about movies and books

It stars…
It's set in…
It tells the story of… / It's about…
It was directed by…
It was released in…
It came out in…
It was published in…
The main character is…
The soundtrack was amazing.
The special effects were a little disappointing.
The sequel is even better / not as good.
It's a moving / inspiring / great / exciting / funny story.
I'd definitely recommend it.
I couldn't put it down.
It made me feel…
Unfortunately, I thought it was…

2 Enjoy the Ride

Students in Colombia cross the Rio Negro canyon using cables to get to school.

IN THIS UNIT, YOU...

- talk about getting around.
- read about an unusual hobby.
- learn about how to live and travel cheaply.
- watch a TED Talk about "happy maps."
- write a story about a trip you have made.

2A Getting from A to B

VOCABULARY Travel

1 MY PERSPECTIVE

Work in pairs. Discuss the questions.

1 What does this quote mean to you?
"Travel is the only thing you buy that makes you richer."
2 What are the benefits of travel? Do you want to be a traveler? Why?
3 Look at the photo and read the caption. Would you like to go to school like this? Why do you think the children don't have a safer way of traveling? How do you get to school?

2 Work in pairs. Discuss the questions.

1 How many ways of getting around can you think of? Make a list.
go on your skateboard, take the bus...
2 Look at your list. Which form of transportation is the:
- cheapest?
- fastest?
- most relaxing/stressful?

3 Complete the sentences with these pairs of words.

cruise + excursion	commute + ride	expedition + voyage
flight + destination	ride + route	trip + backpacking

1 When my parents __________ by car, they give me a __________ to school.
2 RY5608—that isn't our __________. It's flying to the same __________ but it's a different airline.
3 Some passengers on the __________ stayed on the ship, but we went on an __________ around the old port.
4 We had an amazing __________! I'm glad we were __________ and didn't stay in a hotel. We saw more of the outdoors that way.
5 When I went for a bike __________ yesterday, I took a different __________. I get bored going the same way all the time.
6 The __________ to the Antarctic lasted a year. After a difficult month-long sea __________, the scientists started their research.

4 Cross out the item in each list that does not collocate with the verb(s).

1 **catch/miss** my bus, my train, ~~my car~~
2 **get** home, lost, school, from A to B
3 **get on/off** the bus, the car, the plane
4 **get to know** your way around, a trip
5 **get to** work, home, school
6 **go for** a trip, a bike ride, a drive
7 **go on** a flight, a journey, a travel
8 **take** a taxi, an hour, two miles

5 Complete the sentences with a word from Activity 3 or 4. Then finish them so they are true for you.

1 My __________ to school takes...
2 The best way for visitors to __________ to know my city is by...
3 If I __________ public transportation, I prefer to travel by... because...
4 The last long trip I __________ on was to...
5 If I could take a __________ anywhere, I'd choose... as my destination.

LISTENING

6 Listen to three people describe how they go to school. Complete the table. 8

	Where they live	How they travel	Time / distance they travel	What they do on the way
1 Santiago Muñoz				
2 Chosing	*The Himalayas*			
3 Daisy Mora				

7 Listen again. Who (Santiago, Chosing, or Daisy): 8

1 travels the farthest?
2 doesn't take long to get to school?
3 stays at school for a long time?
4 gets up early to get to school on time?
5 takes public transportation to get to school?
6 travels with a parent?
7 has a dangerous trip to school? (2 people)
8 is going to have an easier way to get to school soon?

GRAMMAR Adjectives ending in *-ed* and *-ing*

8 Read the sentences in the Grammar box. Underline the adjectives. Which adjectives describe the trips? Which adjectives describe how the people feel?

Adjectives ending in *-ed* and *-ing*

a *You might think it takes you a long time to get to school, but Santiago Muñoz has one of the most exhausting school commutes in the world… He's excited about having more time to spend with friends and getting more sleep!*

b *They don't talk much, but it is never boring. It takes them six days and at the end they are exhausted.*

c *For some students living along the Rio Negro, their trip to school is absolutely terrifying… If Daisy is scared, she doesn't show it!*

Check page 130 for more information and practice.

9 Choose the correct option to complete the sentences.

Participial adjectives are adjectives that are made from verbs. They usually end in *-ing* or *-ed*.

1 Adjectives that describe how a person feels end in *-ing* / *-ed*.
2 Adjectives that describe the thing that makes you feel an emotion end in *-ing* / *-ed*.

Students on the train in Kyoto, Japan

10 Match the *-ed* adjectives (1–8) with their meanings (a–h). Then complete *-ing* adjectives.

-ed adjective	meaning	*-ing* adjective
1 terrified	*e*	*terrifying*
2 exhausted		
3 annoyed		
4 disappointed		
5 depressed		
6 shocked		
7 worried		
8 confused		

a surprised because of something bad that happened suddenly
b unhappy and a little angry about something
c unhappy because something was not as good as you hoped or because something did not happen
d thinking about bad things that might happen
e very scared
f very sad and without hope
g unable to think clearly about or understand something
h very tired

11 Choose the correct option. Then work in pairs and tell your partner about one or two experiences you have had.

1 a destination you were looking forward to seeing but were a little *disappointed / disappointing* about when you got there

I was excited about a school excursion to the History Museum, but it was really boring. Everyone was really disappointed.

2 a *terrified / terrifying* experience you've had on a car trip
3 a day when you did so much walking that you were completely *exhausted / exhausting* at the end
4 the longest and most *bored / boring* trip you've ever been on
5 a trip when you were very *worried / worrying* that you wouldn't get to the destination on time
6 an *annoyed / annoying* delay on public transportation that you really didn't need
7 a *depressed / depressing* trip somewhere when you had a horrible time
8 an expedition that you'd be very *excited / exciting* to go on

12 Work in groups. Share your stories from Activity 11. Whose experiences have been the most exciting / boring / exhausting / frightening / disappointing?

2B Urban Explorers

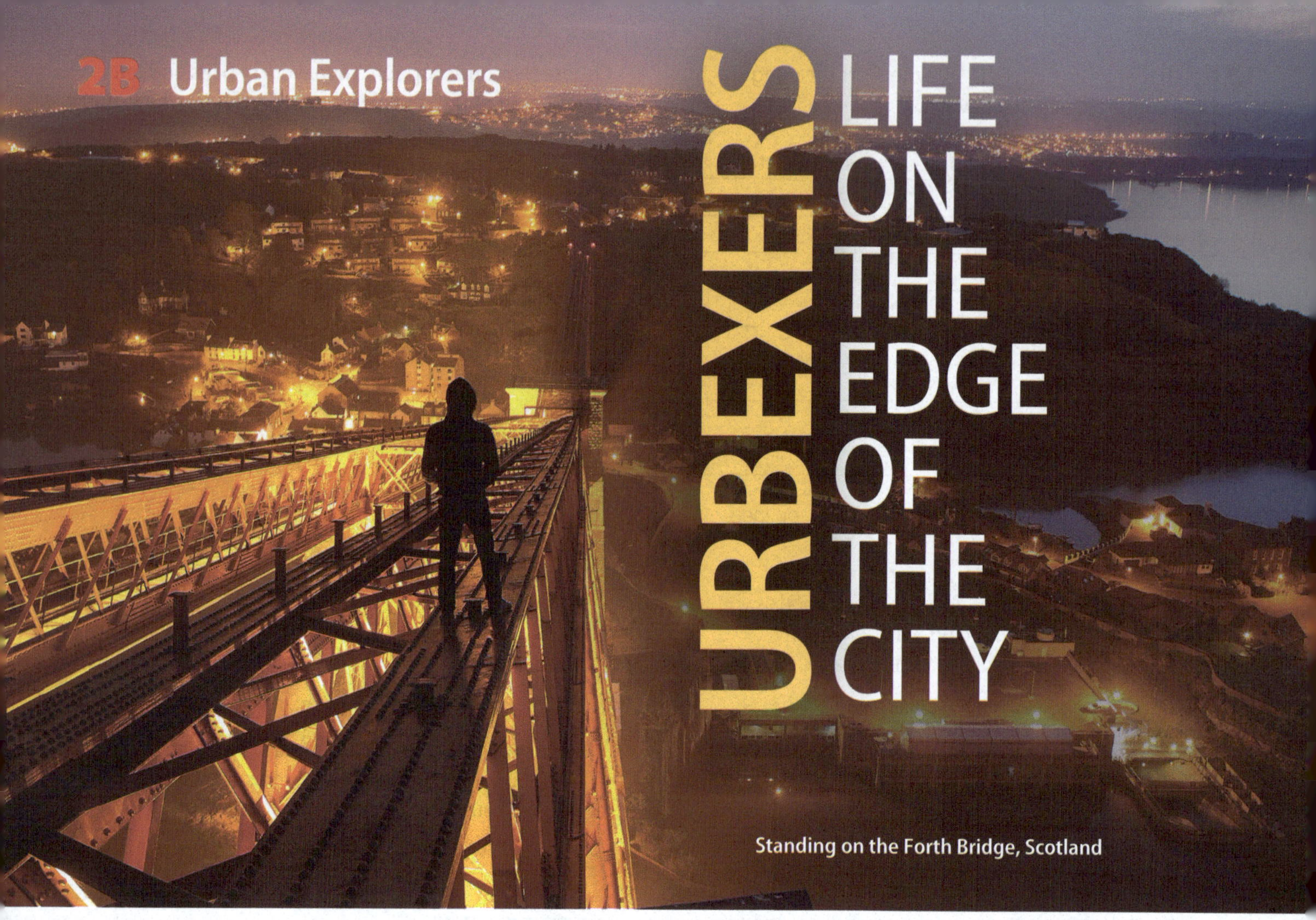

URBEXERS LIFE ON THE EDGE OF THE CITY

Standing on the Forth Bridge, Scotland

VOCABULARY BUILDING Compound nouns

1 What places do visitors to your city or a city near you usually visit?

2 Use words in columns A and B to make compound nouns. Check the spelling in a dictionary.

	A		B
1	sight	**a**	site
2	a walking	**b**	station
3	a subway	**c**	transportation
4	a shopping	**d**	seeing
5	a construction	**e**	mall
6	public	**f**	tour
7	urban	**g**	roads
8	rail	**h**	top
9	a sky	**i**	park
10	a roof	**j**	exploration
11	an amusement	**k**	scraper
12	a view	**l**	point

3 Listen and check your answers to Activity 2. Underline the stressed part of each compound noun. Is there a general rule about where the stress is? 9

4 Which of the compound nouns in Activity 2 are things visitors might do, use, or visit? Which are buildings? Which are places the public doesn't usually go?

5 Use the compound nouns in Activity 2 to make eight sentences about your town or city.

READING

6 You are going to read an article about urban explorers (urbexers). Write three questions you'd like to find out about them. Does the article answer your questions?

7 Choose the correct ending to complete the sentences.

1 The article begins by talking about options for tourists because:
a they are good examples of urban exploration.
b they are very different from what urbexers do.
c the writer wants to recommend some ways of exploring cities.

2 The places that urban explorers visit are:
a always underground.
b not used anymore.
c not usually attractive to many people.

10 How do you get to know a city you've never been to before? For most people, the typical tourist options are enough. Take a bus tour to see the sights or, if you're feeling energetic, consider a walking tour. To get a taste of city life, use public transportation.

But there are people who want more than the standard tourist options. They are *urbexers*—urban explorers. They're interested in discovering parts of the city we normally see as less beautiful, the places tourists are not supposed to see: ghost subway stations that have been closed for years, shopping malls and amusement parks at night, abandoned* factories, construction sites, tunnels, and railroads. It's not for everybody. You can't be scared of heights or small spaces and you have to be willing to take risks.

Bradley Garrett is one of them. Urbexers don't follow the same routes as everyone else: "I've been to Paris six times and I've seen more of the city underground than I have above ground," he says. "If somebody asked me for a good restaurant, I'd have no idea."

It wasn't until Bradley and his urbexer friends had climbed to the top of London's tallest skyscraper, the Shard, and had managed to visit all of the city's fourteen abandoned subway stations that the police stopped them from exploring as a group. Bradley was studying urbexers for a book he was writing when they had to stop.

Bradley's best experience as an urbexer was in Chicago with friends when they climbed the Legacy Tower, a 72-story skyscraper. "We were sitting on a rooftop looking up at this building when someone suggested we try to get up. So we walked in and just got in the elevator after some residents had opened the door. When we made it up to the roof, it was the most incredible view I've ever seen."

Why do urbexers do it? Many enjoy the excitement of putting themselves in danger. Some enjoy the feeling they get from being alone in abandoned places. "I feel I'm the only person in the world," says Zhao Yang, a 29-year-old Chinese urbexer who explores places where people used to work, like old industrial sites and abandoned hospitals. Like many urbexers, Zhao is an avid photographer who takes his smartphone to record what he sees, and, like many, he also writes a blog about his experiences, but he prefers to explore alone.

This can be dangerous, of course, but if you're interested in exploring city spaces, there are safe ways of doing it. For example, it's easy to look at a map, identify an area that is new to you, and go there. Another way is to try to get lost in your own town. Or you could just set off for a walk without planning your route. Who knows what you might find!

abandoned *left; no longer used*

3 Bradley Garrett:
- **a** knows Paris very well.
- **b** doesn't like high places.
- **c** wouldn't be a very good guide for traditional tourists.

4 Bradley and his friends:
- **a** weren't allowed to go to London's abandoned underground stations.
- **b** can't explore together anymore.
- **c** didn't climb the Shard.

5 Garrett's trip to the top of the Legacy Tower was:
a easy. **b** lonely. **c** well planned.

6 Zhao Yang:
- **a** investigates abandoned factories.
- **b** explores with friends.
- **c** doesn't want to tell anyone about his experiences.

7 The article ends by:
- **a** describing more activities that urban explorers do.
- **b** recommending other ways of exploring cities.
- **c** explaining the health benefits of urban exploration.

CRITICAL THINKING Selecting information

Writers have to think about the kind of information that will interest their readers.

8 **Read the Critical Thinking box. Which questions does the article answer about urbexers and urban exploration?**

1. Does urban exploration happen all over the world?
2. How long have people been exploring in this way?
3. How many people do it?
4. If I want to explore my local urban area, what can I do?
5. Is the word "urbexer" in the dictionary?
6. What are some of the stories that urbexers have?
7. Why is urban exploration attractive to some people?
8. What kind of places do urbexers visit?
9. What personal qualities do urbexers need?

9 **Work in groups. Discuss the questions.**

1. Did the article answer all your questions in Activity 6?
2. What other information would you like to learn?
3. How could you find out the answers to the questions that weren't answered?

10 **Do you think the author did a good job? Did he choose the information that was interesting to you?**

Sydney Opera House and the city, Australia

2C Sydney on $20

GRAMMAR Narrative forms

1 Work in pairs. Can you remember Bradley Garrett's adventure at the Legacy Tower? Retell the story using these words.

rooftop	the elevator	view

2 Check your ideas in Activity 1 with the article on page 25.

3 Choose the correct options to complete the sentences in the Grammar box.

Narrative forms

a *It wasn't until Bradley and his friends* **had climbed / were climbing** *to the top of the Shard and* **used to manage / had managed** *to visit all of the city's abandoned underground stations that the police* **stopped / were stopping** *them from exploring as a group.*

b *Bradley* **studied / was studying** *urbexers for a book he* **wrote / was writing** *when they had to stop.*

c *"We* **had sat / were sitting** *on a rooftop when someone* **suggested / used to suggest** *we try to get up the Legacy Tower. So we* **walked / were walking** *in and just* **had gotten / got** *in the elevator after some residents* **had opened / were opening** *the door."*

d *Zhao Yang explores places where people* **were working / used to work***, like old industrial sites and abandoned hospitals.*

Check page 130 for more information and practice.

4 Read the sentences in the Grammar box and complete these rules with *simple past*, *past continuous*, *past perfect*, or *used to*.

When we tell stories or talk about actions or events in the past:

1. we use the __________ to describe an incomplete action or event when another action happened. The actions are often connected with *when*, *while*, or *as*. We also use it to give background information. It is not used with stative verbs (*know*, *love*, etc.).
2. we usually use the __________ to describe completed actions in the past. If actions happen one after another, we use this tense.
3. we use the __________ to emphasize that one past action finished before another past action. The actions are often connected with *after*, *before*, and *already*.
4. we usually use __________ to talk about situations, habits, and routines that were true in the past but are not true anymore.

5 Read about freeganism. What are the advantages of living like this? Would you like to live like this? What are the disadvantages?

Freeganism is a way of living and traveling that costs almost nothing. It's simply using your skills so you don't have to pay for things. People who practice freeganism are called "freegans," and they try to buy as little as possible because they want to save money and reduce their impact on the environment. They choose to eat food that has been thrown away and find alternatives to sleeping in hotels and paying for transportation when they travel.

6 Becky Khalil was a freegan in Australia for some time. Choose the correct option to complete what she says about traveling as a freegan in Sydney.

I (1) *used to think / was thinking* that Australia was a really expensive place, and the first time I (2) *went / had gone there*, I worked to pay for my living expenses. But while I (3) *had stayed / was staying* in Australia last time, I (4) *found / used to find* another way to live. I (5) *used to use / had already used* my working visa on my first trip, so I couldn't get a job this time. To make things worse, someone (6) *was stealing / had stolen* all my money during a train ride. So I (7) *became / had become* a freegan. Before, I (8) *used to buy / was buying* too much food and threw a lot of it away, but this time I (9) *had eaten / ate* leftover food from friends and shops, like day-old bread. I (10) *didn't spend / hadn't spent* anything on accommodations, less than $100 on travel, and less than $20 on food for six weeks!

7 Complete the rest of Becky's story with the best form of the verbs.

Most of the time, friends of mine (1) __________ (let) me sleep on their couches, but before my trip I (2) __________ (contact) a company that organizes "house-sitting" jobs, so sometimes I took care of houses when the owners were on vacation. To save money on bus fares, I (3) __________ (get) rides with people I knew, and while I (4) __________ (travel) around the country, I usually decided to camp. Once I went to sleep under the stars because I (5) __________ (be) too tired to put my tent up. Finding cheap or free food was much easier than I (6) __________ (expect) it to be. Even in winter, I enjoyed it because I (7) __________ (live) with other freegans and we (8) __________ (become) friends and helped each other. At the end of each day, stores gave us anything they (9) __________ (not sell). Believe it or not, we (10) __________ (eat) extremely well!

8 **PRONUNCIATION** *Used to*

Listen to these sentences. How is *used to* pronounced? Practice reading the sentences. 11

1 Our grandparents never used to throw their food away.
2 Did people use to travel a lot when your parents were young?
3 **A** Do you enjoy traveling by plane?
B I used to, but not anymore.

9 Complete the sentences in your own words. Then work in pairs and compare your sentences.

1 Before this lesson I didn't know...
2 When I was younger, I used to...
3 I didn't use to... (but I do now).
4 The last time I... was when...
5 I didn't spend any money when...
6 I bought... while I was...

10 Prepare notes about a trip you have taken that was memorable in some way. Use these questions to help you plan what you are going to say.

- Where did you go? Did you use to go to the same destination regularly, or was this the first time?
- How did you travel?
- When did you make the trip?
- Who did you go with?
- What memorable things happened? What were you doing when they happened?
- How did you feel about the trip in general?

11 **CHOOSE** Choose one of the following activities.

1 Work in pairs. Tell your stories to each other. Ask each other questions to find out more.
2 Present your story to the class.
3 Write your story. Read each other's stories and choose your favorite.

“If you think that adventure is dangerous, try routine. It’s deadly.”

DANIELE QUERCIA

Read about Daniele Quercia and get ready to watch his TED Talk. ▶ 2.0

AUTHENTIC LISTENING SKILLS

Understanding accents

When you travel abroad or listen to people on TV and the internet, you will hear foreign and regional accents in English. It's helpful to practice listening to different accents so you can enjoy listening to people from all over the world.

1 **Listen to the beginning of the TED Talk, at first said by a native English speaker and then by Daniele Quercia, a native Italian speaker. Compare the pronunciation of the underlined sounds.** 🎧 12

"I have a confession to make. As a scientist and engineer, I've focused on efficiency for many years."

2 **How do you say these sentences? Listen to Daniele and a native speaker to compare.** 🎧 13

1. I lived in Boston and worked in Cambridge.
2. I teamed up with Luca and Rossano.
3. They also recalled how some paths smelled and sounded.

3 **MY PERSPECTIVE**

Which of these statements do you agree with? Why?

1. Learners should try to sound like native speakers of English.
2. Sometimes it's easier to understand other non-native speakers of English than native speakers.
3. Your foreign accent in English is an important part of your identity, so be proud of it.

WATCH

4 **What do you usually see on your way to school? What can you hear? What can you smell?**

5 **Watch Part 1 of the talk. Answer the questions.** ▶ 2.1

1. What journey helped Daniele see that travel isn't just about efficiency?
   - **a** moving from Boston to Barcelona
   - **b** a bicycle race he took part in
   - **c** his commute to work
2. How was the new route different from the old one?
   - **a** It went along Massachusetts Avenue.
   - **b** It had less traffic.
   - **c** It was shorter and quicker.
3. What does Daniele say about mapping apps?
   - **a** They encourage people to explore more.
   - **b** They give you too many choices about which way to travel.
   - **c** They are very similar to computer games.

6 **Watch Part 2 of the talk. Choose the correct option to complete each sentence.** ▶ 2.2

1. Daniele changed his research to look more at how people *experience / get around* the city.
2. The red path on the map is the *shortest / most enjoyable* one.
3. They collected data by asking people to *play a game / take a test*.
4. The first map that they designed was of *Boston / London*.

5 Their research now is in developing maps based on smell, sound, and *memories / sights*.
6 Their goal is to encourage people to take *the best path / many paths* through the city.

7 VOCABULARY IN CONTEXT

a Watch the clips from the TED Talk. Choose the correct meaning of the words and phrases. ▶ 2.3

b Think of examples of the following things. Then work in pairs and compare your examples.

1 a place that's *surrounded by* nature
2 a time when you felt *shame*
3 somewhere that only has a *handful of* stores
4 a situation that makes you feel *shy*
5 a time you *teamed up with* someone

CHALLENGE

Work in pairs. Daniele asks, "What if we had a mapping tool that would return the most enjoyable routes based... on smell, sound, and memories?" Think of places near where you live that:

- have an interesting smell.
- make you think of an interesting sound.
- remind you of a memory.

Tell your partner about them.

8 Work in groups. Discuss the questions.

1 How does Daniele think that his mapping app will make people's lives better?
2 Daniele's London map shows routes that are short, happy, beautiful, and quiet. Which kind of route would you prefer to use to get around your city? Why?
3 Why might these people be interested in using this kind of mapping app? Give reasons for each one.
   - a tourist spending a week in a new city
   - a courier who delivers letters and packages quickly for companies by bicycle
   - a student
   - a taxi driver
4 Would you like to have this mapping app on your smartphone? Why?

9 Work in pairs. Look at a map of your town or a city that you know well. Plan two one-hour walking routes.

- Route 1. This must include as many beautiful sights and interesting places as possible.
- Route 2. This must include the places most likely to interest teenagers who are visiting the city.

10 Work in groups. Compare your routes and discuss the questions.

1 As a tourist, what tour would you enjoy most? Why?
2 What other types of (guided) tours could you offer?

2E You Can't Miss It

SPEAKING

1 Work in pairs. Discuss the questions.

How do you find your way when you are lost? Have you ever used a map, GPS, or app to help you, or do you prefer to ask someone?

2 Listen to two conversations. Complete the table. 14

	Conversation 1	Conversation 2
1 Do the speakers know each other?		
2 Where do they want to get to?		
3 How are they traveling?		
4 How far is it?		
5 What will they do if they get lost?		

3 Look at the map and listen again. Match a letter from the map with each of these places. 14

1 where the first conversation takes place
2 the science museum
3 the movie theater
4 Melanie's house

4 Use one word to complete the expressions. Listen again to check. 14

1 Can you ____________ me? I'm trying to ____________ to the museum.
2 It's a long ____________ from here. About a fifteen-minute ____________ .
3 Go up Northway Street for about five minutes ____________ you get to the supermarket on your left. Then take the first… no, the second ____________ .
4 You can't ____________ it.
5 Can you give me ____________ to your house?
6 So if the station's ____________ you, you'll need to turn right.
7 At the ____________ of the street you'll see a movie theater in front of you.
8 ____________ on Northway Street until you get to a supermarket on your right. Just after ____________ , there's a street on the left.

5 Label the sentences in Activity 4 with the correct category (A–D) from the Useful language box.

6 Work in pairs. Ask for and give directions between places on the map.

7 Work in groups. Give directions to each other from school to destinations around town. Listen and say what you think the destinations are.

Useful language

A Asking for directions

Excuse me. Can you tell me how to get to…? / Do you know the way to…?

B Giving directions

Go all the way up there until you get to…

At the traffic lights, go straight / turn right.

After 200 yards, take the first exit off the traffic circle.

C Talking about landmarks and destinations

Go past a… on your left / right.

The train station is on your left.

D Talking about time and distance

It's not very far from here.

It's less than half a mile from there.

WRITING A story

8 Work in pairs. Read the writing task below. Then tell your partner about a time when you got lost.

Write a story that ends with the sentence: *After so many hours feeling completely lost, I ended up just where I needed to be!*

9 Read the story on page 149. When did the writer feel uncertain?

1 talking to his cousin
2 at the bus stop
3 on the bus
4 when he got off the bus
5 on the motorcycle
6 at the boat

10 **WRITING SKILL** *just*

Match the sentences (1–5) with the meaning of *just* (a–e).

1 My cousin had just returned from an island called Koh Tao.
2 An old man pointed to a bus that was just about to leave.
3 I was just falling asleep when the driver shouted, "Koh Tao!"
4 I couldn't see the sea, just a quiet road.
5 I ended up just where I needed to be!

a only
b recently
c exactly
d almost
e very soon (*with be about to*)

11 You are going to write a story about a trip that ends with one of these three sentences. Choose your ending.

- That was one of the worst trips of my life.
- I hadn't expected to have such an exciting trip.
- Getting to school had never been so complicated.

12 Prepare to write your story.

1 Use the questions in the Writing strategies box to write the details of your story.
2 Think about the verb forms you will need to tell the story.

13 Write your story. When you have finished, share it with other people in the class. Whose stories sound like the best/worst experiences?

Writing strategies

Writing a story

Use a paragraph plan like this when you write a story:

Paragraph 1: Set the scene
Where does the story start?
Who is the story about?
When does the story take place?

Paragraphs 2 and 3: Main events
What happened?
How did you feel?
What happened next?

Paragraph 4: The end
What happened in the end?
How did you or other people feel?
What do you remember most about the events?

Koh Tao is a beautiful island in Thailand. Its name means "Turtle Island."

3 Active Lives

IN THIS UNIT, YOU...

- talk about the reasons for doing sports.
- read about how sports are saving Africa's lions.
- learn about runners.
- watch a TED Talk about swimming at the North Pole.
- write an opinion essay about sports.

Bike base jumping in Canyonlands National Park, Utah

3A Pushing the Limits

VOCABULARY Sports

1 Work in pairs. Look at the photo and read the caption. Why do people do sports like this? Have you ever done an "extreme sport"? Would you like to try one? Why?

2 Put these words into the correct category. Use a dictionary if necessary. How many more words can you add to each category?

bounce	~~climbing~~	coach	court	diving
field	gymnastics	karate	kick	net
opponent	pass	referee	rink	rope
sailing	spectator	the 100-meter dash	throw	track

Sports	People	Places	Equipment	Actions
climbing				

3 Write five sentences about sports using the words in Activity 2.

In tennis, you have to hit the ball to your opponent's side of the court.

4 Collocate these verbs with corresponding words and phrases.

achieve	beat	do	encourage	go
play	represent	score	train	win

1. a prize / a trophy / the gold medal
2. climbing / sailing / cycling
3. golf / tennis / an important role
4. gymnastics / yoga / your best
5. people to work as a team / children to exercise more
6. for the event / before the race / hard
7. your goal / your personal best / your ambition
8. your school / your country / the team
9. a goal / ten points
10. your opponent / the champion

5 Work in pairs. Read the statements. Which sport(s) are they about?

1. The field is where I met all my friends. And I **feel proud when I'm representing my team** in tournaments.
2. Being out on my boat **gives me a real sense of freedom**. It's always played an important role in my life.
3. When I'm going up a mountain, it's about **pushing my own limits**, not **winning trophies or breaking records**.
4. I'm doing it to **raise money** for a children's charity. I've been training for months, but I've still got a long way to go!
5. I want to **encourage** the younger players to have some fun on the court.
6. To be honest, I don't enjoy it much—it's pretty boring. I only do it to **stay healthy**.

6 **MY PERSPECTIVE**

Do you do any sports for the reasons in bold in Activity 5? Can you think of other reasons for doing sports?

Ashima Shiraishi on *Slashface*, a V13 bouldering problem in Hueco Tanks Historic Site, Texas

LISTENING

7 Look at the photo of a young climber, Ashima Shiraishi, and read the caption. What do you think the V scale measures?

8 Listen to a podcast about Ashima. Answer the questions. 15

1 Why does she enjoy climbing?
2 What has she achieved?

9 Listen again. Are these sentences *true* or *false*? How do you know? 15

1 Ashima started climbing when she was a teenager.
2 She has been a professional climber for a year.
3 She always uses ropes when she climbs.
4 She has climbed in several countries, including Japan and South Africa.
5 She is the only female athlete to successfully climb a V14 problem.
6 She is the youngest person to successfully climb a V15 problem.
7 She recently had an accident, but it hasn't stopped her from climbing.
8 She does her homework late in the evening because she has to train hard.

GRAMMAR Simple past and present perfect

10 Read the excerpts from the podcast in the Grammar box. Underline the verbs in the simple past and circle the verb in the present perfect.

Simple past and present perfect (1)

a *Ashima **has traveled** to many countries looking for more and more difficult climbs.*
b *In 2014, she **went** to South Africa and **completed** the "Golden Shadow" problem.*

11 Answer the questions about the sentences in the Grammar box.

1 Is it clear when Ashima traveled to *many countries*? Is it important here?
2 Do we know when she went to South Africa? Is it important here?
3 Which timeline illustrates sentence a? Which timeline illustrates sentence b?

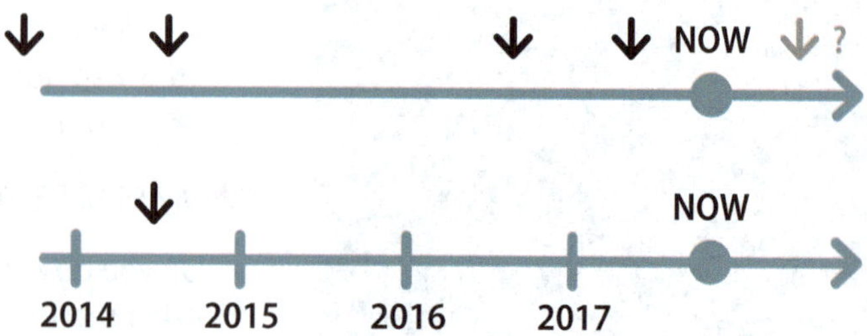

Simple past and present perfect (2)

a *Ashima discovered climbing at the age of six, and she's* ***loved*** *it ever since.*
b *She* ***has traveled*** *to many countries in her young life, looking for more and more difficult climbs.*
c *She's just* ***achieved*** *an even more amazing record.*
d *Earlier this year, Ashima* ***climbed*** *"Horizon," a V15 climb in Japan.*
e *Shortly after that, she fell and injured her back, but she* ***has recovered*** *and is now climbing again.*

Check page 132 for more information and practice.

12 Match the sentences in the Grammar box (a–e) above with the rules (1–5).

Simple past

The simple past is used to talk about:

1 completed actions in the past. The time is often stated, e.g., *last week*, *yesterday*, *in 2017*, etc.

Present perfect

The present perfect is used to talk about:

2 actions which started in the past and continue to the present. We often use *for* and *since* to say how long the action has continued.
3 actions in the past which are connected to a present situation.
4 past experiences, when the exact time isn't stated. Any time expression is connected to the present, e.g., *until now*, *never*, *in my life*.
5 recent actions when the exact time isn't stated. We often use *just* to emphasize that it happened very recently.

13 Choose the correct options to complete the article.

Speed climbing is a race against the clock. Climbing as a sport (1) *was / has been* around for a long time, but competition speed climbing (2) *became / has become* popular only a few years ago. Competitors try to climb a fifteen-meter wall (about 49 feet) as quickly as they can. When they reach the top, they must hit a button to stop the clock.

When the sport (3) *started / has started*, climbers (4) *used / have used* walls with different heights and holds but, since 2007, all the walls (5) *were / have been* exactly the same. The men's world record holder is Danyl Boldyrev, who (6) *broke / has broken* the record with a time of 5.6 seconds in 2014.

Competitive climbing (7) *wasn't / hasn't been* in the last Olympic Games, but the organizers of the Games (8) *just accepted / have just accepted* it as a sport for the 2020 Tokyo Olympics.

14 Put the verbs in the correct form of the simple past or present perfect to complete the conversations.

1 A (you / play) tennis recently?
B No. I (injure) my arm in March, and I (not / play) any sports since then.
A That's a shame. When I (see) you in the competition last year, you (be) really good.

2 A What sports (you / do) when you were younger?
B Many different ones—soccer, volleyball, swimming. I (always / love) sports.
A So what do you do now?
B (I / just / start) mountain biking. That's my latest interest.

3 A (you / ever / win) a medal or a trophy?
B Yes, several times. I (play) baseball for several years, and my team is very good.
A Wow! I didn't know that.

4 A (you / ever / do) karate?
B No, but I'd love to. A friend (try) it last year, and he (enjoy) it.
A It's not something that (ever / interest) me.

5 A (you / watch) any games yet this year?
B No, I haven't. But my dad (go) to all of them.

15 Work in pairs. Talk about your own experiences with sports. Use the questions in Activity 14 to help you, and continue the conversation.

3B Conservation through Sports

A Maasai warrior competes in the high jump event during the Maasai Olympics at the Sidai Oleng Wildlife Sanctuary, Kenya.

Can sports protect AFRICA'S LIONS?

VOCABULARY BUILDING Phrasal verbs

1 Underline the phrasal verb and its synonym.

1 More and more people are taking up *capoeira*. People often start doing it after seeing it on the street.
2 If you don't want to participate now, you can just watch, and join in another time.
3 Even professional athletes warm up before running. Our bodies need time to prepare for sports.
4 I wanted to keep up with the main group of runners, but it was impossible to stay with them.
5 Surprisingly, he's knocked out the second-best world athlete and could beat the world champion in the final!
6 On Sunday, Brazil takes on Germany. Can the Brazilians challenge the Germans for a place in the quarterfinals?
7 I gave up tennis in 2015. I had to stop playing because of a hand injury.
8 I don't exercise much during the week, but I work out at the gym on Sundays.

2 Complete the questions with the correct form of a phrasal verb from Activity 1.

1 Do you like to __________ sports, or do you prefer to be a spectator? Why?
2 Has your team ever __________ a better team?
3 If you could __________ a sport, what would you try? Why?
4 What sports have you __________ ? Why did you stop?
5 What's the best way to __________ before running?
6 Do you ever go to a gym to __________ ? Do you enjoy it?

3 Work in pairs. Ask and answer the questions in Activity 2.

READING

4 Read the article. Why were the Maasai Olympics started?

5 Complete the paragraphs with the topic sentences (a–f).

> A **topic sentence** summarizes the main idea of the paragraph. Topic sentences are usually the first sentence of the paragraph.

a The African Wildlife Foundation got together with Maasai leaders to come up with a plan.
b The Games are not just for the men, however.
c One of Africa's most famous animals needs protection.
d Maasai tribes have been hunting lions as trophies for hundreds of years.
e Have the Games been a successful way to help conservation efforts in Kenya and Tanzania?
f Preparations for the next Games have been heating up, and everyone involved is getting excited.

16 1 ______. In the 1940s, there were an estimated 450,000 lions across Africa, but since then numbers have decreased dramatically, to around 20,000 today. Reasons include a loss of habitat as the human population has grown, and the trade in lion body parts. However, another threat to the lions may soon be a thing of the past.

2 ______. In Maasai culture, killing lions has been an important tradition among the men because it shows their physical strength and skill. The Maasai also hunt lions when the lions kill their cows. Unfortunately, this has brought the lion population to dangerously low levels. Conservationists have believed for some time that the number of lion killings can be reduced without destroying the Maasai culture. But how?

3 ______. The idea was to replace lion hunting with a sports event. The Maasai Olympics were born, and *manyattas*, or villages, from across the region were invited to join in. Since 2012, they have held three Maasai Olympics. Young men take part in six running, throwing, and jumping events, which all reflect Maasai culture. For example, the javelin competition is similar to the traditional skill of throwing a spear*, and the high jump is similar to Maasai dancing.

4 ______. Including women in the events is very important because the women can influence the men's behavior. If the women are more aware of lion conservation, they can discourage the men from hunting. At the 2014 Games, there were two running events for women and the winners received the same prizes as the men.

5 ______. The coaches in each *manyatta* have already chosen their athletes for the team, and they are training hard. The competitors take their preparation very seriously. Every day they warm up before exercising in groups. Although the final is over a year away, the Games have already started, as *manyattas* take on one another in friendly competitions before the main event.

6 ______. A survey among Maasai men shows that attitudes have changed. Although nineteen percent of the people asked haven't even heard of the Maasai Olympics, the majority of them say that the Games have made them less interested in killing lions. And even though trophy hunting still goes on, they see sports as an effective alternative. As one of the athletes said, "We used to celebrate lion hunting, but this program has shown us a better celebration."

spear *a long, sharp stick you throw as a weapon*

6 Read the article again. Choose the correct option to complete these sentences.

1 Lion populations have become smaller because:
a the animals have less space to live in the wild.
b of a number of reasons.
c the Maasai have hunted them too much.

2 Hunting:
a is the biggest danger to the lions.
b is how Maasai men show how brave they are.
c has been a part of Maasai culture for a long time.

3 All of the events in the competition:
a involve throwing.
b are like traditional Maasai activities.
c include all the villages.

4 Women are involved in the competition:
a as much as the men.
b because they asked to compete.
c to help in the goal of reducing lion hunting.

5 The *manyattas*:
a haven't chosen their athletes yet.
b get all the hopeful athletes to train.
c have already started competing.

6 The Maasai Olympics:
a are changing the way people think.
b have stopped the Maasai from hunting lions.
c are less interesting to the Maasai than killing lions.

CRITICAL THINKING A balanced view

It is important to give both sides of an argument, even if the writer wants to persuade readers that one opinion is correct. Including points that support the opposite argument shows that the writer has thought about them and makes the argument more persuasive.

7 Does the writer give a balanced view of the Maasai Games? Underline sentences that support your answer.

8 Work in pairs. Read the statements (1–5). Do you agree or disagree? Why? Try to present a balanced view.

1 People can learn important life skills by playing sports.
2 Sports always help people feel better about themselves.
3 Sports are a good way to help people who don't have much money or education to achieve their ambitions.
4 Sports aren't about winning. They're about participating and doing your best.
5 Athletes earn too much money.

9 Work in groups. Discuss the statements in Activity 8.

3C Marathon Men and Women

Kenyan Eliud Kipchoge competes in the 2016 Rio Olympics marathon.

GRAMMAR Present perfect and present perfect continuous

1 Read the sentences in the Grammar box. Underline examples of the present perfect. Circle examples of the present perfect continuous.

Present perfect and present perfect continuous

a *Maasai tribes* ***have been hunting*** *lions as trophies for hundreds of years.*
b *Since the 1940s, numbers* ***have decreased*** *dramatically, to around 20,000 today.*
c *Preparations for the next Games* ***have been heating up****, and everyone involved is getting excited.*
d *The coaches in each manyatta* ***have*** *already* ***chosen*** *their athletes for the team.*
e ***Have*** *the Games* ***been*** *a successful way to help conservation efforts in Kenya and Tanzania?*

Check page 132 for more information and practice.

2 Match the sentences in the Grammar box with the rules (1–5).

The present perfect:

1 emphasizes the fact that an action is complete.
Sentence ________

2 emphasizes the present result of the action, i.e., *How many? / How much? / How often?*
Sentence ________

3 is used with stative verbs, e.g., *want, know, believe, be.*
Sentence ________

The present perfect continuous:

4 emphasizes the fact that an action is incomplete.
Sentence ________

5 emphasizes the duration of an action, i.e., *How long?*
Sentence ________

3 Choose the correct options to complete the paragraph about Kenyan marathon runners.

Kenyans know how to run fast. Kenyan men (1) *have run / have been running* seven of the ten fastest marathons in history. It's a similar story for the women: Jemima Sumgong has finally (2) *given / been giving* Kenya its first Olympic gold in the marathon, and Kenyan women hold more of the records than anyone else. So how long has the title of world long-distance champions (3) *belonged / been belonging* to Kenya? Interestingly, although the country (4) *has sent / has been sending* athletes to competitions, such as the Olympics, since 1956, it (5) *hasn't won / hasn't been winning* races for all of that time. So what have they (6) *done / been doing* more recently to make them so good? Well, about 40 years ago, training camps started in small towns in the mountains, like Iten, and they (7) *have become / have been becoming* major centers for sports. Since then, this area (8) *has created / has been creating* more world champions than anywhere else in the world.

4 Complete the questions about Catherine Ndereba.

RUNNER PROFILE
CATHERINE NDEREBA

Many people believe that Catherine Ndereba, or "Catherine the Great," is the greatest female marathon runner ever.

1. how long / Catherine / run?
   She started when she was just a girl.
2. she / always / love running?
   Yes, she has had a passion for it since she was in school.
3. how many marathons / she / win?
   Many! She won the Boston Marathon four times between 2000 and 2005.
4. she / win / any Olympic medals?
   Yes. She's never won gold, but she came second in the marathon in 2004 and 2008.
5. what / she / do / recently?
   Since retiring in 2014, she's been helping to train young Kenyan runners.
6. how far / she / run / this week?
   Only about 50 kilometers (31 miles)—much less than when she was competing.

5 Complete the interview with these time expressions. Then listen and check your answers. 17

already	ever	for	just
never	since	since	yet

A José, you've (1) __________ arrived here in Kenya, haven't you?

B Yes, I've only been here (2) __________ four days.

A Have you (3) __________ been to Kenya before? Why have you come?

B I've (4) __________ been here before. I've loved running (5) __________ I was a boy, and I've been competing for a couple of years. But I'm not improving. I haven't won any races (6) __________ this year.

A And you're hoping that training here will help?

B Exactly. A running friend of mine has (7) __________ been here twice to train and he's been a lot faster (8) __________ then.

6 **PRONUNCIATION** *For*

a Listen to the sentences (a-c). Notice how *for* is pronounced. 18

- **a** Catherine has been competing for 21 years.
- **b** I've only been here for four days.
- **c** I've been competing for a couple of years.

b Practice saying these sentences. Pay attention to the pronunciation of *for*. Then listen and check. 19

1. I've only been here for a week.
2. You've been playing that game for too long.
3. He's been getting ready to go out for 40 minutes.
4. We've had this car for over ten years.
5. I've been learning English for a long time.

7 **CHOOSE**

Choose one of the following activities.

1. Work in pairs. Interview each other about sports and hobbies that you enjoy. Use the questions below and any others you can think of.
   1. What is one hobby or sport you enjoy?
   2. How long have you been doing it?
   3. Have you taken part in any competitions?
   4. Have you been training for any competitions recently?
   5. What are the secrets to doing your sport or hobby well?
2. Write about your sport or hobby for a class blog. Use the questions above to give you ideas.
3. Find out about an athlete you admire and write a short profile about him or her.

AUTHENTIC LISTENING SKILLS

Signposts

Signposts are words and expressions that speakers use to help the listener understand where the argument is going: what they are going to say next or what they have just said. For example: *I'm going to tell you about…, The main thing is…, First of all…, Let's finish by looking at….*

1 Read the Authentic Listening Skills box. Then listen to these excerpts from the TED Talk. Underline the signposts. 20

1 Today I want to talk to you about swimming across the North Pole, across the most northern place in the whole world.
2 And the message was very clear: climate change is for real, and we need to do something about it. And we need to do something about it right now.
3 But the most important thing was to train my mind to prepare myself for what was going to happen.

2 Listen to four more excerpts from the talk. Complete each signpost with one word. 21

1 I'd just like to end by just __________ this: it took me four months…
2 And I say to them, I think we need to do three __________. The first…
3 The __________ thing we need to do is…
4 But the most __________ thing we must do is…

WATCH

3 Work in pairs. Discuss the questions.

1 Does it take you a long time to get into the ocean or a swimming pool?
2 Do you prefer swimming in indoor swimming pools, lakes, or the ocean? Why?
3 Would you describe yourself as a confident or strong swimmer? What's the farthest you've ever swum?

4 Watch Part 1 of the talk. Match the numbers (1–8) with the reasons we hear about them (a–h). ▶ 3.1

1 23%	**5** -1.7°
2 27°	**6** hundreds
3 5°	**7** 1
4 0°	**8** 5

a the number of people in Lewis's team who went with him to the North Pole
b the number of times Lewis had imagined swimming across the North Pole
c the number of years Lewis trained for the swim
d the amount of Arctic sea ice that melted in the two years before the swim
e the temperature of an indoor swimming pool
f the temperature of water when it freezes
g the temperature of the sea at the North Pole
h the temperature of the sea when the Titanic sank

5 Watch Part 2 of the talk. It describes Lewis's practice swim. Are these sentences *true* or *false*? How do you know? ▶ 3.2

1 He felt cold in the water.
2 He got out of the water after five minutes.
3 His fingers were bigger than normal when he got out of the water.
4 He was less worried about swimming for twenty minutes after doing the practice swim.
5 David was confident that Lewis could do the swim.

6 Watch Part 3 of the talk. Choose the correct option to complete each sentence. ▶ 3.3

1 Lewis believes that we need to *break the problem of climate change into smaller parts / look at climate change as one problem.*
2 Even children in poor countries *have an effect on climate change / understand climate change.*
3 Lewis *tells / asks* us what decisions we need to make to create a sustainable world.

7 **VOCABULARY IN CONTEXT**

a Watch the clips from the TED Talk. Choose the correct meaning of the words and phrases. ▶ 3.4

b Think of an example of these things. Then compare your examples in pairs.

- somewhere you can swim in *fresh water*
- a time you wore a special *costume* or suit
- someone who can *barely* swim
- a time you had a *swollen* ankle or wrist
- something you *believe in* strongly

8 Read the comments. Which are in favor of Lewis Pugh's swim? Which are against it?*

1 "Lewis Pugh was very lucky that he didn't die. Nothing is worth risking your life like that."
2 "Swimming at the North Pole was a powerful way of showing people the effect of climate change."
3 "The effects of climate change in the Arctic were already very well known before he did his swim."
4 "The journey to the North Pole was long and expensive, and probably wasn't good for the environment. Wasn't there an easier way to raise awareness?"
5 "The personal story of his training and his fears and difficulties make the message about climate change more memorable and real."

*These comments were created for this activity.

9 Work in pairs. Discuss the comments. Which do you agree with most? Why?

10 Work in pairs. Discuss the questions.

1 What do you think we can do about climate change?
2 What do you already do about climate change?

CHALLENGE

Work in groups. Choose another important issue. Use these questions to plan a sporting event to raise awareness of it.

1 What issue is important to you as a group?
2 What sport will you use to raise awareness?
3 Where will you hold the event?
4 How will you advertise it?

3E School Sports

WRITING An opinion essay

1 Work in pairs. Discuss the questions.

1 How many hours a week do you play sports in school?
2 Does a break for sports help you focus on other subjects?
3 Are sports mandatory for high school students in your country?
4 Would you like to do more or fewer sports in school? Why?

2 Read the essay topic below. Which questions (1–5) do you have to answer?

"Gym should be a mandatory subject at school, with the same importance as other subjects like Math and English." Do you agree or disagree with this statement?

1 How many countries have mandatory sports in school?
2 Are sports as important as Math and English?
3 What kind of sports do most students enjoy?
4 Do schools have enough space for students to play sports?
5 Why are sports and exercise important for young people?

3 Read the essay on page 150. Are the questions you selected in Activity 2 answered?

4 Work in pairs. Read the essay again. Discuss the questions.

1 What reasons does the writer give to support the argument? Underline them.
2 What arguments does the writer give with the opposite view? Circle them.
3 Which points do you agree with most and least?
4 Can you think of any other arguments for or against the writer's opinion?

5 WRITING SKILL Giving your opinion

a Read the statements. What do you think? Use the Useful language box and make notes about your opinions on two or three of the statements.

1 The government should stop people from doing dangerous sports like boxing.
2 There are more disadvantages than advantages for a country when it holds international sporting events like the Olympic Games.
3 There are good reasons why some professional athletes make more money than doctors, teachers, and nurses.
4 It is better to encourage children to practice noncompetitive sports (e.g., yoga) than to play competitive sports.
5 The world of sports is a better place these days because of all the money that has come into it from business and advertising.
6 Young people often see professional athletes as heroes. Some people think that those athletes have a responsibility to be good role models.

b MY PERSPECTIVE

Work in groups. Compare your opinions about the statements in Activity 5a.

Useful language

Giving your opinion

Personally, I think that…
I strongly believe that…
I do not think that…
Of course,…
There is no question that…
I would say that…
It's true that…
In my opinion,…
In my view,…

6 Choose one of the statements in Activity 5a and write an essay giving your opinion. Think about the questions you must answer. Make sure each paragraph has a topic sentence. Write about 150 words.

Paragraph 1 Introduce the topic by describing the situation and clearly stating your opinion.
Paragraph 2 Give at least two points that support your opinion.
Paragraph 3 Give one or two points against your opinion.
Paragraph 4 Summarize the main points and give your opinion again.

7 Read another student's essay. Is his or her opinion clear? Do you agree with it?

Useful language

Agreeing

I totally agree with you.
That's true.
That's a good point.
He's right about that.
He's got a good point.
You're not wrong there.

Disagreeing

Yes, but…
I'm not sure I agree.
Maybe, but…
I agree up to a point, but…
I see what you're saying, but…
I understand what you mean, it's just…

SPEAKING

8 Listen to a conversation between three friends. Which statement from Activity 5a are they discussing? 22

9 Listen again. Which of the expressions in the Useful language box do you hear? 22

10 Read about a competition. Which three sports would you like your school to win? Why?

Your school has entered a competition to win modern equipment and new facilities for **three** sports. Winners can develop existing sports at the school, or choose equipment for new sports. The school with the best argument for its choice of sports will win. Each school can only send one proposal.

11 Work in pairs. Discuss your choice of sports with your partner. Decide on three sports you would like to propose and the reasons why.

12 Work with another pair. Decide on the three sports you would all like to propose. Present your proposal to the class.

4 Food

IN THIS UNIT, YOU...

- talk about food and cooking.
- read about Filipino street food.
- learn why you might start eating insects.
- watch a TED Talk about becoming a weekday vegetarian.
- write a social media update.

4A Learning to Cook

VOCABULARY Describing food

1 In pairs, find a dish or food in the photo, or suggest one that:

1 looks **delicious**.
2 you think probably tastes **disgusting**.
3 looks like **junk food**.
4 is very **unhealthy**.
5 contains lots of **vitamins**.
6 would make good **fast food**.
7 is made from **raw** ingredients.
8 is highly **processed** food.
9 has a **well-balanced** mixture of ingredients.
10 is often **steamed**.
11 would be suitable for **a vegetarian.**
12 contains **wheat**.

2 Find a word in bold in Activity 1 that is an opposite of:

1 natural.
2 fried.
3 a meat-eater.
4 delicious.
5 cooked.

3 What's the difference between:

1 *fresh* vegetables and *raw* vegetables?
2 *fast* food and *junk* food?
3 *cooked* food and *processed* food?
4 *boiled* vegetables and *steamed* vegetables?
5 a *strong* flavor and a *spicy* flavor?

4 Think of an example for each category below. Then compare your ideas with a partner. How similar were your answers?

I love having a hamburger and French fries sometimes. I probably have that once or twice a month.

1 a type of junk food you think is delicious
2 an ingredient that contains lots of vitamin C
3 food from your country that people from other countries might find disgusting
4 a dish that contains raw meat or fish
5 a type of processed food that is popular in your country
6 a well-balanced meal that you know how to cook
7 a type of fast food that is suitable for vegetarians
8 something containing wheat that you'd enjoy right now

5 **MY PERSPECTIVE**

1 Which of these "bad habits" annoy you most? Which are the most unacceptable where you live?
- talking with your mouth full
- being a noisy eater
- never offering to do the dishes
- not finishing your main course, but eating dessert
- talking about your healthy diet all the time
- eating while you're shopping in the supermarket

2 Are there any other bad habits that annoy you?

A robot created by Moley Robotics cooks crab soup.

LISTENING

6 Listen to a podcast about food. Do the two speakers agree about cooking in schools? 23

7 Listen again. Which speaker, Terry (T) or Mali (M): 23

1. is going to cook after the show?
2. will do the dishes today?
3. says that the secret to being a good cook is to start young?
4. says students are going to have cooking classes?
5. believes that schools have more important things to focus on than cooking?
6. says that school is a good place to teach children about healthy food?
7. plans to learn to cook?
8. has a brother who cooks?

8 Work in pairs. Discuss the questions.

1. Is cooking a required school subject in your country?
2. What dishes can you cook?

GRAMMAR Future plans, intentions, and arrangements

9 Look at the Grammar box. Match the future uses (1–7) with the sentences from the Grammar box (a–g).

1. decisions that we make at the moment of speaking
2. arrangements between people
3. hopes, expectations, beliefs, and plans
4. plans and intentions
5. ideas that are only possible, not certain
6. after *if* and time expressions like *when*, *until*, *after*, and *as soon as*
7. future scheduled events

will, may/might, going to, present continuous, simple present

a *OK, I'**ll** do the dishes if you want.*

b *I think children **will** learn some simple dishes at about eight years old.*

c *Children should learn about basic food preparation before they **leave** school.*

d *They **may** teach them about the dangers of a poor diet in those lessons, too.*

e *I've recently decided I'**m going to** learn one new recipe each week.*

f *My brother'**s showing** me how to make vegetable lasagna at his house tomorrow.*

g *Next week, the podcast **goes** out at the same time and it's all about eating raw food.*

Check page 134 for more information and practice.

10 Match the forms (a–e) with the future uses (1–7) in Activity 9.

a *going to*
b *may/might*
c present continuous
d simple present
e *will/won't*

11 Choose the correct option.

According to a recent survey, 60% of today's 18- to 25-year-olds in Britain are leaving home without being able to cook five simple recipes.

Ana I don't want that to be me, because I think home cooking means a healthier diet, so (1) *I'm going to / I may* learn. My friend's aunt is a chef, and she's agreed to teach me. My lessons (2) *start / will start* next Thursday. She says she (3) *teaches / might teach* me to make spaghetti Bolognese, but (4) *I'll / I might* probably ask her if we can do something vegetarian because I don't like touching raw meat.

Fumio I've never cooked in my life, and I'm never (5) *cooking / going to cook*, either. (6) *I'm moving / I'll move* in with friends next week, and they're all learning to cook. I'm sure (7) *they'll practice / they're practicing* their skills on me when (8) *I'm / I will be* hungry.

Mohammed I've never thought about it, but I probably (9) *don't / won't* learn unless (10) *I'm needing / I need* to. Right now I live at home, but when I live on my own, (11) *I might / I'm going to* get more interested in cooking. It doesn't look very hard, though, so I'm sure (12) *I'm picking / I'll pick* it up fast.

12 MY PERSPECTIVE

Work in pairs. When you leave home, will you be more like Ana, Fumio, or Mohammed? Tell your partner why.

13 Complete the article with the best form of the verbs. Use *will, may, going to,* or the simple present.

People say that cooking is fun, but I (1) ______________ (do) everything I can to not cook when I (2) ______________ (leave) home. If, like me, you can't even cook an egg, you (3) ______________ (probably / be) disappointed with anything you make at home. But, bad home cooking (4) ______________ (disappear) in the near future. Moley Robotics has designed a kitchen robot that (5) ______________ (cook) any dish in the world as well as a professional chef.

It looks like two human arms and it works by "learning" the hand and arm movements of professional chefs as they work. The company (6) ______________ (record) celebrity chefs cooking fantastic meals and the arms can copy these instructions in people's homes. You will be able to start the machine before you (7) ______________ (get) home by choosing what to eat from thousands of recipes on your phone. That's if you can afford it: it (8) ______________ (go) on sale soon for $12,500. Despite the price, the makers think that in years to come robots (9) ______________ (make) all home food. Personally, I find the idea of robot arms in my house very strange, so I think I (10) ______________ (spend) my money on restaurants instead.

14 Work in pairs. Discuss the questions.

1 Do you think there will be robot chefs in the future? If so, will you use one? Why?
2 Do you think they will help us eat better?
3 How is your diet preparing you for a healthy future? What will you eat less or more of?

4B Street Food

A food stall on Mactan Island in the Philippines

VOCABULARY BUILDING Compound adjectives

1 **Read about compound adjectives. Then choose the correct option to complete the sentences (1–5).**

> Compound adjectives are formed with two words. They often have a hyphen (-). Many compound adjectives are formed from the past or present participles of verbs.
>
> *It's better to eat* ***oven-baked*** *food that hasn't been fried in oil.* (The food has been **baked** in the **oven**.)
>
> *You'll keep coming back for more* ***great-tasting*** *lemonade.* (The lemonade **tastes great**.)

1 I fried the chicken in deep oil.
It's *deep-fried* / *deep-frying* chicken.
2 That salad looks good.
It's a *good-looked* / *good-looking* salad.
3 What's the ingredient that tastes sweet?
What's the *sweet-tasted* / *sweet-tasting* ingredient?
4 The tomatoes are filled with rice.
They're *rice-filled* / *rice-filling* tomatoes.
5 I don't think they've cooked this chicken enough.
It's *undercooked* / *undercooking* chicken.

2 **Complete the sentences with one of these compound adjectives.**

homemade	modern-looking	old-fashioned
overcooked	well-known	

1 I've eaten in so many restaurants recently. It's great to get back to some good ____________ food.
2 You've never heard of *tiramisu*? It's a ____________ Italian dessert.
3 We had lunch in a lovely ____________ restaurant in the historic center of town.
4 The restaurant is very traditional but it has a ____________ menu. I'd love to go there someday.
5 Be careful not to leave it in the oven for too long. It gets dry if it's ____________ .

3 **Choose a dish that is popular where you live. Write three sentences to describe it using compound adjectives.**

Churros are sweet-tasting, deep-fried things that we eat for breakfast in Spain.

24 Walk down the street in most big cities and you'll find a Middle Eastern grill selling kebabs and falafel. Without a doubt, you'll also find a restaurant selling burgers or Mexican tacos. If you look for spicy food, there's a good chance you'll find Indian or Thai food. You might even find Vietnamese curry for takeout. But you probably won't find food from the Philippines. That's strange, because Filipinos make the best street food in the world.

One reason Filipino food is so good is that there's so much variety! You only have to look at the country's rich history to see why. The Philippines have been influenced by Chinese, Malay, Arab, and Spanish cultures, to name a few. Filipinos took these influences and mixed them in their own way. A popular street breakfast illustrates this very well: take some Chinese rice porridge*, mix in some chocolate (the Spanish introduced cocoa to the islands), then add some 100 percent Filipino salted fish. That's *champorado* with *tuyo*, and it'll wake you up! So, Filipino food is a wonderful mix of many countries' ingredients and styles.

You'll recognize many dishes for this reason. *Lumpia*, for example, are delicious spring rolls, very similar to the ones on a Chinese menu. However, there are a few characteristics of Filipino cuisine that make it unique. Seafood is everywhere in this nation of 7,000 islands. *Ukoy* is a popular prawn* dish; the prawns are mixed with vegetables in egg and flour, fried until they are golden, and served with spicy vinegar. You may discover that the food isn't as hot as in countries like Thailand, but it has flavorful dishes with many great-tasting ingredients in each bite. The best-known dessert of the islands is *halu halo*—it contains cooked banana, sweet beans, coconut, fruit, sweetened milk, sugar, and ice. A milkshake like no other!

You'll find the best *adidas* (grilled chicken feet) in Manila at a food stall called Maong's Grill. Filipinos don't let anything go to waste and make the most delicious snacks out of every part of the animal. At Maong's, for example, you can also get grilled chicken head and chicken intestine*. In many parts of the world, street food started as food for people who weren't wealthy enough to have their own kitchens, and here in the Philippines they do it best.

So why has the world not discovered Filipino street cuisine? Perhaps it's because some of its tastiest dishes are very unusual, so you have to be open to trying new things. But adventurous young people are exploring world food more than ever, so this is going to change, and in a few years, we'll all be eating Filipino food. For now, though, the best place to experience it is still on the streets of Manila.

porridge *a soft food made with water or milk and grain (e.g., oats or rice), eaten hot for breakfast*
prawn *shrimp*
intestine *the part of an animal that processes and digests food*

READING

4 Work in pairs. Discuss the questions.

1 If you're out in the city or in your town, what do you eat? Are there many choices?
2 What are the characteristics of "street food"?

5 Read the blog. What are two characteristics of Filipino street food?

6 Match the dish (1–5) with the idea that it illustrates (a–e).

1 *champorado with tuyo*
2 *lumpia*
3 *ukoy*
4 *halu halo*
5 *adidas*

a Filipino food often puts many flavors together.
b Some dishes are similar to dishes from other countries.
c The cuisine shows the simple origins of street food.
d A lot of Filipino food uses local ingredients, like seafood.
e The food shows the multicultural past of the country.

7 Work in pairs. Discuss the questions.

1 Have you ever tried Filipino food? What dishes would you like to try? Which ones would you avoid?
2 The writer believes that "in a few years, we'll all be eating Filipino food." Do you agree? Why?
3 Are you an adventurous eater? What strange things have you eaten?
4 What other types of food are you interested in trying?

8 It is useful to increase your vocabulary by trying to understand new words in texts. Find words in the blog with these meanings.

1 food that you buy in a restaurant but don't eat there (paragraph 1)
2 individual components of a meal (paragraph 3)
3 animals from the ocean that we eat (paragraph 3)
4 a small meal (paragraph 4)
5 a place in the street used for selling food and other things (paragraph 4)
6 a style of cooking, such as a national style (paragraph 5)

9 What food would you use to promote your country or region? Are there any dishes you would not mention because they might not sound attractive to tourists?

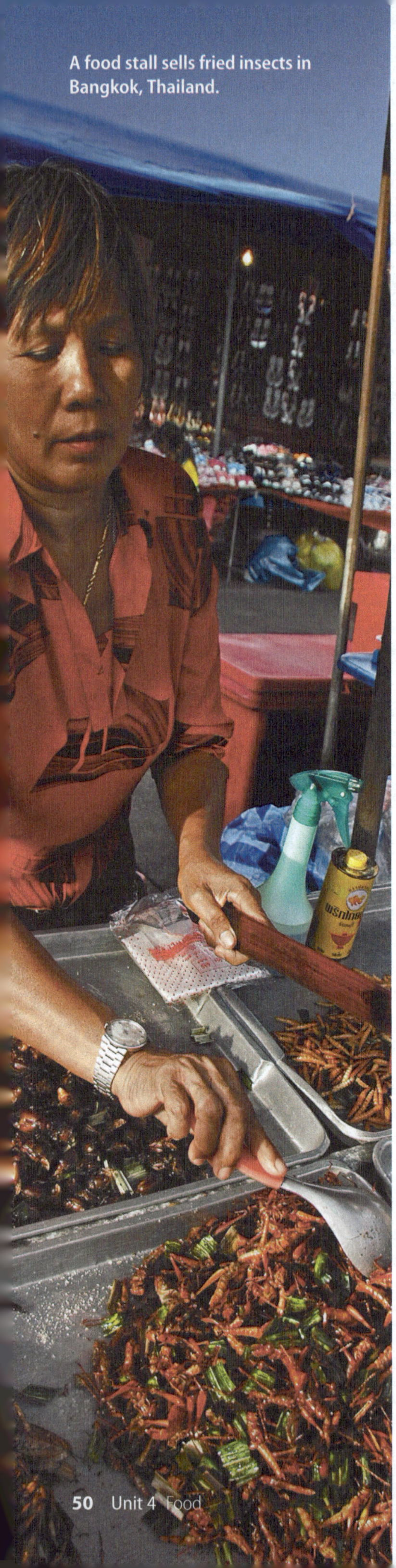

A food stall sells fried insects in Bangkok, Thailand.

4C Feed the world with... bugs?

GRAMMAR Making predictions

1 Read the excerpts (a–f) in the Grammar box. Use them to complete the summary below.

***will, may/might, going to,* future continuous, future perfect**

a *By 2050, the human population* ***will almost certainly have grown*** *to nine billion*

b *we* ***may be able to find*** *our protein from somewhere else*

c *They think we* ***will run out of*** *food*

d *we* ***will*** *all soon* ***be eating*** *insects*

e *we can see that figure is* ***going to*** *rise*

f *We* ***won't have*** *enough of these resources*

There are more than seven billion people on the planet, and (1) _____ . (2) _____ , and experts are worried. (3) _____ . People in developed countries get most of their protein from animals like chickens and cows, but these animals need a lot of land, water, and food to live. (4) _____ as the world's population grows and more people want to eat this kind of meat. But (5) _____ . There's a chance that (6) _____ .

Check page 134 for more information and practice.

2 Activity 1 talks about a problem. How could insects be the solution?

3 How likely is it that the events in bold in the Grammar box will happen? Match the excerpts (a–f) with the probabilities (1–3).

1 certain—100% **2** probable—80 to 100% **3** possible—10 to 80%

4 Complete the rules for making predictions (1–6) with these verb forms. Then match the rules with the excerpts (a–f) in the Grammar box.

Use:

future continuous	future perfect	*going to*	*may/might*	*will* (x2)

1 _____________ to make predictions when there is a clear reason in the present for the prediction. Excerpt _________

2 _____________ to make predictions that we believe are true, often with verbs like *think*, *expect*, *imagine*, and *know*, adverbs like *definitely*, and expressions like *I'm sure*. Excerpt _________

3 _____________ to talk about future things that are certain to happen. Excerpt _________

4 _____________ if we are less certain that the prediction is true. Excerpt _________

5 the _____________ to talk about an action that you know or think will be in progress at a certain point in the future. Excerpt _________

6 the _____________ to talk about an action that will be finished before a particular time in the future. Excerpt _________

5 Complete the voicemail with either the future continuous or future perfect form of the verbs.

"Just wanted to let you know what we (1) ___________ (do) this weekend. Remember the World Food Fair last year? We're going again! If it's like last year's, by the end of the weekend I (2) ___________ (try) all sorts of strange snacks. Apparently, this year, they're promoting insects, but I (3) ___________ (not eat) any ants, even if they are covered in chocolate! What about you? (4) ___________ (you do) your school project? Do you think you (5) ___________ (finish) before Monday morning? Good luck! I (6) ___________ (not finish) mine by then!"

6 **PRONUNCIATION** Sentence stress with the future continuous and future perfect

a Listen and check your answers to Activity 5. 25

b Listen to the positive and negative sentences again. How does the stress change? 26

1. Just wanted to let you know what we'll be doing this weekend.
2. If it's like last year's, by the end of the weekend I'll have tried all sorts of strange snacks.
3. I won't be eating any ants, even if they are covered in chocolate!
4. I won't have finished mine by then!

c Work in pairs. Practice reading the voicemail.

7 Read about a possible solution. Choose the best form of each verb to complete the text.

Researcher Marcel Dicke gives several reasons why insects (1) *are going to / won't* provide us with a lot of the protein we need. First, farming insects is efficient: "Give cows ten kilograms of food and you will (2) *be getting / get* only one kilogram of beef, but locusts can give you nine kilograms of locust meat."

Second, you will (3) *be already eating / have already eaten* hundreds of meals containing insects in your life, whether you like it or not! Next time you eat processed food, you (4) *will / may* probably be eating insects. A lot of fruit gets damaged by insects, so it (5) *won't go / isn't going* to the supermarkets, but (6) *is going to / may* be used to make processed foods like tomato soup.

Third, insects are already a popular form of good, healthy food. Up to two billion people in Asia, Africa, and Latin America will (7) *be enjoying / have enjoyed* an insect recently. Even so, Dicke expects that other people will (8) *find / be finding* it hard to get used to the idea of eating insects. One possibility is that food manufacturers (9) *are going to / might* start introducing processed insect protein into their products. Dicke predicts that, by 2020, we (10) *are going to buy / will be buying* them, knowing that we are eating insects.

8 **MY PERSPECTIVE**

Work in pairs. Discuss the questions.

1. What are the advantages of eating insects?
2. Do you think you will be eating them in the future?

9 Work in groups. Create an insect recipe using the prompts.

- Our dish is going to use… (type of insect)
- It's going to be a… (type of food)
- Other ingredients will include…
- We think it will look more attractive if we…
- We'll be promoting it in… (places)
- When you eat it, make sure you…
- We're sure it will… (predictions)

10 **CHOOSE** Choose one of the following activities.

1. Work in groups. Have a food invention competition. Persuade other groups to buy your dish from Activity 9.
2. Write the recipe and instructions for your dish in Activity 9.
3. Find out how people around the world eat insects. Give a short presentation.

Crispy, fried insects

4D Why I'm a Weekday Vegetarian

> "If all of us ate half as much meat, it would be like half of us were vegetarians."

GRAHAM HILL

Read about Graham Hill and get ready to watch his TED Talk. ▶ 4.0

AUTHENTIC LISTENING SKILLS

Pausing

When people are speaking to an audience, they often pause to break their sentences up into short sections, or chunks. This makes it easier for listeners to follow. Speakers often pause:

- at the end of sentences.
- where there is a comma or other punctuation.
- to separate adverbial phrases (e.g., expressions about time or place).
- before an important word or phrase.
- between the subject of a sentence and its verb when the subject is long.

1 **Listen to the beginning of the TED Talk. Mark the pauses.** 27

About a year ago, | I asked myself a question: "Knowing what I know, why am I not a vegetarian?"

2 **Mark where you think Graham will pause in the next two sentences. Then listen to check.** 28

After all, I'm one of the green guys: I grew up with hippie parents in a log cabin. I started a site called TreeHugger—I care about this stuff.

WATCH

3 **Work in pairs. Make a list of reasons that somebody might be a vegetarian (e.g., "It's good for your health.").**

4 **Watch Part 1 of the talk. Put the problems with eating meat in the order that Graham mentions them. Which problem doesn't he mention?** ▶ 4.1

a It is bad for the planet.
b The animals suffer in poor conditions.
c It is expensive.
d It is unhealthy.
e People are eating more and more meat.

5 **Complete the facts about eating meat. Then watch Part 1 again and check your answers.** ▶ 4.1

1. If you eat one ________ every day, it can increase the possibility of dying by a third.
2. We keep ________ animals for meat each year in factory-farm conditions.
3. Meat causes more emissions than all ________ .
4. Beef production uses 100 times more ________ than most vegetables do.
5. We are eating ________ meat as in the 1950s.

6 **Watch Part 2. Choose the correct option.** ▶ 4.2

1. Why does Graham say to the audience: "Imagine your last hamburger"?
   a He wants them to see what a difficult decision becoming a vegetarian is.
   b He wants to help the audience become vegetarian.
   c He wants them to feel sorry for him.
2. Which of these rules is part of Graham's solution?
   a Only eat fish on the weekend.
   b Don't eat meat on Saturdays and Sundays.
   c Reduce the amount of meat you eat by 70 percent.

3 Which part of Graham's solution is he happiest about?
- **a** He's not creating so much pollution.
- **b** He has more money.
- **c** He's healthier.

7 **Work in pairs. Graham says that "we as a society are eating twice as much meat as we did in the '50s." How has diet changed in your country in the last 100 years?**

8 **VOCABULARY IN CONTEXT**

a **Watch the clips from the TED Talk. Choose the correct meaning of the words and phrases.** ▶ 4.3

b **Answer the questions. Compare answers in pairs.**

1. Do you do any hobbies where there is a *risk* of hurting yourself?
2. What is the *combined* age of your family?
3. Do you ever want to do things that are *in conflict with* what you should be doing? What?
4. Have you ever *come up with* a way of making money? What?
5. Have you ever done any *damage* to another person's possessions?

CRITICAL THINKING Persuading

There are many ways that speakers can use to persuade their listeners to do things. They can:

- **a** describe personal experiences that others can relate to.
- **b** make it sound achievable.
- **c** offer choice and flexibility.
- **d** point out the personal benefits of doing it.
- **e** ask themselves and the audience questions.
- **f** ask listeners to imagine a situation.

9 **How does Graham try to persuade his audience? Match the excerpts with techniques (a–f) in the Critical Thinking box. Each excerpt may use more than one technique.**

1. Knowing what I know, why am I not a vegetarian?
2. Any of these angles should have been enough to convince me to go vegetarian. Yet, there I was—chk, chk, chk—tucking into a big old steak.
3. Imagine your last hamburger.
4. I'd commit to doing it later, and not surprisingly, later never came. Sound familiar?
5. I've been doing it for the last year, and it's great. It's called Weekday Veg.
6. On the weekend, your choice. Simple. If you want to take it to the next level...
7. It's okay to break it here and there.
8. Best of all, I'm healthier, I know that I'm going to live longer, and I've even lost a little weight.

10 **Work in pairs. Discuss the questions.**

1. Which of Graham's reasons for becoming a weekday vegetarian are the most convincing?
2. Would you consider becoming a weekday vegetarian (if you aren't already)? How easy or difficult do you think it would be? Why?
3. If you are a vegetarian, do you think part-time vegetarianism is a good thing?

CHALLENGE

Do a survey. Find out what other people in the class think about becoming a weekday vegetarian.

4E Future Plans

SPEAKING

1 **Listen to three people talking about something they would like to change in their life. Which speaker, João, Emily, or Kei, is not happy about:** 29

a money? **b** their home life? **c** their diet?

2 **Listen again. Which of the expressions in the Useful language box do you hear?** 29

3 **Work in pairs. Use expressions from the Useful language box to discuss some of your hopes and goals.**

4 **Look at these instructions for helping other people achieve their goals. What goals from Activity 3 could a classmate help you with?**

1 Ask them to describe the problem as they see it. Ask what they want to change. Make sure they say exactly what their goal is, (e.g., not *eat less chocolate*, but *eat no more than one bar of chocolate a day*).
2 Ask them what is stopping them from achieving their goal.
3 Ask them to set a time limit for their goal. How long do they need to achieve their goal?
4 Together, talk about what they will do to achieve their goal. Ask them to list the advantages of achieving their goal and to commit to them.

5 **Work in pairs. Follow the instructions and take turns helping each other to achieve the goals you identified in Activity 4.**

- You want to eat more healthily. (What do you want to cut down on?)
- You think you and your family should eat more organic food, but your parents say it's expensive.
- You want to give up a bad habit, (e.g., biting your nails, drinking soft drinks).
- You don't get along with someone and want to have a better relationship.
- You want to travel (where to?) but need to save money for the trip. You find it hard to save money.

Useful language

Talking about hopes and goals

I expect to...
I think I might...
I'd really like to...
I'm aiming to have... by next month.
I'm interested in -ing.
I'm looking forward to -ing.
I'm thinking about / of -ing.
In the long / short term, I'm going to / hoping to / planning to...

La Boqueria food market, Barcelona, Spain

WRITING A social media update

6 Work in pairs. Look at the types of trips and discuss the questions.

a biking vacation	a cooking vacation	a photography expedition
a school trip	a volunteering trip	

1 What activities would you expect to do on these trips?
2 Which trip would you prefer to go on? Why?

7 Read the social media update on page 150. Which of these activities has Lali already done? Which is she hoping to do? Which is she going to do?

1 **get to** Leh *already done*
2 **quickly visit** the Red Fort
3 **walk around** Delhi streets
4 **travel slowly** between Delhi and Leh
5 learn to cook **nice** food
6 go **walking**
7 **talk to** people for a project
8 **see** a festival

8 **WRITING SKILL** Interesting language

a Read the update on page 150 again. Find words that Lali uses instead of the words in bold in Activity 7. Why does she use these words?

b Find the words in the update that Lali uses instead of these words.
1 big (line 2)
2 hot (line 3)
3 cooler (line 4)
4 tiring (line 5)
5 very (line 6)

9 Choose one of the trips below, or a trip you would like to take one day, and plan a social media update.

- a trip to a region in your country with its own special local cuisine
- a visit to the house of a friend or relative where you tried a new dish
- a trip abroad when you ate some interesting food

10 Write your social media update. Use phrases from the Useful language box. Make it interesting to read.

- Is it a vacation, expedition, school trip, or some other type of trip?
- What have you already done?
- What are you going to do? What else are you hoping to do or see?

11 Read your classmates' updates. Whose trips sound the most interesting? Whose food sounds the most delicious?

Useful language

Writing a social media update

We finally… after…
What a beautiful place / long journey!
It's such a / an adjective + noun *(noisy city, huge country).*
The food was so + adjective *(tasty, spicy, fresh, etc.).*
The weather's wonderful / boiling / freezing.
I'm hoping to…
I want to… while I'm here.
We might… if there's time.

5 Work

IN THIS UNIT, YOU...

- talk about jobs and describe working life.
- read about a real-life superpower.
- learn about jobs that no longer exist.
- watch a TED Talk about finding the best person for a job.
- write a job application letter.

A painter works on a colorful underpass in Munich, Germany.

5A New Ways of Working

VOCABULARY Describing work

1 What skills, abilities, and personal qualities do people need to work successfully in the 21st century? Is it more than just qualifications?

2 Work in pairs. Think of a job:

1. that is popular, so the job market is **competitive**.
2. in which you need to be **flexible** (able to adapt to changing situations).
3. that's **well paid** (you get a good salary).
4. **in the** construction **industry**.
5. where employees **work long hours** (50 hours a week or more).
6. that you would find very **stressful**.
7. that has good **career prospects**.
8. in which you would be **in charge of** many people (responsible for them).
9. that is physically **demanding**, so you need to be healthy.
10. that needs **creative** people with new ideas and new ways of doing things.

3 Use the words and phrases in bold in Activity 2 to complete the paragraph.

A survey about the reasons people leave their jobs shows some surprising results. You might think that people want more money, so they move to jobs that are (1) ____________ or prefer an easy life, but in fact this is not always the case. Many employees are happy to (2) ____________ in (3) ____________ jobs, where they are (4) ____________ large teams, working with important clients. In return, they want exciting (5) ____________ in their chosen (6) ____________. Work only becomes (7) ____________ if employers refuse to listen to their workers' needs or don't trust them with responsibility. For example, employees with a long commute may want more (8) ____________ working hours. The lesson for business? To keep good employees, you need to trust them and listen to them.

4 Put the lines in order, 1–9. The first and last lines have been done for you.

a I've always wanted to **work in** *1*
b **charge of** the boys' football teams. It wasn't a very **well-paid**
c **for** organizing a football tournament. Since that job, I've never been **out**
d **work** at the sports center, where I was **in**
e **job** as a coach. I'm currently **working**
f **job,** but it was very satisfying—I was **responsible**
g **of work.** Now I have got **a full-time**
h **the sports industry**. I got qualified as a personal trainer and got **part-time**
i **on** a fitness program for one of my clients who is a professional athlete. *9*

5 Work in pairs. Discuss the difference between these terms.

1. *part-time* and *temporary* work
2. to work *in* something and to work *on* something
3. to have a *full-time job* and to *work long hours*

6 **MY PERSPECTIVE**

Write about the career path you would like to take. Work in pairs and compare your plans. Who has the clearest idea of what they want to do?

I'm not sure what industry I'd like to work in yet, but I'm looking for a well-paid job that tests my abilities…

LISTENING

7 Work in pairs. Imagine you are a company manager. Which of these ideas would make your employees most productive? Put them in order with 1 as the best idea.

a Give employees a share of the company.
b Give everyone a day every month to volunteer for a charity.
c Let workers choose their work hours.
d Let everyone decide if they want to work from home or in the office.
e Let each person decide when to take vacations.

8 Listen to a podcast about the world of work. Which of the ideas in Activity 7 are mentioned? Which employer uses them, Hamdi Ulukaya or Jenny Biggam? 30

9 Listen again. Complete each excerpt with the missing verb. 30

1 Ulukaya started the business a few years ago, and it has ___gone on___ to become a multibillion-dollar company.
2 Does he just __________ to be nice, or is this actually good management?
3 He __________ feeling grateful to his workers for helping him start the business.
4 Do you think he might __________ giving so much of the company away?
5 Jenny Biggam decided to __________ treating her workers like children.
6 They are __________ to make coming to work a happier experience.
7 What kind of boss would you like? Don't __________ to call in and tell us!

GRAMMAR Verb patterns: verb + *-ing* or infinitive with *to*

10 Look at the completed sentences in Activity 9. Are the verbs you wrote followed by *-ing* or the infinitive?

Verb patterns: verb + *-ing* or infinitive with *to*

a *Do you think other companies will* ***go on treating*** *their workers the same?*
b *Making work enjoyable* ***means creating*** *a more productive company.*
c *Some managers* ***remember to show*** *their employees how much they appreciate their work.*
d *I* ***regret to inform*** *you that we can't afford to employ you anymore. I'm so sorry.*
e *I* ***stopped to buy*** *a coffee on the way to work.*
f *If it's taking so long to get to the office,* ***try working*** *from home for a few days.*
g *Hamdi Ulukaya will never* ***forget making*** *his first million dollars.*

Check page 136 for more information and practice.

11 Work in pairs. Look at the verbs in bold in the Grammar box. Compare them with the sentences in Activity 9. Discuss how their meanings change.

go on + *infinitive with to means "to do something after doing something else"*

go on + -ing *means "to continue"*

12 Complete the paragraph with the correct form of the verbs.

Sometimes being a good boss means (1) ____________ (give up) important personal things. I remember (2) ____________ (hear) about a company that lost a lot of money. If they wanted the company to go on (3) ____________ (do) business, they had to stop (4) ____________ (employ) some of the workers. But the director of the company didn't want to say to some of his employees, "I regret (5) ____________ (tell) you that we have to let you go." He wanted (6) ____________ (keep) everyone employed and motivated. So, he tried (7) ____________ (talk) to the workers. Together, they decided to reduce their salaries and to give up paid vacations. He didn't forget (8) ____________ (include) himself in the cuts. In fact, he remembered (9) ____________ (lead) by example and took the biggest salary cut of all. The company went on (10) ____________ (survive) the bad times and is now doing very well.

13 Complete the topics with the correct form of the verbs. Choose three or four of the topics and make notes about them. Discuss your notes in pairs.

1 something you meant ____________ (do) this morning
2 a mistake you regret ____________ (make)
3 the job you'll go on ____________ (do) in the future
4 an item of clothing you've tried ____________ (wear)
5 a bad habit you've stopped ____________ (do)
6 something you never remember ____________ (do), which annoys your family
7 a person you'll never forget ____________ (meet)
8 something you forgot ____________ (do) which meant ____________ (do) a lot more work later
9 a day you remember ____________ (enjoy) when you were a very young child
10 a sport or game you tried ____________ (do) but found too hard

14 **MY PERSPECTIVE**

Work in pairs. Discuss the questions.

1 What do the companies described in this lesson have in common?
2 Which company would you prefer to work for? Why?
3 What hopes do you have about the places you will work at in the future?

A worker checks her smartphone sitting on a swing in the offices of PT Tokopedia in Indonesia.

5B An Unusual Job

VOCABULARY BUILDING Ways of seeing

1 **Read the sentences (1–7). Underline a verb related to seeing. Then match the verbs with their definitions (a–g).**

1 The police spotted him leaving the parking lot in a van. *f*
2 She stole from three stores and they caught her on camera.
3 He only glanced at the woman but he knew who she was immediately.
4 I waved at her but I don't think she noticed me because she didn't stop to say hello.
5 The person in the photo was identified as Adam Smith.
6 Officers observed people leaving and entering the building entrance throughout the night.
7 I recognized an old friend at the train station, even though I haven't seen her for years.

a became aware of someone or something
b looked quickly at someone or something
c saw someone and was able to say who they were
d knew who the person was because you had seen them before
e saw someone doing something wrong
f saw someone or something because you were looking for them
g watched someone or something carefully in order to learn information

2 **Rewrite the sentences, replacing all the words in bold with the correct form of one verb from Activity 1.**

1 I didn't **know it was** Christophe at first—he's grown a beard since the last time I saw him.
2 I only need to **look** at a phone number **briefly** and I can remember it.
3 How many of these people can you **put a name to**?
4 I looked for you at the park but I didn't **see** you. Where were you?
5 If my parents **see** me playing games when I should be doing homework, they take my laptop away.
6 He learned the job by **watching and studying** what the other staff members did.
7 I **saw** that the window was open when I heard a loud noise outside.

READING

3 **Work in pairs. Discuss the questions.**

1 Do you find it easy to recognize people you have only met once?
2 How good are you at remembering names?
3 Can you recognize people from their voice?

4 **Read the article. Complete the descriptions of super-recognizers.**

1 To be a super-recognizer, you must be very good at ________________.
2 Super-recognizers work mostly ________________.

5 **Read the article again. Are the sentences *true* or *false*?**

1 The article mentions two problems with CCTV.
2 One answer to these problems is to install more cameras.
3 Super-recognizers don't need to look at a face for long in order to identify it.
4 The police use super-recognizers to prevent violent situations from developing.
5 If you are good at recognizing faces, you will probably have a good general memory.
6 To become a super-recognizer, you need years of training.

6 **Work in pairs. Discuss the questions.**

1 Would you like to be a super-recognizer? Why?
2 Do you think it is possible to develop your skills at recognizing faces, or is it something that you can't change?

CRITICAL THINKING Exaggerating

Sometimes writers exaggerate (describe things so that they seem a lot better / worse / more important than they really are) to make their point. It's important to be able to recognize when the author is exaggerating and when they are stating facts. For example, to say that there were lots of people at a party, you might say that there were *hundreds* of people, when in fact, there were not that many.

7 **Work in groups. Which of these excerpts from the article are probably exaggerating facts? Why does the writer do this in each case?**

1 You are being watched.
2 Many large cities have thousands of security cameras.
3 ...people with the amazing ability to remember thousands of faces.
4 Collins was able to identify a total of 190 troublemakers.
5 Collins admits he can't even remember a shopping list.
6 ...if you're looking for a job where you are allowed to watch TV all day...

8 **Work in pairs. Discuss the questions.**

1 Do you think the job name "super-recognizer" is an exaggeration? Why?
2 Think about a job you would like to do. Write three sentences to exaggerate it. Tell your partner. Whose job sounds most interesting?

A Real-Life, Crime-Fighting Superpower!

31 You are being watched.

Next time you're in a busy city center, look up. The chances are there will be a CCTV * camera somewhere nearby. Many large cities have thousands of security cameras: on buildings, next to roads, even in public buses and trains. They are supposed to prevent crime, but there is a problem. No matter how many cameras are in place to catch people breaking the law, criminals can't always be identified. For one thing, the police can only put a name to a face if they have a file on that person. Also, even if the criminal is known to the police, the CCTV image is often of such a poor quality that it is impossible to recognize them.

Impossible for most people, that is, but not if you're a "super-recognizer." These are people with the amazing ability to remember thousands of faces and pick them out from a crowded street, even if they only see them for a moment. At soccer games, for example, the police must spot troublemakers immediately, before they start fighting, and this means acting fast. The 152 super-recognizers employed by the London police can do this, and they get results.

The police didn't need to worry, for example, when there was trouble in the streets in 2011. Officers sat in CCTV control centers, observing the scenes on TV and picking out known criminals for their colleagues on the ground. Just one member of the team, Gary Collins, was able to identify a total of 190 troublemakers! The police later arrested many of them; others weren't allowed to go back on the streets.

You might think that with a memory this good, super-recognizers must be good at remembering lots of things, but Collins admits he can't even remember a shopping list. "I have to write that down," he says. Scientists believe that the ability to recognize faces is different from other kinds of memory, and uses a special part of the brain. Damage to that area of the brain can cause "face blindness," where people can't recognize faces at all. Having said that, most of us are really good at recognizing faces. We are even able to identify people we know from the back of their heads and from the way they walk, something computers are unlikely to do in the near future. However, we can't all do it as well as professionals like Gary Collins, who do it better than 99 percent of the population.

You might also be in the top one percent and not even know it. So, if you're looking for a job where you are allowed to watch TV all day, you should find out whether you're a super-recognizer and join the police!

CCTV *closed-circuit television—a camera system used for watching activity in some places*

5C Job Evolution

GRAMMAR Present and past modals

1 Work in pairs. Discuss the questions.

1. The concept of super-recognizers did not exist a few years ago. Make a list of new jobs that were not around until very recently.
2. What jobs from the past no longer exist, or are disappearing? Make another list.
3. Look at your lists. What do you think "job evolution" means?

2 Look at the sentences in the Grammar box. Which sentence describes:

1. obligation?
2. no obligation?
3. permission?
4. prohibition?
5. ability or possibility?
6. no ability or possibility?
7. advice?
8. deduction or speculation?

Present and past modals

a *At soccer games, the police* ***must*** *spot troublemakers immediately.*

b *Gary Collins* ***was able to*** *identify 190 troublemakers.*

c *If you're looking for a job where you* ***are allowed to*** *watch TV all day…*

d *…you* ***should*** *find out whether you're a super-recognizer.*

e *…others* ***weren't allowed to*** *go back on the streets.*

f *"Face blindness"… where people* ***can't*** *recognize faces at all.*

g *The police* ***didn't need to*** *worry when there was trouble in the streets.*

h *With a memory this good, super-recognizers* ***must*** *be good at remembering lots of things.*

Check page 136 for more information and practice.

3 What sentences in the Grammar box refer to the present? Which refer to the past?

4 Complete the table with the words in bold from the sentences that refer to the present.

Meaning	Present
obligation	*have to,* (1) ________ *, need to*
no obligation	*don't have to, don't need to*
permission	*can,* (2) ________
prohibition	*must not, can't, isn't / aren't allowed to*
ability or possibility	*can, is / are able to*
no ability or possibility	(3) ________ *, isn't / aren't able to*
advice	(4) ________ *, ought to*
deduction or speculation	(5) ________ *, may, might, can't*

5 Match these past forms with a meaning from the table in Activity 4.

didn't have to *managed to* *needed to* *weren't able to*

6 Complete the paragraphs about jobs that no longer exist.

can	can't	couldn't	don't have to
had to	have to	needed	shouldn't

They say that the world is changing faster now than at any time in history. We (1) ____________ do things that were unimaginable just a few years ago. Twenty years ago, you (2) ____________ send photos from your phone, for example, and you (3) ____________ carry a map before GPS existed. These changes affect everything. Smartphones mean people (4) ____________ buy cameras anymore, so camera companies (5) ____________ survive and employees (6) ____________ find new jobs. Technology is changing the way we live, but also the way we work.

Many professions are changing or disappearing entirely due to technology, but you (7) ____________ think that job evolution is a recent thing. Many old jobs you have probably never heard of (8) ____________ to make way for new ones because of advances in technology.

7 Work in pairs. Look at the photos. What jobs do you think these people are doing?

8 Read the article to find out what the jobs are. Then choose the correct options to complete the sentences.

Here are two jobs from the past we have forgotten existed:

Icemen and icewomen (1) *had to / weren't allowed to* deliver heavy blocks of ice to wealthy families who (2) *are able to / could* afford to buy it to keep their food cold. This was before every home had a fridge. If you (3) *didn't need to / couldn't* buy ice, you (4) *had to / didn't manage to* find another way to keep your food fresh.

In the UK, if you (5) *must / needed to* wake up early, you (6) *could / ought to* pay a knocker-up. Their job was to wake people up by tapping on bedroom windows with a long stick. They (7) *didn't manage to / weren't allowed to* leave until they were sure their customers were awake. But why is it that the knocker-up (8) *couldn't / didn't have to* be awakened?

9 Complete the paragraphs with one word in each blank. Contractions count as one word.

Until very recently, there were many jobs you (1) ____________ do, that we're all (2) ____________ to do nowadays thanks to computers. Travel agents still exist of course, but there (3) ____________ be many people who still book their vacations the old-fashioned way. The internet means we (4) ____________ pay a professional to book our airline tickets or hotels.

Is it possible that some very common jobs may soon disappear? Companies like Google have shown that driverless vehicles (5) ____________ work, but at the moment the law says that automated cars and buses aren't (6) ____________ to drive on most public roads. However, if technology can make them safe, they (7) ____________ be allowed on the roads. In fact, some people think that we (8) ____________ to replace all drivers, for safety reasons. Perhaps one day we will look back and wonder how we (9) ____________ to drive safely without robots at the wheel!

10 **CHOOSE** Choose one of the following activities.

1 Work in groups to play a game. Think of a job. Let the other people in the group take turns asking ten *yes/no* questions to guess the job.

A *Do you need to travel long distances?*
B *Yes.*
A *Are you a pilot?*
B *No, but I do have to work in an airplane.*

2 Work in pairs. Together, choose a job. Then, on your own, write as many sentences as you can in two minutes about things that you have to do in this job. Compare lists. Score one point for each obligation that you both wrote. Score two points for obligations that your partner doesn't have. The winner is the player with the most points.

3 Find out about another job that has disappeared. Write a paragraph about it.

AUTHENTIC LISTENING SKILLS

Understanding contrasts

We often compare and contrast ideas when we are explaining things. When you listen, try to identify these contrasts. Speakers often show that you are about to hear contrasting ideas by:

- using words like *but; however; not x, y; in spite of this; on the other hand*, etc.
- repeating structures, replacing some words with their opposites.

1 **Read the Authentic Listening Skills box. Then listen and complete these excerpts. Which contrasting technique does Regina use?** 32

1 A series of odd jobs ______________ indicate inconsistency, lack of focus, unpredictability. Or, it ______________ signal a committed struggle against obstacles.

2 Graduating from an elite university takes a lot of hard work and sacrifice. ______________ if your whole life has been engineered toward success, how will you handle the tough times?

2 **Listen to two more sentences from the talk. Complete the sentences, then practice reading them with intonation that shows the contrasts.** 33

1 If your whole life has been engineered toward success, how will you handle the tough times? . . . But on the flip side, what happens when ______________ ?

2 They don't think they are who they are in spite of adversity, they ______________ .

WATCH

3 **Which of these reasons do you think are important for choosing candidates for a job? Put them in order from most to least important.**

a their personality
b their qualifications
c their work experience
d how many jobs they have had in the past
e references from other employers
f the university they attended
g a sense of humor

4 **Watch Part 1 of the talk. Regina describes two types of candidates, A and B. Do these expressions belong to A, B, or both?** ▶ 5.1

1 destined for success
2 had to fight
3 Ivy League
4 job hopping
5 odd jobs
6 perfect résumé
7 qualified
8 state school
9 "the Scrapper"
10 "the Silver Spoon"

5 Work in pairs. Would you hire the Scrapper or the Silver Spoon? Why?

6 Watch Part 2 of the talk. Choose the best option. ▶ 5.2

Regina has learned that a resume with lots of jobs on it doesn't always show a person who is not (1) *focused* / *well educated*. She believes that the Scrapper should have (2) *success* / *an interview*. For example, Steve Jobs (founder of Apple) (3) *had* / *didn't have* a good resume. He (4) *didn't finish* / *finished* college, had (5) *a few* / *many* different jobs, spent time abroad, and had dyslexia.

7 Watch Part 3 of the talk. Choose the options that are not true according to Regina. ▶ 5.3

1 Dyslexia, a learning difficulty that makes it hard to read and spell,
- **a** affected 35 percent of the entrepreneurs in one study.
- **b** was a problem that held entrepreneurs back.
- **c** meant entrepreneurs were better at listening and paying attention.

2 Scrappers
- **a** often don't feel that they are in control of their own lives.
- **b** are not scared by business challenges because they have dealt with much harder things.
- **c** can cope by seeing the funny side of difficult situations.

3 Regina
- **a** used to drive the president's assistant to work every day.
- **b** had a colleague in her first job who gave her good advice.
- **c** once worked as a singing waitress.

8 **VOCABULARY IN CONTEXT**

a Watch the clips from the TED Talk. Choose the correct meaning of the words and phrases. ▶ 5.4

b Think of an example for each of these things. Then work in pairs and compare your examples.
- a technical *term* used in a sport or hobby that you do
- an *assignment* that a teacher gave you that you enjoyed doing
- a situation that *turned out* better than you expected
- a skill that many people find tough but you think is a *piece of cake*
- a friend or family member who you know you can always *count on*

CHALLENGE

Regina says that successful entrepreneurs "don't think they are who they are in spite of adversity, they know they are who they are because of adversity." Work in groups and discuss the questions.

1 Have you ever experienced adversity?

2 Has adversity helped you become who you are?

3 Do you know anyone who has had to deal with adversity in their life?

5E Going for the Job

SPEAKING

1 Look at the photo. In some countries, students have part-time jobs like this while they are in school, and some work during vacations. Is this the same in your country?

2 Work in pairs. Look at the job ads on the left. Which job would you prefer? Why? What other types of jobs could you do to make money?

3 Listen to a job interview. Which job in Activity 2 is the interview for? Would you give Roberta the job? Why? 34

4 Listen again. Which expressions in the Useful language box do you hear? What does Roberta say after each one? 34

5 **PRONUNCIATION** Showing confidence

These are some tips to sound confident in conversation:

- Speak slowly.
- Avoid using filler phrases such as "I mean" and "well."
- Use an even tone of voice so your statements do not sound like questions.

a Listen to the sentences. Do the speakers sound confident or insecure? What makes the speakers sound insecure? 35

1 I'm very good at handling multiple projects.
2 I'm kind of good at handling multiple projects.
3 The graph shows a decrease in book sales.
4 The graph shows a decrease in book sales.

6 Work in pairs. Take turns interviewing each other for one of the jobs advertised in Activity 2. Use the phrases in the Useful language box and these questions.

- Can I ask you why you're interested in this job?
- What experience do you have that could be useful in the job?
- What personal skills do you have that you think would help you?
- Is there anything you want to ask me?

SANTA CRUZ FRUITS—summer workers needed in the Colchagua Valley

Would you like to work outdoors as part of our friendly team? Are you a hard-working person who wants to stay fit? Join this family-run fruit farm during our busy summer season. Good pay, and free fruit every day!

Part-time waiters at AquaParks

Popular water park looking for enthusiastic staff to work at our restaurant. No waiter experience necessary, but applicants must be polite and well dressed. Must speak English. Hours 11:30am to 4:00pm, Tuesday to Sunday. Openings now until September. Free entry to water park for family and friends.

Personal care assistant

50-year-old wheelchair user looking for a reliable caregiver during the summer while regular provider is on vacation. The right person will be happy to help with household tasks, such as cleaning and cooking, as well as grocery shopping, etc. Must be relaxed and happy and have a sense of humor. About five hours' work daily, with plenty of free time.

WRITING A cover letter

7 Read the cover letter on page 151. Which information (1–7) does Aya include?

1 details of when she is available to work
2 experience she has that is relevant to the job
3 her interests
4 personal qualities she thinks are relevant to the job
5 her reasons for wanting the job
6 her reason for writing the letter
7 her academic degrees

8 **WRITING SKILL** Hedging

When you talk about your own positive qualities, it is important not to sound arrogant.

a **Find sentences in Aya's letter that give us the information below. How are the sentences in the letter different?**
1 I am perfectly qualified for the job.
2 I have a lot of experience.
3 I am an awesome cook.
4 I get along with everyone.
5 I am really smart, so I'm a fast learner.

b **Rewrite these sentences to sound less arrogant.**
1 My Chinese is perfect and I have a good level of Japanese.
2 I am an amazing driver.
3 My grade point average was impressive.
4 I had a lot of responsibility in my last job. I was basically in charge.
5 I am an extremely creative thinker.

9 Write a cover letter for one of the other jobs in Activity 2 or a job of your choice. Follow the organization and writing conventions of the letter on page 151.

10 Work in a group with students who applied for the same job. Read the other students' letters. Who is the best candidate?

Useful language

Talking about skills and personality
I'd say I was very…
I wouldn't say that I was…
I'm willing to…
I'm usually very good at…
I like to think I'm not afraid to…
I know I can sometimes…
I've had a lot of experience…
I'm working on…

Being positive about the job
I've always wanted to…
I think this job would give me…

Asking about the job
What does the job involve?
I was just wondering if I would have to…?
Are we allowed to…?

6 Superhuman

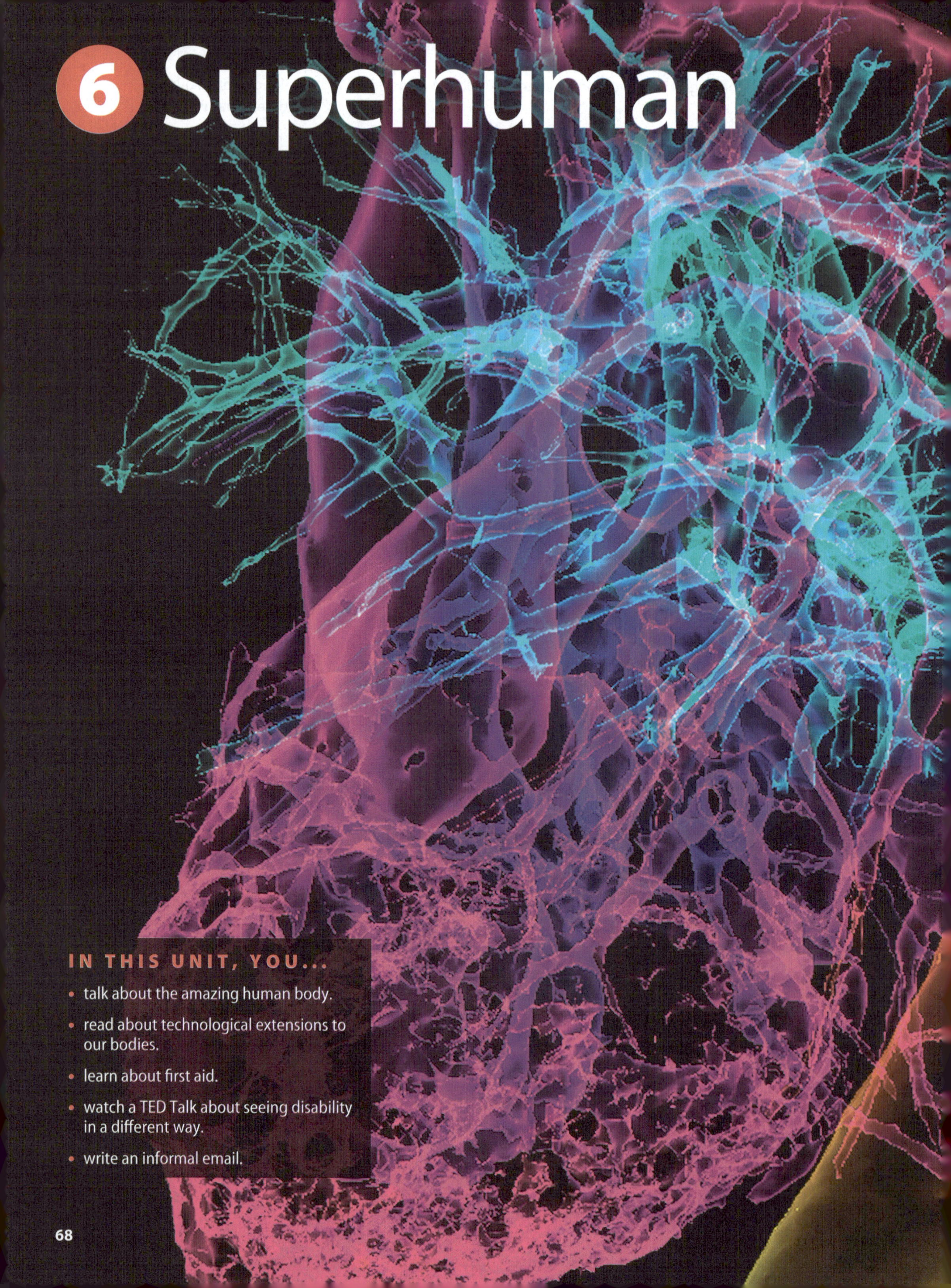

IN THIS UNIT, YOU...

- talk about the amazing human body.
- read about technological extensions to our bodies.
- learn about first aid.
- watch a TED Talk about seeing disability in a different way.
- write an informal email.

6A Amazing Bodies

VOCABULARY The human body

1 Do you know any interesting facts about the human body?

2 Use the numbers in the boxes to answer the questions in the quiz. There is one number in each box that you don't need.

1	5	27	70	100	18,000	96,000	86,000,000,000

The heart and blood The heart moves blood and oxygen around the body.

1 How much blood passes through an adult heart each time it beats? (ml)
2 How long are all the blood vessels in the body if you put them all in a line? (km)
3 What percentage of the oxygen we breathe in do the lungs absorb? (%)

The brain and senses These tell us about our environment.

4 How many cells are in the human brain?
5 What percentage of the brain do we use? (%)
6 What is the surface area of the skin of an adult male? (sense of touch) (cm^2)
7 How many areas are there on the human tongue? (sense of taste)

9	17	50	206	300–1,000	435

The bones and skeleton The skeleton supports the body.

8 What is the difference in your height if you measure how tall you are in the morning and again in the evening? (mm)
9 How many bones are there in an adult body?
10 What is the world record for the number of bones one person has broken?

Food and digestion Digestion is how our bodies get nutrients from food.

11 How far does food travel through the body? (meters)
12 How many different types of bacteria live in our digestive system?

3 Complete the sentences with these pairs of words.

beat + skin	blood + oxygen	bone + bacteria
breathe + lung	muscles + tongue	skeleton + cell

1 I enjoyed the Biology exam. We had to label the bones on the human ______________ and draw a red blood ______________ .
2 She has a cough and she's finding it hard to ______________ . She may have a ______________ infection.
3 The doctor says I've broken the ______________ , but she's more worried that ______________ have gotten into the cut.
4 It isn't true that the ______________ vessels under your skin look blue because they don't contain much ______________ .
5 I know there are several places where you can feel your heart ______________ under your ______________ , but I can never find them!
6 There are eight ______________ in the ______________ . They work together so we can speak and eat.

4 **MY PERSPECTIVE**

Work in groups. Which facts in Activity 2 did you find most interesting?

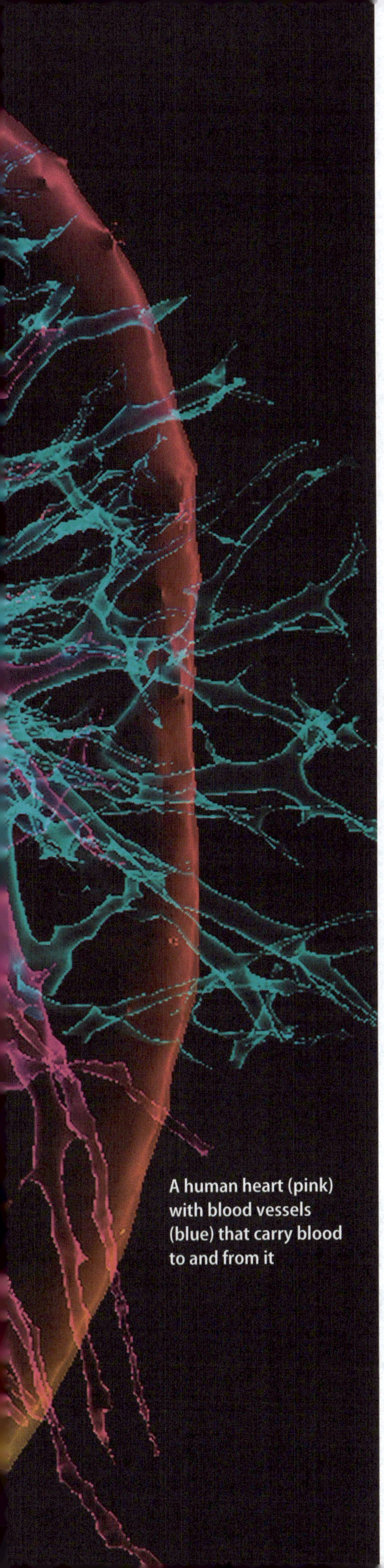

A human heart (pink) with blood vessels (blue) that carry blood to and from it

LISTENING

5 Listen to a radio show about the human body. Which areas do the speakers talk about? 36

- the heart and blood
- the brain and senses
- the bones and skeleton
- food and digestion

6 Listen again. Choose the correct option (a–c) to complete the sentences. 36

1 The backbone has changed over time…
a so we can travel long distances.
b so it can hold our head up.
c so we can run, climb, and swim better.

2 If you have a healthy diet, you may have ______ bacteria in your body.
a more
b less
c no

3 People who live in the Andes and the Himalayas…
a breathe in more air than most people.
b show that evolution can happen quickly.
c carry more oxygen in their blood.

7 Work in pairs. Discuss the questions.

1 Do you walk more than, less than, or about the same as most people you know?
2 How do you take care of your body (e.g., your bones, heart, lungs, and skin)? What about your diet?

GRAMMAR Zero and first conditional

8 Look at the sentences in the Grammar box. Which are talking about possible future situations? What are the other sentences describing?

Zero and first conditional

a *Our bodies* ***don't look*** *very impressive if we* ***compare*** *them with other animals.*

b *If you* ***listen*** *to today's show, you'****ll find*** *out why the human body is extraordinary.*

c *Unless you* ***take*** *the car everywhere, you* ***might walk*** *up to 115,000 miles in your lifetime.*

d *You* ***will have*** *difficulty breathing if you* ***go*** *to high altitudes.*

e *If you* ***think*** *evolution always happens very slowly,* ***think*** *again.*

Check page 138 for more information and practice.

9 Look at the Grammar box again. Complete each sentence about zero and first conditional sentences.

1 Zero conditional sentences talk about *general facts / possible future situations.*
2 First conditional sentences talk about *general facts / possible future situations.*
3 Conditional sentences have *one clause / two clauses.*
4 Zero and first conditional sentences have a *present / future* tense in the *if*-clause.
5 In zero conditional sentences, we usually use the *simple present / future with "will"* in the result clause (e.g., sentences ______ and ______).
6 In first conditional sentences, we use a *present / future* form in the result clause (e.g., sentences ______ and ______).

Danuru Sherpa uses his iPhone to talk to his family at Ama Dablam Camp 1, Nepal.

7 Not all conditional sentences use *if. However / Unless*, which means *if not*, can also be used.

8 In zero or first conditional sentences, an imperative, (e.g., sentence ______), or a modal verb, (e.g., sentence ______) can also be used.

10 Choose the correct options to complete the paragraph.

There's so much health advice these days, how do you know what to believe? They say that if (1) *you're / you will be* worried about your heart, you (2) *should / will* exercise every day. But then again, you (3) *might / will* hurt yourself if you (4) *may do / do* sports. And they said that (5) *if / unless* you (6) *avoid / might avoid* eating fatty foods, you (7) *get / will get* heart disease. But now it's sugar we should be worried about! (8) *If / Unless* we (9) *continue / will continue* to drink sugary drinks, (10) *do / will* we all get diabetes? I'm so confused!

11 Complete the advice with the correct form of the verbs.

1 You ______________ (get) sick if you ______________ (keep) having late nights.

2 Broken bones ______________ (heal) themselves if patients ______________ (not move) them for several weeks.

3 That cut looks bad. If you ______________ (not clean) it well, you ______________ (get) an infection.

4 Have you cooked that chicken long enough? You ______________ (not kill) the dangerous bacteria unless you ______________ (cook) it well.

5 Diseases ______________ (spread) easily unless people ______________ (wash) their hands regularly.

6 If you still ______________ (have) a headache tomorrow, ______________ (make) an appointment with the doctor.

12 Work in groups. What should you do if:

1 you cut your finger?

2 you have a high temperature (over 28° C or 100° F)?

3 a classmate feels sick?

4 a cyclist is hit by a car and cannot move?

5 you find someone in the street who is not breathing?

13 Work in groups. Imagine you are going camping, far from medical help. Plan your first aid kit. What will you include? Why?

We'll need adhesive bandages if people cut themselves.

6B More Than Human?

READING

1 Read the definition of a *cyborg*. What cyborg technology can you think of, fictional and real?

> cyborg (n.) *a person who has added extra tools or machines to themselves so that they can improve their own abilities*

2 Read the article. Choose the best summary.

1 Cyborg technology is already used to help people with disabilities.
2 In the future, everyone will have cyborg superpowers.
3 Surprising as it may seem, cyborg technology is not new, and not unusual.

3 Read the article again. Answer the questions. Then compare your answers with a partner.

1 Why doesn't Michael Chorost like the word *cyborg*?
2 What unusual ability does Michael Chorost have? Why is it good?
3 Hugh Herr lost his legs. What two unexpected advantages of this are mentioned?
4 What technologies that many people already use does the writer mention?
5 How is writing a "cyborg technology"?

4 **MY PERSPECTIVE**

Work in pairs. Discuss the questions.

1 In what ways are you a cyborg?
2 What jobs that your brain could do have you given to technology?
3 Are there any disadvantages of using technology as an extension of our abilities?

VOCABULARY BUILDING Verbs describing ability

5 There are several verbs in the article that mean *make something easier/possible* or *difficult/impossible* or *unnecessary*. Use the clues to find the verbs in the article.

1 a ___ ___ ___ ___ (paragraph 1)
2 l ___ ___ ___ (paragraph 2)
3 e ___ ___ ___ ___ ___ (paragraph 4)
4 h ___ ___ ___ (paragraph 5)
5 p ___ ___ ___ ___ ___ ___ (paragraph 5)
6 k ___ ___ ___ (paragraph 5)
7 s ___ ___ ___ ___ (paragraph 6)

6 Match the verbs from Activity 5 with their verb patterns. Use the article to help you.

make something easier/possible
(1) ____________ / (2) ____________ + someone + *do*
(3) ____________ / (4) ____________ + someone + *to do*

make something difficult/impossible or unnecessary
(5) ____________ / (6) ____________ /
(7) ____________ + someone + *from* + *-ing*

7 Put the words in the correct order. Add *to* and *from* if necessary.

1 enable / glasses / people with poor eyesight / see better
2 allows / go to school / have a cold / if / this medicine / you / you
3 disabled people / helps / the robot suit / walk again
4 doing exercise / prevents / gaining weight / you
5 becoming addicted / hopes / will stop / the advertisement / the government / to cigarettes / young people
6 having to run / in the rain / treadmills / save / you
7 if / know / lets / the nurses / stops breathing / this machine / the patient

8 List six advantages of smartphones. Can you think of any disadvantages? Compare your list with a partner.

They let you stay in touch with your friends when they're far away.

CRITICAL THINKING Bold claims

9 Work in groups. Read about bold claims. Then discuss the questions.

> A bold claim is a statement that something is true, even if many people do not agree. For a bold claim to convince readers, it needs to have a good argument for why it is true.

1 The article suggests that everyone is a cyborg. What is the writer's argument for claiming this is true?
2 How could you argue that someone who wears glasses or carries a cell phone is not a cyborg? Do you think "we are all cyborgs"?
3 Which of these other statements, if any, are bold claims?
   a Technology is very much part of who Michael Chorost and Hugh Herr are.
   b The first time a human used a rock as a tool to open a nut, they created an extension of their hand.
   c Writing is a cyborg extension of the brain.

A World of Cyborgs

37 Without technology, Michael Chorost wouldn't hear anything. Electronic implants* in his brain allow him to hear enough to have a phone conversation. Technically, Michael is a cyborg—part man, part machine—but he doesn't like that term: "it brings up images of superhuman abilities." In science fiction, the cyborg is stronger than normal humans; think about Robocop or Darth Vader, for instance. "The future is not about giving our bodies ways to do things they already do," Chorost says. "It's about giving our bodies entirely new things."

In Michael's case, for example, his disability has an unusual benefit. Thanks to his implants, he's able to turn his hearing off. This lets him concentrate better. If only the rest of us could do that!

Hugh Herr lost both legs in a mountaineering accident, but that didn't stop him from climbing. Artificial legs offer advantages he wouldn't have if he had his old legs. His small artificial feet can get into smaller gaps in the rock. And in normal life, when he's feeling small, he can make himself taller! Don't you wish you could change your height? Now Herr is working on how brain cells can communicate directly with electronics to control muscles.

This may sound like science fiction, but in a sense, we are all cyborgs, and always have been. Technology is very much part of who Michael Chorost and Hugh Herr are, but just because the rest of us don't have implants doesn't mean our gadgets* aren't an extension of our bodies. Would it make any difference if our smartphones were in our arms in the future, for example? The first time a human used a rock as a tool to open a nut, they created an extension of their hand. And glasses and contact lenses are technologies that many of us wear most of the time, and which enable us to see better.

Some experts claim that modern gadgets such as smartphones are different because they help us extend our brains, not just our bodies. For example, they prevent us from forgetting our friends' birthdays, they do difficult calculations for us, and they keep us from getting lost. However, haven't we been using technology to do our thinking for us for hundreds of years? Take a calculation like 312 ÷ 13. I'm sure you can do it in your head, but if you weren't able to, you could use a calculator, or you could also use a pen and paper if you needed to.

Writing is a cyborg extension of the brain that saves us from having to keep a lot of information in our memory, and we've had it for a long time! So, next time you hear someone saying that cyborg technology is the future, tell them it's the past and present, too.

implants *things that have been put into the body in a medical operation*
gadgets *small machines with a particular purpose*

Hugh Herr can climb with his artificial legs.

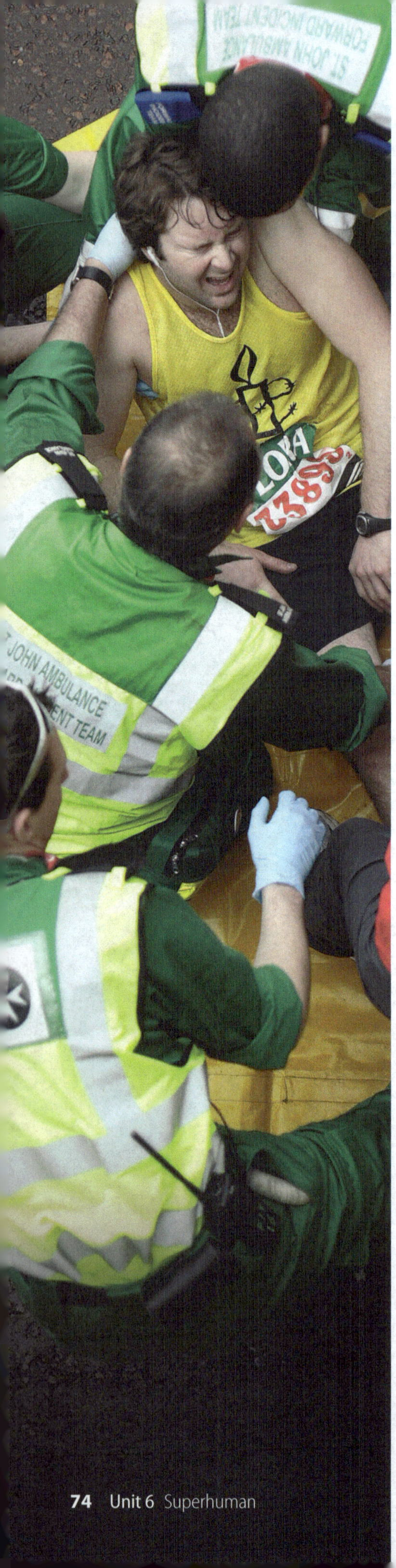

6C First Responders

GRAMMAR Second conditional

1 Work in pairs. Look at the photo, then discuss the questions.

1 What is the emergency?
2 What skills is the team using to deal with it?
3 Do you think you could handle an emergency like this? What first aid skills do you know?

2 Listen to the radio report. Complete the table. 38

	Anmol	Natasha
What was the problem?		
How did they help?		

3 Read this sentence and answer the questions.

More lives would be saved if everyone learned first aid at school.

1 Does everyone learn first aid at school?
2 Do we save all the lives that we could?
3 What verb form is used after *if*?
4 Is the situation in the past?

4 Read the Grammar box. Then choose the correct options to complete the paragraphs.

Second conditional

a *If I* ***took*** *a first aid class, I* ***would*** *know what to do.*
b *Anmol* ***wouldn't*** *know what to do in emergencies if they* ***didn't*** *teach first aid at her school.*
c ***If only*** *more of us* ***knew*** *what to do.*
d *The Red Cross* ***wishes*** *more schools* ***taught*** *these essential skills.*
e ***Could*** *you help if you* ***saw*** *someone in trouble?*
f *If it* ***weren't*** *for you, she* ***might*** *not be alive.*

Check page 138 for more information and practice.

The second conditional describes (1) *imaginary / real* situations, or situations which are (2) *likely / unlikely* in the future. To form the second conditional, use *would* in the (3) *result clause / if clause* and the simple past in the (4) *result clause / if clause*.

Would can sometimes be replaced with (5) *can / could* or (6) *may / might*.

If only or *I wish* can be used when the speaker wants a present situation to be different. These are followed by verbs in the (7) *past / present* form.

5 Choose the correct options to complete this first aid advice.

What would you do if you (1) *saw / see* someone in trouble in the street? Do you wish you (2) *knew / know* more about first aid? Here are a few tips…

First, don't feel that just because you're not a doctor, you can't help. If it (3) *were / would be* you in trouble, (4) *didn't / wouldn't* you want someone just to hold your hand and sit with you? Stay calm and try not to panic.

If you (5) *found / might find* someone who was unconscious (i.e., you couldn't wake him up), you (6) *first / would first* need to check that his airway (mouth and throat) was clear, that he was breathing and that he (7) *have / had* a heartbeat. Look up "Airway, Breathing, Circulation—ABC first aid" to find out more. If you had a phone with you, the second thing to do (8) *was / would be* to call an ambulance.

Finally, do more than just read about it. (9) *Can / Would* you trust doctors if all their medical knowledge (10) *was / would be* from books? Take a first aid class. If someone's life was in your hands one day, you (11) *might / would* have to act fast. Don't leave yourself thinking: (12) "*If / If only* I was a first responder!"

6 **PRONUNCIATION** *I wish* and *If only*

a Listen to the sentences. Underline the stressed words. 39

1. If only I knew what to do.
2. I wish I had a cell phone.
3. I wish I didn't have a cold.
4. I wish I could get to sleep at night.

b Write sentences starting with *I wish* and *If only* that are true for you.

1. an ability you wish you had
2. something you wish your parents let you do
3. a bad habit you wish a friend or family member didn't have
4. something you wish you could change about your town or country
5. something you wish you could do for someone else

c Compare your sentences with a partner. Practice saying them with the correct stress.

7 Complete the conversations with a suitable ending.

1 **A** Oh dear! Are you OK?
B No. I've cut my knee.
A Ooh, it looks bad! If only…

2 **A** I have a really bad earache today.
B Have you made an appointment to see the doctor?
A Not yet. If my mom…

3 **A** I feel sick. If only…
B Oh no! Sit down and have a drink of water.
A I wish…

8 Work in pairs. Practice the conversations.

9 **CHOOSE** Choose one of the following activities.

1. Find out as much as possible about local first aid classes (what you learn, when you can take them, etc.). Tell the class what you found.
2. Research what to do in one of these emergencies. Then write an information poster about it.

bleeding	broken bones	burns
choking	insect stings	a sprained ankle

3. Imagine you are in an English-speaking environment and there is a medical emergency. Role play the situation in pairs or small groups.

A lifeguard on Baga Beach in Goa, India

> “We see and discover the power and joy of seeing the world from exciting new perspectives.”

SUE AUSTIN

Read about Sue Austin and get ready to watch her TED Talk. ▶ 6.0

AUTHENTIC LISTENING SKILLS

Following the argument

Certain words and phrases help us follow the speaker's argument. For example:

Learning to play the game was difficult. ***However,*** *I really enjoyed it.* ***That's why*** *I decided to keep going.*

1 Read the Authentic Listening Skills box. Then listen to an excerpt from the TED Talk. Underline the words that help you follow the argument. 🎧 40

When I started using the wheelchair, it was a tremendous new freedom… But even though I had this new-found joy and freedom, people's reaction completely changed towards me… As a result, I knew I needed to make my own stories about this experience, new narratives to reclaim my identity.

2 Listen and complete two more excerpts. 🎧 41

1. ____________ ____________ I began to dive, in 2005, I realized scuba gear extends your range of activity in just the same way as a wheelchair does… ____________ ____________ ____________, "I wonder what'll happen if I put the two together?"
2. For me, the wheelchair becomes a vehicle for transformation. ____________ ____________ ____________ ____________ ____________, that because nobody's seen or heard of an underwater wheelchair before,… now you have this concept in your mind.

WATCH

3 Read the quote in Activity 1 again. Why do you think Sue describes using a wheelchair as freedom? What reaction do you think her wheelchair had from other people?

4 Watch Part 1 of the talk. Are these statements *true* or *false*? ▶ 6.1

1. At first, Sue didn't enjoy her wheelchair.
2. Other people felt that wheelchairs were a sign of a lack of freedom.
3. Sue didn't let what other people thought affect her.
4. Sue read a story that helped her to see things differently.

5 Watch Part 2 of the talk. Choose the correct option to complete the sentences. ▶ 6.2

1. With her wheelchair, Sue tried to communicate *happiness / strength* as well as freedom.
2. She used her wheelchair to create *music / visual art*.
3. The interest that other people took in Sue's work *excited / surprised* her.
4. Sue says that underwater scuba gear allows people to do things in more places. Wheelchairs are *different / no different*.
5. Sue wanted people to associate wheelchairs with *excitement and adventure / the underwater world*.
6. Sue plays the underwater video to show how *the wheelchair works / amazing her journey has been*.

6 Watch Part 3 of the talk. Which results of her underwater adventures does Sue mention? ▶ 6.3

1 Other people are inspired to challenge themselves.
2 Sue has become a good diver.
3 Wheelchair users can now buy an underwater wheelchair.
4 She has experienced physical freedom.
5 Sue's art makes people think about wheelchairs in a more positive way.
6 She has learned more about the problems that the ocean faces.

7 VOCABULARY IN CONTEXT

a Watch the clips from the TED Talk. Choose the correct meaning of the words and phrases. ▶ 6.4

b Think about:

- ways we can make it easier for wheelchair users to *access* buildings.
- times when you have experienced a *tremendous* sense of freedom.
- the last time you needed to ask a teacher to *extend* a homework deadline.
- the possible learning *outcomes* of this lesson (i.e. what you will learn).
- a reason your eyes would *light up*.
- a *concept* that young children find difficult to understand.

c Work in pairs. Compare your ideas. Which are the most interesting? Why?

8 MY PERSPECTIVE

Work in pairs. Discuss the questions.

1 What ideas about wheelchairs and wheelchair users did you have before watching Sue Austin's talk?
2 Why did Sue decide to go underwater with her wheelchair?
3 Did the video of Sue's underwater wheelchair change your ideas? How?
4 What other activities associated with freedom could be used to challenge people's assumptions about wheelchairs, implants, and artificial body parts? Think about Sue, Michael Chorost, and Hugh Herr (page 73).
5 Is there anything in your life that people think is negative but you consider positive?

CHALLENGE

Sue says that when people see her art, they think, "If you can do that, I can do anything."

Think of a challenge or goal that you would like to accomplish, or have been intending to achieve. If Sue can dive underwater in a wheelchair, can you do your "anything"?

6E Physical Challenges

SPEAKING

1 Work in pairs. Look at the photos and answer the questions.

1 Would you describe yourself as a dancer?
2 Does your country or region have a traditional dance?
3 Do people dress up to do the dance? Do you do it on special occasions?
4 What do you know about the history of the dance?

2 Listen to two people describing one of the photos below. Which photo are they talking about? 42

Useful language

Describing photos

This one shows...
On the right, there's a...
In the middle / background, there's a...
Behind..., you can see...

Making guesses

They look / seem... (+ adjective)
She looks like... (+ noun)
It looks as if... (+ phrase)
It must / might be...
It's obviously...

Being imprecise

It's some / a sort of / kind of...

3 Use a word or expression from the Useful language box to complete the sentences. Listen again and check. 42

1 ______________________ some women dancing.
2 ______________________ costume.
3 ______________________ they're in a show or something.
4 ______________________ during a festival of some kind.
5 ______________________ a stage show in a theater.
6 The feeling is ______________________ happiness.
7 They ______________________ they're really enjoying themselves.
8 ______________________ proud.

4 Work in pairs. Take turns describing the other photo below. Answer the questions.

1 What sort of event are the dancers at?
2 What feelings are they expressing?
3 How do they use their bodies and clothes to show their feelings?

5 Find a photo in this book that you like. Tell your partner which unit it is in. Describe the photo and ask your partner to find it.

WRITING An informal email describing people

6 **Read the email on page 151. Answer the questions.**

1. What's the relationship between Mauricio and Aditi?
2. What does Mauricio want Aditi to do?
3. Which of these questions does not Aditi answer?
   - **a** How do you know this person?
   - **b** What are they like?
   - **c** What do they look like?
   - **d** What is their extraordinary ability?
   - **e** What challenges have they faced?
   - **f** Why do you admire them?

7 **WRITING SKILL** Informal language

a **Read the first paragraph of the email on page 151 again. Find informal words and phrases for these neutral or more formal words.**

1 Dear **2** thank you **3** city **4** accept **5** definitely

b **Match the words and expressions (1–9) with these more informal synonyms and abbreviations.**

ages	at the mo	BTW	in a rush	a bunch of stuff
my place	my stuff	say hi to	thrilled	

1 happy **2** a long time **3** in a hurry **4** send my regards to **5** a lot of things **6** at the moment **7** my bags, suitcases, etc. **8** by the way **9** my house

c **Rewrite the sentences so that they sound more informal and friendly. Use contractions where necessary.**

1. Dear Gurpreet, Thank you for your email. It has been such a long time since we spoke, so I was happy to get your news. How is life with you?
2. By the way, while I'm traveling I'll need somewhere to keep my bags and everything. I was wondering if I could keep them at your house. I should warn you—there's a lot!
3. Anyway, I must go now; I am in a hurry to finish an essay at the moment. I'll definitely write again soon. Give my regards to Yuki. Yours, Ana.

8 **Reply to Mauricio. Share some of your news and tell him about someone you admire. Use phrases from the Useful language box and informal language.**

9 **Read your classmates' emails. Who would you like to know more about?**

Useful language

Ways of starting an email

Hi ___ / Hello ___
How are things?
Sorry I haven't written for a while.
Thanks so much for your email.
It was great to hear about…
It was great to get your news.

Ways of ending

Please write soon.
Don't forget to call me!
Anyway, I have to run because…
Say hi to your brother for me.
Give my love to…
Lots of love,
All the best,
Bye for now,
Talk to you soon!

7 Shopping Around

IN THIS UNIT, YOU...

- talk about alternatives to buying new things.
- read about people who did not buy anything for a year.
- talk about the services in our towns and cities.
- watch a TED Talk about a new material.
- write an announcement.

Train Night Market, Bangkok, Thailand

7A Money and Me

VOCABULARY Money and shopping

1 Work in groups. Discuss the questions.

1 What have you spent money on recently?
2 What do you enjoy buying? Are there any shopping experiences you don't like?
3 When you are choosing what to buy, do you think about cost, quality, the brand or company name, and where it was made?

2 Work in pairs. Check that you understand the words and phrases in bold.

1 I'm careful about what I **spend my money on**. I don't **waste** it on useless stuff.
2 I spend time **shopping around** online. I always try to get **a good deal**.
3 My family **donates** a little **to charity**, but I can't **afford** to **give** money **away** yet!
4 Sometimes my sister **lends** me **money** when I need to **borrow** some. She knows I'll **pay** her **back**.
5 I hate **being in debt** to anyone. I prefer to **pay off my debts** as soon as I can.
6 I'll always visit a store if it's having a **sale**. I love **browsing** for **bargains**.
7 If something I want is **on sale**, I buy it quickly in case it **sells out**.
8 It's worth **paying more for** things if they're fashionable **brands**. **Logos** on clothes are worth a lot to me.
9 If I get a gift I don't like, I try to **take** it **back** and **get a refund**.
10 I'm more interested in finding a job I enjoy than one where I can **earn a lot**.

3 Work in pairs. Discuss the statements in Activity 2. How closely do they describe your or your family's attitude to money and shopping?

4 Work in pairs. Discuss the difference between these terms.

1 *spend* and *waste* money on something
2 *earn* and *win* money
3 *lend* and *borrow* money
4 a *sale* and a *bargain*
5 *shop around* and *browse*
6 a *brand* and a *logo*

5 Work in pairs. Complete these opinions about money and shopping with the correct form of one of the words or phrases in bold from Activity 2.

Akiko: I try to get the best (1) __________ I can, by waiting for (2) __________ on the things I need, and always (3) __________ around. I hate buying things then finding them on (4) __________ in other stores. If that happens, I take them (5) __________ and get a (6) __________. People who spend more on famous (7) __________ are silly—it's such a waste of (8) __________! I've been saving so I can pay (9) __________ my college (10) __________.

Guillermo: Money's for (11) __________, not saving. Why waste half your life looking for (12) __________? I love shopping, and I spend hours (13) __________ in clothing stores, but I won't worry if I don't get the cheapest deal before something (14) __________ out. I borrow money from my parents. I usually (15) __________ them back, but I also help my sister out by (16) __________ her money. When I'm older, and (17) __________ a salary, I want to continue to (18) __________ to charity.

6 MY PERSPECTIVE

Work in pairs. Discuss whose attitude toward money and shopping is better, Akiko's or Guillermo's? Why?

LISTENING

7 Listen to three people talking about alternatives to normal shopping. What do the alternatives have in common? 🎧 43

a They mean spending less money.
b They benefit the environment in some way.
c They involve reusing things that people don't want anymore.

8 Listen again. Of the three speakers, who: 🎧 43

a doesn't want to create unnecessary waste?
b doesn't have to leave the house to shop?
c finds that the quality of what they buy is higher than normal?
d has experienced negative attitudes toward what they're doing?
e lives too far from the place to take advantage of it?
f mentions a disadvantage to their alternative way of shopping?

9 **MY PERSPECTIVE**

Work in pairs. Which of these items would you consider buying secondhand or borrowing? Why?

art for your bedroom	books or magazines
clothes and shoes	computers and other electronics
music	presents for other people
sports equipment	other (what?)

GRAMMAR Passive voice

10 Read the sentences (a and b) and answer the questions (1–4).

a *A driver delivers the food right from the farm to our door.*
b *The food is delivered right from the farm to our door.*

1 What tense are both sentences?
2 What is the subject of sentence a? What is the object?
3 What is the subject of sentence b? Is there an object?
4 What is emphasized in sentence b?

11 Look at more sentences in the passive voice in the Grammar box. What tense is each one?

Passive voice

a *People have told me a T-shirt I'm wearing is nice, but when I say I bought it in a secondhand store, **I've been given strange looks!***
b *Good quality, well-made things **can be found**.*
c *These clothes **weren't thrown away**.*
d *The way it works is the things in the shop **are donated** by the customers.*
e *I wish a "lending store" **had been set up** around here.*
f *We **were shown** at school how the environment pays a price for our food.*

Check page 140 for more information and practice.

12 **Work in pairs. Look at the reasons for using the passive voice on page 140. Discuss why the sentences in the Grammar box use the passive.**

13 **Change the sentences into the passive voice. Leave out the agent if it's not important.**

1. Secondhand stores have always bought and sold things people don't want anymore.
2. However, in the past, people found only the most common things in these stores.
3. Generally, only experts and collectors discovered special objects.
4. For example, where could you find secondhand camping equipment before computer engineers had invented the internet?
5. Now people use search engines to find the right thing, at the right price, in the right place.

14 **Use the correct active or passive form of the verbs to complete the article.**

There are several advantages to buying and selling online. First of all, instead of visiting secondhand stores by car or on foot, searches (1) ______________ (can do) from the comfort of your living room. When the internet (2) ______________ (invent), sellers suddenly had buyers from around the world, whereas before, most goods (3) ______________ (buy) by people in the local area. Also, secondhand goods (4) ______________ (not only sell) by professionals with a business and a store anymore. Anyone (5) ______________ (can earn) money from home. Since online selling began over twenty years ago, millions of items (6) ______________ (send) to people thousands of miles away.

Secondhand shopping is big business. Over the last 25 years, many websites (7) ______________ (create) just to resell unwanted things, but the most successful, eBay, is also one of the oldest; it (8) ______________ (establish) in1995 as AuctionWeb. An item (9) ______________ (put) up for sale and the person who (10) ______________ (offer) the most money for it is the "winner." Other websites show "for sale" announcements, where things (11) ______________ (advertise) and an agreement (12) ______________ (make) between the buyer and seller.

15 **Play in pairs. Think of examples for each of the categories. The pair with the most examples wins. Think of things that:**

- have been borrowed.
- have never been used.
- aren't sold any more.
- were made by hand.
- were made in another country.
- were designed for a different purpose than the one they are currently used for.

16 **With your partner, add another category to the list in Activity 15 and find one or more examples. Challenge the rest of the class to guess what the category is.**

7B Waste Not, Want Not

READING

1 Work in pairs. Discuss the questions.

1 What do you spend your money on that you consider essential? What are your luxuries?
2 What would you miss most if you didn't buy anything for a year?

2 Work in pairs, A and B. Student A, read about the roommates. Student B, read about the family. Answer the questions (1–4). Then tell your partner what you learned.

1 Why did they decide to spend nothing for a year?
2 Did they really spend *nothing* during the year? What did they pay for?
3 What skills did they learn?
4 How difficult was it for them?

3 Work in pairs. Answer the questions without looking at the text. Then read both stories to check your answers.

1 What do the roommates and the family have in common?
2 How were the two experiments different?
3 Both used the internet. How did this help them achieve their goal?

VOCABULARY BUILDING Adverbs

4 Identify the adverbs in the sentences from the article (1–4). Then answer the questions (a and b).

1 They stopped getting their hair cut professionally.
2 Jen also learned how to create a website, where she met people who were similarly anti-consumerist.
3 They tried not spending temporarily for a month before deciding to do it for a whole year.
4 Jen had to work hard to think of ideas for the boys.

a Which adverbs are regular and which are irregular? How do you know?
b Which of the adverbs modify a verb, and which modify an adjective?

5 Make adverbs from these adjectives.

1 actual	6 fast
2 busy	7 healthy
3 complete	8 independent
4 eager	9 occasional
5 good	10 realistic

6 How many ways can you complete these sentences? Use adverbs from Activity 5.

1 I don't think I could stop buying clothes for a year. I think it would be…
2 I spent most of last week…
3 It's hard to save money and still…
4 After a long day of shopping, I…
5 I'm not very interested in shopping, so I…

7 MY PERSPECTIVE

Work in groups. Discuss the questions.

1 In your opinion, what were the best ideas from each "buy nothing" experiment?
2 Do you think you could do what the roommates and Jen's family did? Why?
3 Do you think you would be more or less happy if you stopped spending? Why?

CRITICAL THINKING Reading between the lines

> It is often possible to get a lot of meaning from a text, even if it is not actually stated. For example, in the sentence *She asked her friend whether she liked her new dress, but her friend said nothing,* we understand that the friend probably didn't like the dress.

8 Work in pairs. Use the information in the stories and your own interpretation to discuss the questions.

1 Were the decisions to live without spending for a year a choice or a necessity?
2 What have the roommates and the family achieved for themselves as a result of their experiments?
3 For what reasons, other than the ones given, do you think they created a blog and a website?
4 What do you think has been the effect of their stories on other people?

9 Read the statements. Who do you think said them, Geoffrey or Jen? How do you know?

1 "Everything in our life changed in the past year."
2 "I found buying new clothes really easy to give up."
3 "I was spending so much every month, no matter how much I made it never seemed like I was getting ahead."
4 "I am just one person… I can only do what I can do. You have to be the change you want to see in the world."
5 "It's so useful to know that if your toaster stops working, you don't have to throw it away, you can repair it."
6 "We even made our own Christmas tree."
7 "Maybe we didn't save much money, but it's great that we have changed our consumerist lifestyle."

NOTHING FOR A YEAR

44 How hard is it to live without spending money? Read these stories of two Canadian roommates and a British family who decided not to buy anything for a whole year.

THE ROOMMATES Geoffrey invited a friend to share his apartment. His new roommate had to throw away a lot of things to squeeze into a smaller bedroom, and Geoffrey made room by getting rid of some of his possessions. They realized how much they owned and how little they actually needed.

They decided to do an experiment: could they live for a year without buying anything unnecessary? As well as having to create space, Geoffrey was worried about money, and they both felt uncomfortable with their consumerist* lifestyle. Would they be happier not buying so much? They started a blog to explain their plan and track their progress.

Of course, some things you just can't do without, such as food. But instead of occasionally going to a restaurant and having food prepared for them, now they always cooked at home. They stopped getting their hair cut professionally. And rather than taking public transportation to work, they walked or rode their bikes. They learned how to grow vegetables so they could eat fresh food for free.

It wasn't always easy. Geoffrey says that after a long day at work, preparing dinner was sometimes the last thing he wanted to do. But by sharing the experience with his roommate and their supporters online, and reminding themselves of the benefits of cooking, such as being creative and having a healthy diet, they learned to enjoy it.

consumerist *buying and having lots of things, often things that are not necessary*

THE FAMILY By the time her son William was three, Jen noticed how many plastic toys he had and how often he wanted new things. In stores, he looked eagerly for colorful toys, expecting to take them home. She realized that she and her husband needed to teach their children that there are alternatives to new. So, they stopped buying anything apart from food and essential household items like toothpaste. If they needed something, they could find it secondhand or make it themselves.

Jen started repairing holes in pants, knitting winter hats, and even making soap. Her husband Ben busily fixed toys and other objects. Jen also learned how to create a website, where she met people who were similarly anti-consumerist. They inspired her to keep going.

They tried not spending temporarily for a month before deciding to do it for a whole year. By doing this, they discovered that it would be easier than they expected. Ben already made his own bread and jam, so reducing what they needed from stores wasn't completely unfamiliar. They also agreed on a few exceptions to make things easier, like having the washing machine repaired if it ever broke down (it didn't). The hardest part was finding birthday presents for the children's friends. Jen found making bags and clothes for girls easy, but had to work hard to think of ideas for boys.

They managed to save £2,000, and Jen says they are no longer "drowning in plastic." More importantly, they have changed their habits. She believes that "Each time we make a more thoughtful choice, about what we buy, or don't buy, we are changing the world."

7C Services in My Town

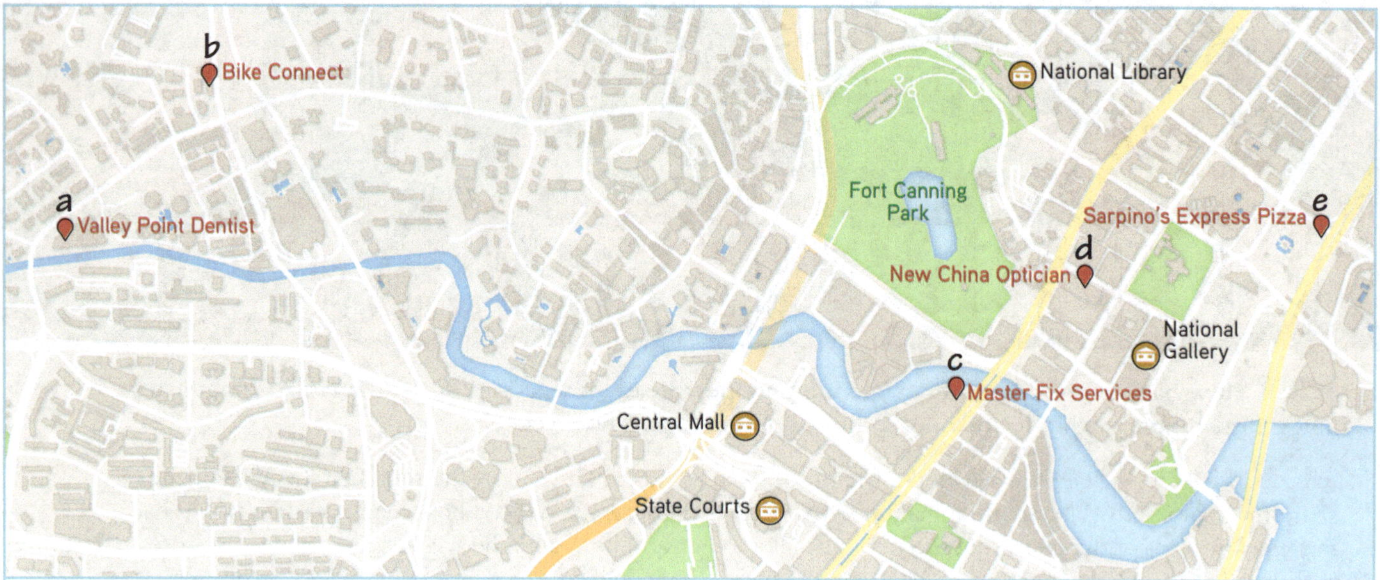

a This is my dentist's office. My brother and I have been going there all our lives.

b My bike often needs repairs. I usually fix it myself, but if it's a big job, I go to Bike Connect. The last time I took it there, I had the brakes changed.

c I had a really nice pair of boots, but the heel was broken. I took them here, but they said they couldn't repair them.

d Last week I had an appointment at the optician, but there's nothing wrong with my eyes.

e We have a family tradition—pizza every Friday. It gives Mom a night off from cooking. Sarpino's pizza is great, but we never go to the restaurant—we always get it delivered.

GRAMMAR *have / get something done*

1 Look at Emma's map of Singapore, where she lives. Find ways that her life is similar to and different from yours.

Emma rides a bike, and so do I.

2 Look at the Grammar box and Emma's map. What does *it* refer to in each sentence?

> ***have / get something done***
>
> **a** *We never go to the restaurant—we always get* ***it*** *delivered.*
>
> **b** *The last time I took* ***it*** *there, I had the brakes changed.*

Check page 140 for more information and practice.

3 Look at the Grammar box again. Answer the questions about sentences a and b.

1. Do we know who delivers the pizza? Who asks them to deliver it?
2. Do we know who changed the brakes? Who asked them to do it?
3. Does *have / get something done* mean:

   a someone does something by accident?
   b you do something for yourself?
   c you ask someone to do something for you?

4 Look back at the text on page 85. Find three examples of *have / get something done.*

5 Use the prompts to write sentences about Emma's life.

1. She and her brother / have / their teeth / check / every six months.
2. Last week she / get / her eyes / test.
3. She wanted / have / her boots / repair.

6 Write sentences about the services you and your family use. Use these words, or your own ideas.

clean / your shoes	cut / your hair
fix / your laptop	wash / the car

My mom gets the car washed at the garage. She says they do it better than me!

7 **PRONUNCIATION** Sentence stress

a Use the prompts to write questions. Use *Have you ever had…?*

1 your groceries / deliver
2 your phone / repair
3 breakfast / bring up to your bedroom
4 a tooth / take out
5 your photo / take / with a famous person

b **Listen and check your answers. Which words are stressed? Repeat the questions.** 45

8 **Complete the sentences about "the one percent." Use *have* or *get* and these verbs in the correct form.**

NOTE: "The one percent" means the richest people.

arrange	carry	choose	clean
cut	manage	plan	walk

You know you're in "the one percent" when you:

1 ______________ your clothes ______________ for you every morning.
2 ______________ your birthday parties professionally ______________ when you were a child.
3 ______________ your hair ______________ by a hair stylist at home since you were little.
4 ______________ your shoes ______________ for you.
5 ______________ your dogs ______________ when you don't feel like doing it.
6 ______________ your social media ______________ by online experts.
7 ______________ your vacations ______________ by your personal travel agent.
8 ______________ your bag ______________ to school.

9 **Work in groups. Discuss the questions.**

1 Is there one service you couldn't do without? Why?
2 If you had a lot of money, what would you get done for you? What would you do yourself?
3 What effect do these changes have on the services that people use? Give examples.
   - More of us are living in cities.
   - People move because of their jobs and don't live so close to their families.
   - Some people have more money to spend on luxuries.
   - People have more access to technology.

In a city, you can have more things done for you. For example, you can have your groceries delivered.

10 **CHOOSE** Choose one of the following activities.

1 Make a map like Emma's showing the services you and your family use. Present it to the class.
2 Tell a classmate about unusual services that people use.
3 Write an opinion essay (see page 42) on this topic: "These days people are having more things done for them. Soon we won't have to leave the house." Do you agree?

Skyline of the center of Singapore behind a market in Chinatown

7D Grow Your Own Clothes

> "In the future, what would you choose to grow?"
>
> **SUZANNE LEE**

Read about Suzanne Lee and get ready to watch her TED Talk. ▶ 7.0

AUTHENTIC LISTENING SKILLS

Reformulating

One way to make a new or complicated idea easier to understand is by reformulating, or saying it again using different words. Notice in this example how the second sentence helps to explain what *static* means:

And this is a static culture. You don't have to do anything to it.

1 Look at the Authentic Listening Skills box. Then listen to this excerpt from the talk. Which word in the first sentence is made clearer by the second sentence? 🎧 46

What excites me about using microbes is their efficiency. So we only grow what we need.

2 Match each sentence (1–3) with the sentence that follows it (a–c). Then listen to the excerpts to check. 🎧 47

1 Bubbles will appear on the surface of the liquid.
2 What I can't yet do is make it water-resistant.
3 We need to maintain an optimum temperature for the growth.

a So if I was to walk outside in the rain wearing this dress today, I would immediately start to absorb huge amounts of water.
b So this is telling us that the fermentation is in full swing and the bacteria are feeding on the sugar nutrients in the liquid.
c And I use a heat mat to sit the bath on and a thermostat to regulate it.

WATCH

3 Work in pairs. Discuss the questions.

1 Look at the labels on the clothes you are wearing. Are they made of cotton, wool, leather, plastic, or other materials?
2 What are the advantages and disadvantages of these materials?
3 Are there any materials you wouldn't wear? Why not?
4 Which materials are most easily biodegradable? Which don't biodegrade easily?
5 Look at the jacket Suzanne is wearing and the one behind her. What do you think they are made of?

4 Watch Part 1 of the talk. Use some of these words and numbers to complete the recipe for making the fabric. ▶ 7.1

2–3	3	5	10	30	bath	hot
liquid	pieces	salt	sheets	sugar	tea	

1 Start by making the __________ (30 liters).
2 Then add some __________ when it is still hot.
3 Pour the liquid into a __________ where it can grow.
4 When it is less than __________ °C, add the microbes.
5 You can keep it outside when the weather is __________ .
6 Bubbles will start to appear on the surface after about __________ days.
7 Now the microbes have started forming __________ of cellulose.
8 The material is about one inch thick after __________ weeks.

5 Watch Part 2 of the talk. Choose the correct options to complete the summary. ▶ 7.2

When the material is ready, you first need to (1) *dry* / *wash* it. Then, because it is mostly (2) *bacteria* / *water*, you leave it on a piece of wood to dry. The finished product will be (3) *darker* / *thinner* than before. It will either be like (4) *paper* / *plastic* or like (5) *cotton* / *leather*. You can cut it and sew it like normal clothes, or you can shape it when it (6) *has been colored* / *is still wet*. The main problem is that the material absorbs (7) *heat* / *water*, making it (8) *dangerous* / *weak*. So, Suzanne still has work to do before the material is really useful.

6 Watch Part 3 of the talk. Which of these things does Suzanne say? ▶ 7.3

1. Using microbes to make fabric means you can make clothes very cheaply.
2. Old clothes made from cellulose could be turned into food.
3. You could throw your clothes away without worrying about the environment.
4. Cellulose will one day replace cotton, leather, and other materials.
5. This process may be used in furniture design.
6. It may be used to heat buildings.
7. Suzanne is destroying the jacket she has on today by wearing it.

7 Work in pairs. Make lists of the advantages and disadvantages of Suzanne's material.

8 VOCABULARY IN CONTEXT

a Watch the clips from the TED Talk. Choose the correct meaning of the words and phrases. ▶ 7.4

b Think of examples of these things. Then compare them with a partner.

- something you *spread* on bread or toast
- three materials that are *transparent*
- a *bug* you would be afraid to hold in your hands
- an object that is *precious* to you
- something you do where *efficiency* matters

CHALLENGE

1 Suzanne's material is sustainable because it can be grown from things that don't run out or damage the environment. It is also biodegradable, so it will not create waste.

a What things do you buy that are:
- sustainable?
- biodegradable?

b What things that you buy are not so good for the environment? Why?

c Do you think about environmental issues when you buy these things?

clothes	soap, shower gel, makeup, etc.
food and snacks	other things

2 Suzanne asks: "In the future, what would you choose to grow?"

Think of things that might one day be created using Suzanne's material, or other natural processes. What would you be happy buying if it was made from grown material like this? Why?

7E Buying and Selling

SPEAKING

1 Work in pairs. Look at the photo and discuss the questions.

1 Does the store in the photo look like your kind of store?
2 What was the last piece of clothing you bought?
3 Would you ever buy clothes as a present for someone else? Would you buy shoes online?

2 Listen to three conversations. Which takes place in a: 48

a men's clothing department?
b women's clothing department?
c shoe department?

3 Listen again and complete the expressions. Then match each expression with an equivalent in the Useful Language box. 48

1 It's OK, I'm just ________ .
2 Have you got these in a ________ ?
3 I'm ________ something more classy.
4 I'm a ________ .
5 We ________ it in red.
6 Where ________ ?
7 Does ________ ?
8 It really ________ .
9 I'll ________ it.

Useful language

Shopping for clothes

It's OK, I'm just browsing.
I want something more classy.
I need a size "L."
Do you have these in a larger size?
Is it the right size?
It looks really good on you.
We only have red ones.
Where are the changing rooms?
I'll buy it.

4 Match each sentence beginning (1–6) with an ending (a–f).

Do you have…

1 something like this shirt but with long
2 a plain shirt? I don't like
3 this in a darker shade of
4 a size 12 of the dress in the
5 this in a different
6 any pants without

a color?
b pockets?
c blue?
d sleeves?
e stripes.
f window?

5 Work in pairs. Think of some clothes you want to buy. Take turns being a store assistant and a customer shopping for different items.

6 Perform your conversations in front of another pair. Use *this* and *these* instead of *this sweater/pair of jeans*, etc. The other pair must guess what item you are talking about.

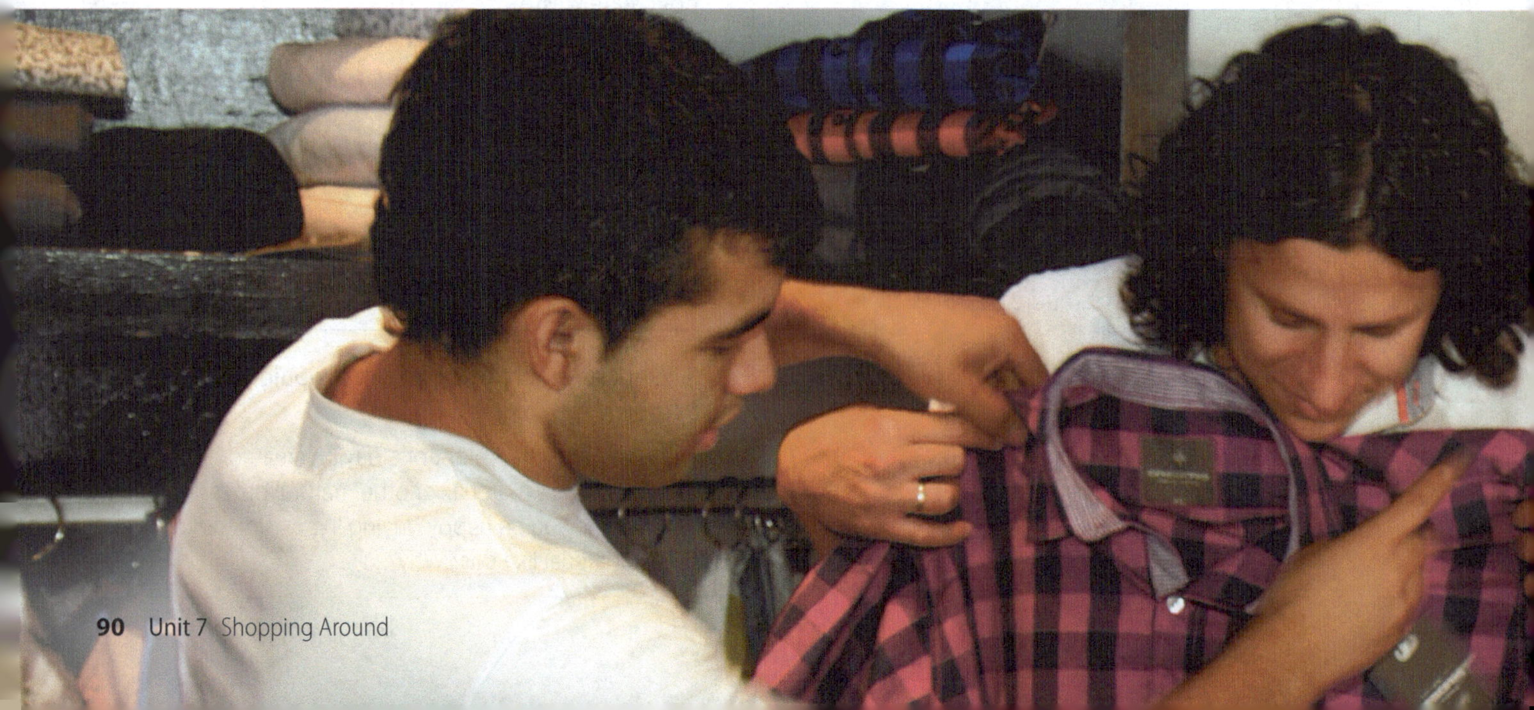

WRITING An announcement

7 **Work in pairs. Discuss the questions.**

1 Do you ever buy or sell things online? What?
2 Do you have any possessions that you could sell secondhand?

8 **In a "for sale" announcement, where would the information (1–9) be: at the beginning, in the middle, or near the end?**

1 a description of the item, including size *at the beginning*
2 details about shipping (how the item will be sent)
3 the age and condition of the item
4 the name of the item
5 the price
6 the reason for selling the item
7 ways you can pay
8 where the seller lives
9 a photo of the item

9 **Read the announcements on page 152. Which information in Activity 8 is included in the first announcement? What important information is missing from the second one?**

10 **WRITING SKILL** Relevant information

a **Look at the Writing strategies box. Read the announcements on page 152 again. Delete the sentences that do not give relevant information.**

b **Match these sentences from online announcements with the type of information in Activity 8 that they introduce.**

1 Bought it new and have had it for…
2 Comes in its original packaging and with instruction manual.
3 Extra large box. I cannot ship. Only bids from Rome area.
4 Measures… in length.
5 Only has… small scratches / marks…
6 Unfortunately, I can no longer use it because…
7 Will accept offers above…

11 **Write an announcement for something you could sell. Use the Writing strategies box and phrases from Activity 10b to help you.**

12 **Read your classmates' announcements. What would you most like to buy?**

Writing strategies

Writing announcements

- Include all the relevant details the readers need to decide if they want to buy the item.
- If any information is not relevant to the buyer, don't include it.
- Keep sentences short (e.g., instead of *This bike is a real bargain*, write *A real bargain!*)
- Use rhetorical questions to attract the reader (e.g., *Looking for earphones with a perfect sound?*)

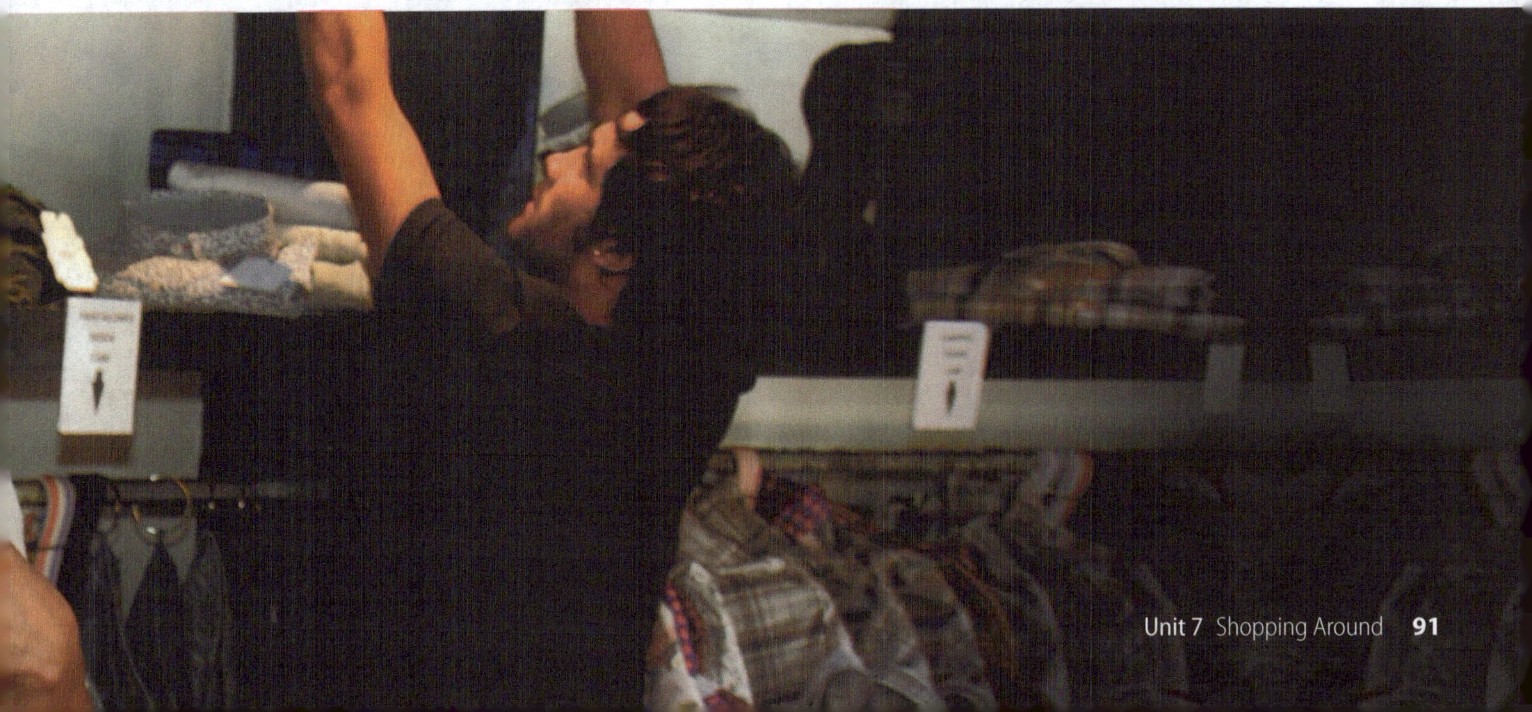

8 Effective Communication

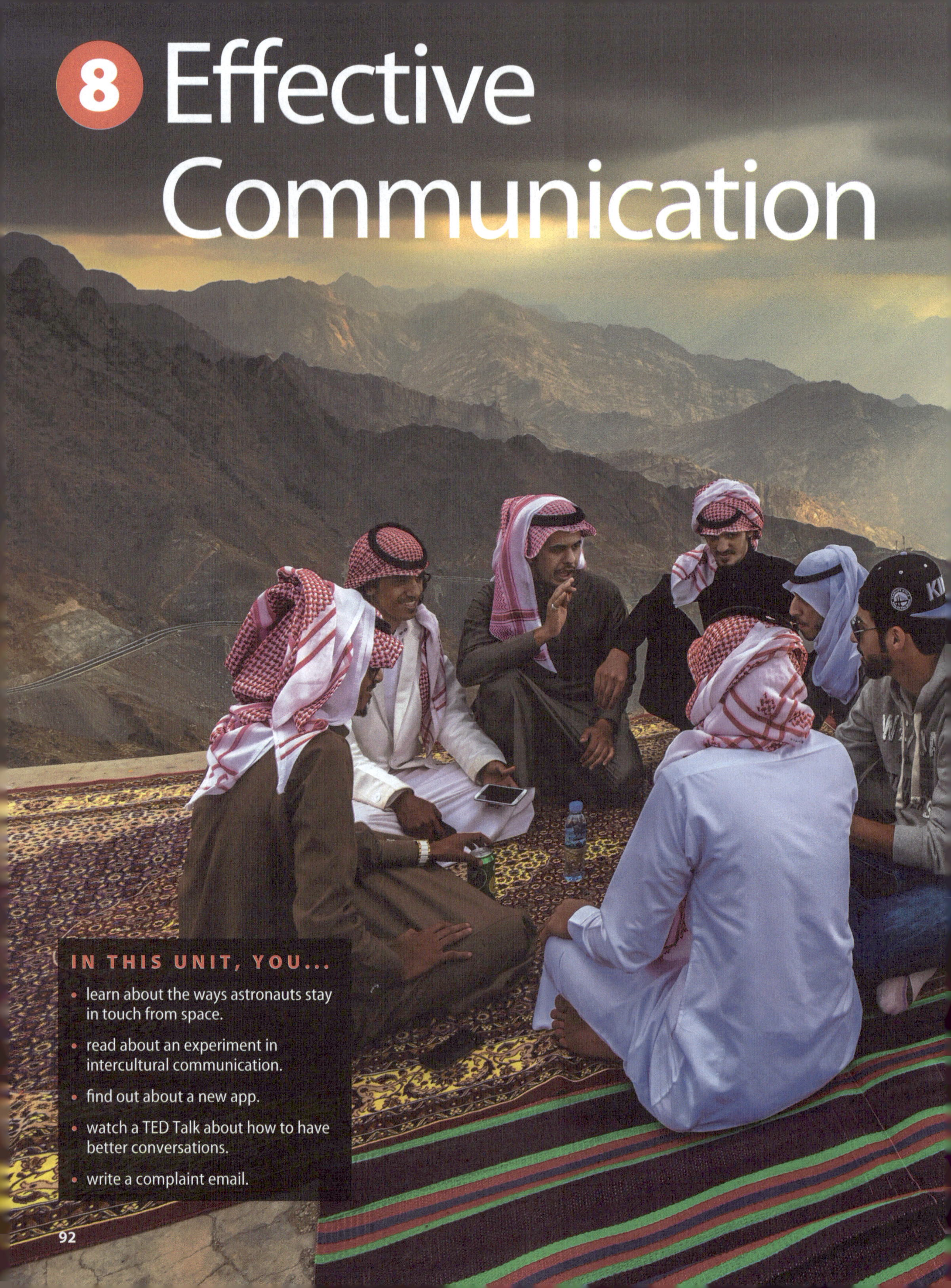

IN THIS UNIT, YOU...

- learn about the ways astronauts stay in touch from space.
- read about an experiment in intercultural communication.
- find out about a new app.
- watch a TED Talk about how to have better conversations.
- write a complaint email.

A group of young men chatting in the Sarwat Mountains, Saudi Arabia

8A Getting Your Message Out

VOCABULARY Effective communication

1 Work in pairs. Look at the photo and read the caption. Discuss the questions.

1 Do men and women talk about different things? What are the differences?
2 Do you use your hands much when you speak? Are you a good listener?
3 What do you talk about with your friends? And with your parents?
4 Do you like talking in large groups or do you prefer one-to-one conversations? Why?

2 Match words in column A with words in column B to make expressions about communication.

A		B	
1	get	**a**	connections
2	interpersonal	**b**	photos
3	make	**c**	skills
4	pay	**d**	distracted
5	share	**e**	attention
6	connect	**f**	my message out
7	get	**g**	with
8	post	**h**	texts
9	respond	**i**	on social media
10	send	**j**	to texts

3 Complete the statements with expressions from Activity 2. Which are about communicating using technology?

1 If I want to make a point, I prefer face-to-face conversations. I don't find it easy to ______________ people if I'm not in the room with them.
2 I know I can't ______________ if I'm looking at my cell phone. I get distracted.
3 I think I have good ______________. My friends say I'm a good listener.
4 I probably ______________ about ten times a day and I respond to my friends' messages right away. It's rude to make them wait.
5 If I want to share a message or a photo, I ______________.
6 I participate in a lot of online forums. It's a great way to ______________ and get my message out.

4 Work in pairs. Discuss the questions.

1 Are the statements in Activity 3 true for you? Change them to make them true.
2 Are any of the comments true for your parents?

I find phone conversations just as easy as speaking face to face, except with my grandfather—he's terrible on the phone!

5 What's the difference between these words?

an argument | a chat | a conversation | a debate | a discussion

6 **MY PERSPECTIVE**

Work in pairs. Discuss the questions.

1 Who do you find it easy to chat with?
2 When was the last time you had a bad argument? Is there anything you could have said to avoid the argument or make it less emotional?
3 Have you ever taken part in a debate? What was the topic?

LISTENING

7 Work in pairs. Discuss the questions.

1. How do you think astronauts on the International Space Station (ISS) communicate with:
   a the mission controllers?
   b their families?
   c the public?
2. How do you communicate with people who live far away?

8 Listen to a conversation between two friends about how Chris Hadfield communicated with people on Earth while he was on the ISS. Match the ways of communicating (1–4) with his purpose (a–f). 🎧 49

1. YouTube
2. video conferencing
3. Twitter
4. online chat forums

a to post photos of Earth
b to send messages to his followers
c to share music videos
d to show experiments in space
e to talk to schools
f to participate in question-and-answer sessions with the public

9 Listen again. Complete the notes with one or two words or a number. 🎧 49

1. David Saint-Jacques and Chris Hadfield are astronauts from ________ .
2. Hadfield's ________ managed his social media accounts for him.
3. He did experiments to show what happens to ________ in zero gravity.
4. He has ________ million followers on Twitter.
5. People loved talking to him while he was ________ .

GRAMMAR Reported speech (1)

10 Read some questions Chris Hadfield was asked during an online chat (1–8). Match them with his responses (a–h).

1. "You'll be away from Earth for five months. Will you get lonely?"
2. "What does it feel like to look down at Earth during a spacewalk?"
3. "Did you take a guitar to space?"
4. "I want to be an astronaut. I'm seven years old. What do I need to do?"
5. "What is it like to sleep without gravity?"
6. "I'm wondering—how often do you hit your head each day?"
7. "Which part of the world looks the coolest from space?"
8. "Where are you right now?"

a "It is beautiful. The colors and textures, the global view, the chance to have Everest and the Himalayas under your feet."
b "There was already one waiting for me! It's been up here since 2001."
c "The most beautiful to me are the Bahamas—you can see every shade of blue there. But honestly, it's difficult to have one favorite place. Everywhere looks amazing."
d "At the moment, we're flying over the west coast of Australia."
e "About once a day!"
f "No! On the ISS there are people on the radio, family are just a phone call away, and I have the other team members to chat with. I also have experiments and work to do."
g "It is wonderful—you can relax every part of your body."
h "You must be healthy (eat your vegetables and do some exercise) and smart (do your homework)."

Astronaut Chris Hadfield plays his guitar on the International Space Station.

Reported statements and questions

"What is it like to sleep without gravity?" → *Someone asked Chris what it was like to sleep without gravity.*

"Will you get lonely?" → *Someone asked him if he would get lonely.*

"Did you take your guitar to space?" → *One person asked whether he had taken his guitar to space.*

"A guitar has been up here since 2001." → *Chris said that a guitar had been up there since 2001.*

"How often do you hit your head each day?" → *He was asked how often he hit his head each day.*

Check page 142 for more information and practice.

11 **In reported direct speech, some changes are made to tenses, pronouns, word order, and punctuation. Read the Grammar box and answer the questions.**

1. When we report statements and questions, verbs usually *stay the same / change to a past tense*.
2. Pronouns and time expressions (e.g., *you, my, now, this*) *often / never* change.
3. When we report *questions with a question word / Yes/No questions*, we use *if* or *whether*.
4. At the end of reported questions, there is a *question mark / period*.
5. In reported questions, the subject is *before / after* the auxiliary verb.
6. In reported questions, the auxiliary verb *do, does*, or *did* is *necessary / not necessary*.

12 **Complete the reported speech with these words.**

could	felt	had	had	was	was

1. "What does it feel like to look down at Earth during a spacewalk?" "It is beautiful."
   One person **asked** what it _________ like to look down at Earth. Chris **replied** that it was beautiful.
2. "I have hit my head about once a day!"
   Chris **admitted** that he _________ hit his head about once a day.
3. "Honestly, it's difficult to have one favorite place."
   He **complained** that it _________ difficult to have a favorite place.
4. "Sleeping without gravity is wonderful—you can totally relax."
   He **claimed** that sleeping without gravity _________ wonderful. He **added** that you _________ totally relax.
5. "To be an astronaut you must be healthy and smart."
   He **explained** that to be an astronaut you _________ to be healthy and smart.

13 **Look at the verbs in bold in Activity 12. Match six of the verbs with the definitions (1–6).**

1. say something in answer to someone else *reply*
2. say something more
3. say something so the listener understands it clearly
4. say that something is true, especially when you are unhappy or sorry about it
5. say that you are not happy about something
6. say that something is true, even when it is not certain

14 **Use the prompts to report more statements and questions about the ISS mission.**

1. "Do you do experiments every day?" someone / ask
   Someone asked Chris if he did experiments every day.
2. "I do, but I don't do many experiments on Saturdays and Sundays." Chris / reply
3. "I can help to educate the public about space exploration with social media." he / explain
4. "How long did it take you to learn how to move around in zero gravity?" one person / ask
5. "I'm still learning!" he / admit
6. "Will it take long to get used to gravity again after living in space?" someone / ask

15 **Work in pairs. Write five questions you would like to ask Chris Hadfield. Take turns interviewing each other as Chris. Then report your interviews to the class.**

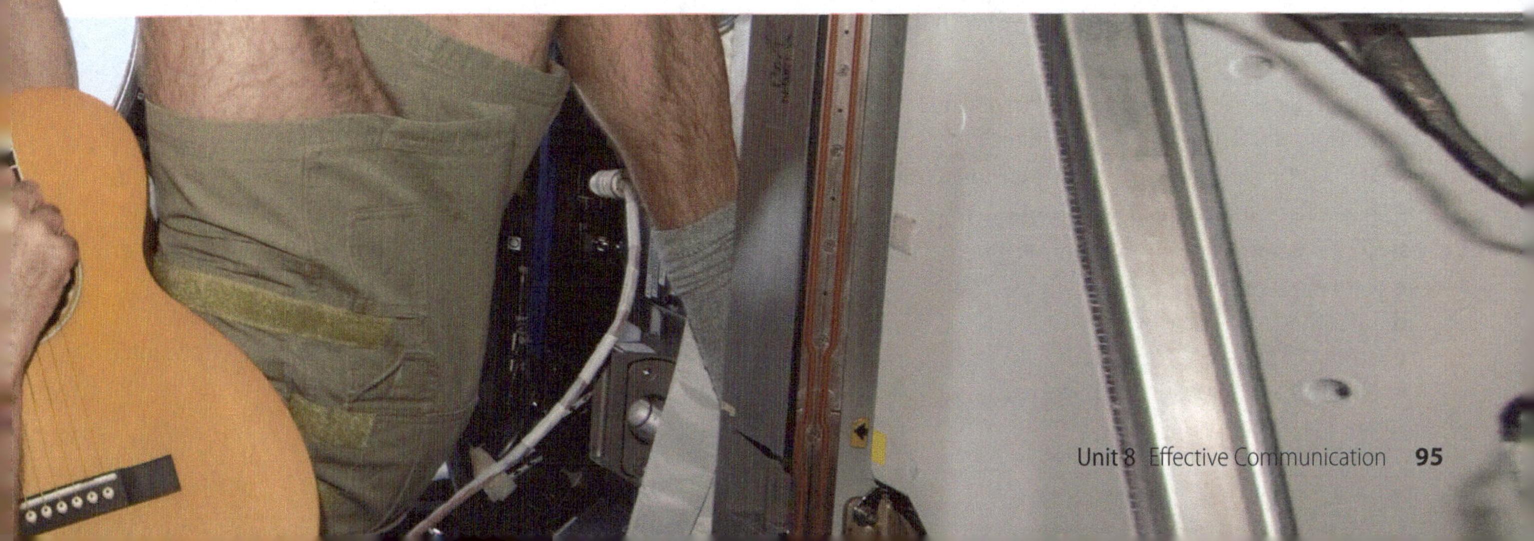

8B Intercultural Communication

READING

1 **Work in pairs. You are going to read an article about what happened when students from different nationalities spent time together. Discuss the questions. Use these adjectives and your own ideas.**

direct emotional formal honest patient polite rude

1 What do you think people in other countries believe about people in your country?
2 How true do you think these views are?

2 **Read the article. Match the headings (a–f) with the paragraphs (1–5). There is one heading you do not need.**

a Let's Get Together
b A Two-Way Thing
c Body Language
d Communication Styles
e Communicating without Words
f Accurate Opinions?

3 **Read the article again. Are the sentences *true* or *false*, or is the information *not given*?**

1 Messages can be communicated in two forms: spoken language and body language.
2 Intercultural understanding is important because different nationalities communicate so often these days.
3 The goal of the experiment was to compare Moroccan and Chinese communication skills.
4 The students were not feeling relaxed about meeting new people.
5 The ideas they had about each other before they met did not match the facts.
6 Hyan Yu was annoyed because Eleni wasn't listening to him.
7 The Chinese students spoke the best English.
8 The most direct group was the Americans.
9 The students had to change their communication styles for the others to understand and accept them.

4 **Match the words from the article (1–6) with their definitions (a–f).**

1 urgent (line 10)
2 background (line 15)
3 stereotype (line 23)
4 fluent (line 29)
5 direct (line 49)
6 passionately (line 50)

a the culture and family someone comes from
b set ideas about people or nationalities, often not true
c with emotion
d important, high-priority
e clear and honest
f able to speak a foreign language well

CRITICAL THINKING Using direct speech

5 **The author uses direct speech in the article. Find four quotes. Why is direct speech used?**

6 **Match the quotes in the article with the points (1–4).**

It is important to:
1 be aware of your own culture and be able to explain it.
2 understand why miscommunication happens.
3 recognize how all communications help understanding.
4 want to know the truth about other cultures.

VOCABULARY BUILDING

Negative prefixes

Make adjectives negative by adding the prefixes *un-*, *im-*, *in-*, or *ir-*.

comfortable → *uncomfortable* *polite* → *impolite*
correct → *incorrect* *responsible* → *irresponsible*

7 **Add the correct prefix to make each adjective negative.**

1 ______patient
2 ______aware
3 ______direct
4 ______usual
5 ______formal
6 ______personal
7 ______regular
8 ______possible
9 ______relevant
10 ______true

8 **Choose the correct option to complete each sentence.**

1 This intercultural experiment was quite *usual* / *unusual*, but everyone needs to be able to communicate with people from different cultures these days.
2 The Americans were surprised at how *personal* / *impersonal* and friendly the Moroccans were.
3 The Moroccans realized their ideas about stereotypes were *true* / *untrue*.
4 Eleni was *aware* / *unaware* she was annoying Hyan Yu.
5 Behavior that is normal in one culture can appear *polite* / *impolite* in other cultures.
6 It's important to be *patient* / *impatient* when you communicate with people from other cultures.
7 Chinese people probably think Moroccans are quite *direct* / *indirect*.

9 **MY PERSPECTIVE**

Work in groups. Discuss the questions.

1 Which of the communication styles in the article is most similar to your country's? Why?
2 What are the best ways to increase intercultural understanding between people from different countries? Which is the most effective?

Rochd and David discuss stereotypes and communication styles.

AN EXPERIMENT IN INTERCULTURAL COMMUNICATION

50

1 ____

We think about communication as someone sending a message and another person receiving it. However, this view suggests that communication is a simple one-way process, when in fact it is very interactive, with many messages being passed in both directions at the same time. These messages are sent and received not just in the words used, but also in more emotional, nonverbal forms such as facial expressions, tone of voice, and body language. In an increasingly interconnected world, the need to understand other cultures is more urgent than ever. So what happens when people from different cultures, who speak different languages, meet?

2 ____

This is what documentary makers Crossing Borders Films wanted to find out. Could young people from different backgrounds develop their intercultural understanding by coming together face to face? Two of their films examine interactions between American, Moroccan, and Chinese students. So what did they learn about each other, and themselves?

3 ____

Before the Moroccans and Americans met, both sides were feeling uncomfortable. What would they think of each other? Both nationalities already had some ideas about stereotypes of the other in their heads. One of the Moroccan students, Fatima, explained, "I need to find out if the images I have of other nationalities are correct." However, when the groups got together, they found that their stereotypes were immediately replaced by the individual personalities of the group members.

4 ____

Not everyone was fluent in English, and sometimes in discussions people felt frustrated that they couldn't express themselves clearly. But misunderstandings were not only caused by language errors. One of the American students who went to China, Eleni, noticed that Hyan Yu always seemed annoyed when he spoke to her. Eleni explained, "My sound to show I'm listening is *'Hm.'* And for Hyan Yu, *'Hm'* is a sign of disrespect." On the other hand, some of the differences in nonverbal communication helped the students to get along better. Rochd, one of the Moroccan students, demonstrated friendship in a Moroccan way by putting his arm around one of the visitors—Americans don't usually do this except with close friends. By spending time together, both sides became more aware of differences and learned to accept them. One of the Moroccan students said, "Maybe we're not communicating a lot of information, but we're connecting."

5 ____

One of the Chinese groups was surprised by how direct the Americans were. Compared to the Moroccans, however, the Americans seemed less direct. The Moroccans were able to argue passionately one minute and laugh together the next. Rochd puts it clearly: "If we didn't speak with emotion, that wouldn't be a Moroccan discussion." Again, simply by understanding that certain ways of interacting seem rude to other cultures, the groups were able to get along better. The young people learned a variety of intercultural communication skills and showed how friendships can give a personal face to a stereotype.

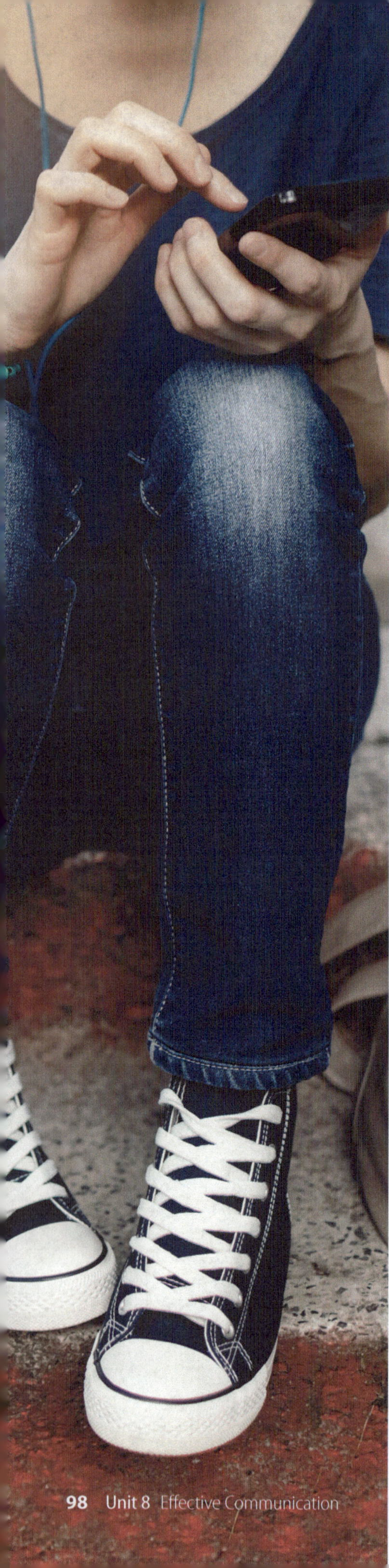

8C Ask Me Anything

GRAMMAR Reported speech (2)

1 Work in pairs. Discuss the questions.

1 What apps do you know that can help people learn languages? How?
2 How will computers help us learn languages in the future?
3 What could you do if you didn't know how to explain what you wanted?

2 Listen to an interview with Nick, who has developed a language learning app. Put the questions in the order you hear them. 51

a Did the users know the app's secret?
b How does the app work?
c What do users need to do if they want to use the app?
d Where does the idea come from?
e What does your company do?
f Will the app be available for English learners soon?

3 Work in pairs. Listen again, then discuss the answers to the questions in Activity 2. 51

4 Work in pairs. Who says these things? Match the speakers (1–5) with the comments (a–j). Then listen again to check. 51

1 the interviewer
2 Nick
3 the app website
4 anyone with an iPhone
5 Javier

a "Yes, of course I can tell you about it!"
b "Can you tell me about the app?"
c "Siri, find a good restaurant near here!"
d "We should use texting as the way people communicate with the app."
e "Text me and I'll help!"
f "If you want to use the app, add this number to your phone contacts."
g "Let's look at an example."
h "It isn't actually a chat bot, it's me."
i "I really think you should try this app. It's great."
j "Remember to come back in five years, because computers will keep on learning."

Verb patterns with reporting verbs

a *The interviewer **asked** Nick to explain where the idea came from.*
b *He **told** Siri to find a good restaurant near there.*
c *Nick **agreed** to talk about his new project.*
d *Nick **suggested** using texting as the way to communicate with the app.*

Check page 142 for more information and practice.

5 Reporting verbs tell us what the speaker is doing, e.g., suggesting. They are sometimes followed by other verbs, but the structure isn't always the same. Match the verbs in bold in the Grammar box with these structures.

1 Some reporting verbs are followed by *to* + infinitive, e.g., ______ .
2 Some reporting verbs are followed by *someone* + *to* + infinitive, e.g., ______ , ______ .
3 Some reporting verbs are followed by the *-ing* form, e.g., ______ .

6 Match the two parts of the sentences.

1 The app **promises**
2 The website **invited** people
3 Nick **offered**
4 Nick **admitted**
5 The first user **recommended**
6 Nick **reminds** us

a being the app.
b to help.
c to add the app's number to their contacts.
d to show how the app works with an example.
e to come back in five years.
f using Nick's app to others on Facebook.

7 Choose the correct options to complete the review of a new app.

A friend (1) *told / suggested* me to download a new app to help me learn vocabulary. He (2) *explained / admitted to* not using it himself, but he (3) *offered / suggested* trying it for a few days. It (4) *promises / reminds* to teach you ten new words every day. The premium version is $5, but if you (5) *invite / suggest* a friend to sign up for it, you get $3 off. (You can also (6) *promise / ask* your parents to pay for it—tell them it's for studying!) It's fun because it turns learning English into a game. Sometimes I (7) *invite / agree* to let my little sister play with it. I (8) *offered / told* to show my English teacher how it works. She thought that some of the vocabulary it teaches isn't very useful. She (9) *reminded / promised* me to do my homework as well, and not to only study with the app. I think she's right—I'd (10) *ask / recommend* spending ten minutes a day on the app, but no more.

8 Work in pairs. Read about the Turing test. Then read the items (1–7) and decide which are the best ones to find out if you are speaking to a human or a bot.

The Turing test is a competition for computer "bots"—programs that try to speak the way humans do. The person taking the test "chats" via text message and interacts with either the bot or with a human. The bot wins if the tester believes they are interacting with a human. These are good prompts to use in the test:

1 Could you give me your definition of love, please?
2 Would you like to ask me anything?
3 Why don't we play chess?
4 Are there any problems in your life you would like to talk about? I'd be happy to listen.
5 Add: 34,789 + 74,203.
6 Actually, I'm also a computer. How does that make you feel?
7 I think you should use more emoticons. It will make you seem more human.

9 Choose the correct verb. Report the sentences in Activity 8.

1 You could *ask it to give* you its definition of love. (ask / offer)
2 You could ____________ you a question. (invite / promise)
3 You could ____________ chess. (admit / suggest)
4 You could ____________ to its problems. (offer / tell)
5 You could ____________ an addition. (recommend / tell)
6 You could ____________ a computer. (admit / ask)
7 You could ____________ emoticons. (invite / recommend)

10 **PRONUNCIATION** Contrastive stress

The same sentence can have different meanings depending on which words are stressed.

a Listen to three sentences. Underline the words that the speaker stresses. 52

1 Nick suggested using texting as the way to communicate with the app. (He didn't tell people to use texting.)
2 Nick suggested using texting as the way to communicate with the app. (No one else suggested it.)
3 Nick suggested using texting as the way to communicate with the app. (He didn't suggest using voice activation.)

b Listen to the first part of the sentence and choose the correct ending: 1, 2, or 3. 53

Ana promised to show me how it worked,
1 Felipe didn't promise me anything.
2 and now she's saying she doesn't have time!
3 not what it looked like.

c Work in pairs. Practice saying the sentences in a and b in different ways. Can your partner provide the correct ending?

11 Work in pairs. Ask and answer questions you would use to find out if you are chatting to a human or a computer.

12 **CHOOSE** Choose one of the following activities.

1 Report the best questions and answers from Activity 11 to your group.
2 Write a summary of the best questions and answers from Activity 11. Use reported speech.

My partner asked me to tell her a joke. I said I didn't know any jokes in English.

3 Search online for a chat bot and have a conversation with it. Tell a partner about your conversation. Decide which chat bot was the best and why.

8D 10 Ways to Have a Better Conversation

“Go out, talk to people, listen to people, and, most importantly, be prepared to be amazed.”

CELESTE HEADLEE

Read about Celeste Headlee and get ready to watch her TED Talk. ▶ 8.0

AUTHENTIC LISTENING SKILLS

Understanding fast speech

Some people speak very fast, often because they are enthusiastic about what they are saying. Groups of words can sound like one long word. To deal with this:

- listen for words you *do* understand.
- try to get the main idea.

1 Read the Authentic Listening Skills box. Listen to the first sentence of the talk. Write down the words you hear. 54

2 Listen again. What does Celeste want the audience to do? Choose the correct option. 54

a Unfriend someone on Facebook.
b Put their hands up.

3 Listen to five more short sentences. Write what you think Celeste says. 55

WATCH

4 Work in pairs. Discuss the questions.

1 When you talk to people you don't know very well, what are "safe" topics to talk about?
2 Which topics should you definitely avoid?
3 Who do you have good conversations with? What do you talk about?
4 What does a good listener do?

5 Watch Part 1 of the talk. According to Celeste, are the sentences *true* or *false*? ▶ 8.1

1 Even the weather and your health aren't safe topics of conversation anymore.
2 Smartphones are helping kids improve their interpersonal skills.
3 Celeste agrees with the advice everyone has heard about how to show that you are paying attention.

6 Watch Part 2 of the talk. Complete Celeste's ten tips for having a better conversation. Use ten of these words. ▶ 8.2

brief	details	experience	flow	know	learn
listen	multitask	open-ended	quiet	repeat	talk

1 Don't __________ .
2 Enter every conversation assuming that you have something to __________ .
3 Use __________ questions. Start questions with *who, what, when, where, why*, or *how*.
4 Go with the __________ . Thoughts will come into your mind and you need to let them go out of your mind.
5 If you don't __________ , say that you don't know.
6 Don't equate your __________ with theirs.
7 Try not to __________ yourself.
8 Leave out the __________ .
9 __________ . It's the number one most important skill that you can develop.
10 Be __________ .

7 **Choose the correct option to complete each tip. Then watch Part 2 of the talk again to check.** ▶ 8.2

1. Be *present* / *available*. Be in that moment.
2. If you want to state your opinion, write *an email* / *a blog*.
3. Because then they might have to stop for a moment and think about it, and you're going to get a much more *complete* / *interesting* response.
4. Don't stop listening when *information* / *stories* and ideas come to you. Let them come and let them go.
5. Be careful about what you claim to be *an expert* / *a listener* in and know for sure.
6. It's not about *who is right* / *you*.
7. We have a point to make, so we just keep *rephrasing* / *repeating* it over and over. Don't do that.
8. People care about you, not the names and *addresses* / *dates*.
9. If your mouth is open, you're not *learning* / *listening*.
10. In short: be interested in *everything* / *other people*.

CHALLENGE

Watch Part 3 of the talk. Celeste says that "everyone has some hidden, amazing thing about them." What is your hidden, amazing thing? Tell a partner. ▶ 8.3

8 **VOCABULARY IN CONTEXT**

a **Watch the clips from the TED Talk. Choose the correct meaning of the words and phrases.** ▶ 8.4

b **Work in pairs. Discuss the questions.**

1. If you want to *avoid* someone, what can you do?
2. What conversations do you enjoy most? Is this *due* to the people you're speaking to, the topic you're talking about, or something else? What?
3. In which professions is good speaking and listening important to *making a living*? How will you make a living?
4. What do you *care about* most in your life?

CRITICAL THINKING Investigating opinions

9 **Work in pairs. Read the comments (1–3). Discuss how Celeste would respond to them.***

1. "Celeste says that people are spending so much time on their phones that they don't develop their interpersonal skills. But if you are messaging people, you are talking to people, just not face to face."
2. "Celeste says we shouldn't compare other people's experiences to our own, but I've always thought that this shows good listening skills—it shows that you really understand how the other person is feeling."
3. "Doesn't it depend on what kind of conversation you are having? Normally both people should be allowed to give their opinions."

*These comments were created for this activity.

10 **Work in groups. Discuss the questions.**

- Which of Celeste's suggestions are going to be most difficult for you to do? Why?
- She says that just making one change is a good start. Which tip will you work on? Why?
- How are you going to put your good intentions into practice?

8E I Hear What You're Saying

SPEAKING

1 Listen to three conversations in which one person wants a change in their situation. Match the conversation with the speaker who wants: 56

a a second chance to do something. Conversation ______
b to get some money back for something they bought. Conversation ______
c to replace something that isn't right. Conversation ______

2 PRONUNCIATION Sympathetic intonation

Being sympathetic means listening to understand how someone feels, and being kind if they have a problem. We show sympathy in the words we use and the way we sound. In general, sympathetic intonation goes up and down more than unsympathetic intonation.

a Listen to the same sentence said twice. Notice how the voice goes up and down in the second, more sympathetic-sounding sentence. 57

I'm really sorry to hear that. I'm really sorry to hear that.

b Listen to the sentences. Does the speaker sound sympathetic (S) or unsympathetic (U)? 58

1 ______ 2 ______ 3 ______ 4 ______ 5 ______ 6 ______

c Listen to the sentences again. Repeat the sympathetic-sounding sentences. Try to sound sympathetic. 58

3 Work in pairs. Choose two of the situations (1–4). Roleplay them with your partner, using expressions from the Useful language box. Take turns being the sympathetic listener.

1 A friend lost a 1,000-word essay. He turned the computer off before he saved it.
2 A teammate can't play in the basketball final because he or she isn't good enough. You are the team captain.
3 A teacher failed a classmate in an exam because she saw him using his cell phone. He says he was only turning the sound off, but you know he was texting someone.
4 You forgot to lock the garage door last night. Your sister's motorcycle was stolen.

Useful language

Showing understanding
I'm sorry to hear that.
Yes, that is frustrating.
That's (such) a shame / pity.
What a pity.
I see.

Disagreeing politely
I hear / see what you're saying, but…
I understand, but…

Preparing the listener for bad news
You see, the thing is…
It's just that…
Unfortunately,…
I'm afraid that…
I'm sorry to say…

WRITING A complaint email

4 **Work in pairs. Tell your partner about any problems you have had buying tickets, clothes, or other items online.**

5 **Read the email on page 152 and answer the questions.**

1 What did Park Seo-yeon want to buy?
2 What problem did she have paying for it? What other problem was there with the product?
3 Was her phone call to the company successful? Why?
4 What three things does she want the company to do?

6 **WRITING SKILL** Using formal connectors

a **Look at the Useful language box. Find these words and phrases in Park's email on page 152. Which heading in the Useful language box could you put them under?**

although	consequently	despite	nevertheless	what is more

b **Complete these sentences in a way that makes sense.**
1 I had to wait to be served for twenty minutes. As a result,...
2 In my experience, customer service in your store is usually good. However,...
3 The phone was not the right color. Also,...
4 Even though the menu didn't look very exciting,...
5 It took us over an hour to buy tickets. In spite of this,...

Useful language

Expressing contrast
in spite of
even though
while
however
even so

Expressing result
as a result
because of this
therefore

Expressing addition
in addition
also
moreover
furthermore

7 **Put the features of a complaint email or letter in the order that they appear in Park's email.**

a a clear demand for a solution
b a description of what happened
c a formal closing
d a formal opening 1
e details of any attachments
f the reason for writing

8 **Choose one of the conversations from Activity 1 and write a complaint letter, or write a letter about an experience you've had. Use these instructions to help you.**

1 Give the reasons for your complaint.
2 Decide what you think the company should do.
3 Underline any expressions from Park's email that you can use in your letter.
4 Make sure you include all the features in Activity 7.
5 Use connectors from Activity 6 to help you organize your writing.

9 **Swap your letter with a classmate. Decide how sympathetic your response should be, then write a reply to your classmate's letter.**

9 Unexpected Entertainment

IN THIS UNIT, YOU...

- talk about forms of entertainment.
- read about young artists.
- learn about FOMO.
- watch a TED Talk about Slow TV.
- write an email describing a place and its culture.

Actors from a theater group take part in the Edinburgh Festival Fringe, Scotland.

9A Entertain me!

VOCABULARY Creative arts

1 MY PERSPECTIVE

Work in pairs. Discuss three of these questions.

1. Look at the photo and read the caption. Is this something you would enjoy watching? Have you seen similar performances?
2. What forms of entertainment do you enjoy? Which ones don't interest you at all?
3. Where can you see art and live entertainment in your area?
4. What are the advantages of watching live performances (theater, dance, music, sports, etc.) over watching at home? What disadvantages are there?

2 Which word does not belong in each group? Why? Use a dictionary if necessary.

1. broadcast / edit / produce / TV program
2. audience / characters / listeners / viewers
3. a theater / a musical / a performance / a play / a production
4. a drawing / a mural / a portrait / a sculpture
5. stadium / exhibition / gallery / studio / venue
6. concert / lyrics / tune / verse

3 Put the words in Activity 2 into these categories: Art, Music, Theater, TV/Radio. Add more words in each category. Then add one new category of entertainment of your choice.

4 Which option is more likely? Why?

1. I love the *lyrics* / *verses* of this song because they say what I'm feeling.
2. She's planning a large *mural* / *sculpture* to decorate the side of the hospital.
3. The president made a ten-minute *broadcast* / *production* to explain the economic situation.
4. More than five million *listeners* / *viewers* watched last night's program.
5. She works in a small *gallery* / *studio* in her garden.

5 Complete the sentences with these pairs of words.

broadcast + viewers	mural + portrait	stadium + concerts
theater + play	tune + lyrics	venues + audience

1. **For me, a good song** is something you can dance to, with a catchy ______________ and memorable ______________ .
2. **If I had some art in my bedroom**, I'd prefer a bright ______________ to a ______________ of someone.
3. **At the moment**, our local ______________ is presenting a ______________ about a murder on a train.
4. **I prefer going to shows** in small ______________ like clubs and halls, where the ______________ is close to the stage. Being so close is a magic feeling.
5. **There's a** football ______________ **near where I live where they sometimes put on** classical music ______________ .
6. *Ranczo* **is a popular** TV show **in my country**. It is ______________ to millions of ______________ around the country.

6 With five of the expressions in bold in Activity 5 make sentences about you.

LISTENING

7 Listen to four conversations. What form of entertainment is each one about? Complete the first row of the table. 59

	1	2	3	4
Form of entertainment				

8 Listen again. Which of the things that are described: 59

a is in a venue?				
b can be enjoyed at home?				
c are recommended by one of the speakers?				
d are known by both speakers already?				
e are about things that are true?				

9 Listen again. Write two more details for each of the forms of entertainment. 59

1 The artist is Italian.

10 Work in pairs. Which of the forms of entertainment described in the conversations would you most enjoy? Why?

GRAMMAR Defining relative clauses

11 Match the two parts of the sentences.

1 He's an Italian artist
2 *Come From Away* is the new show
3 There are some well-written songs
4 If you could recommend just one podcast
5 They were the first band

a I saw live.
b which opened last night on Toronto's Broadway.
c the audience really enjoyed.
d who paints people to look like animals.
e that I should listen to, which would it be?

12 Look at the sentences in the Grammar box. Underline the relative clauses. Which word in bold:

1 could be replaced by *who*? Which one could be replaced by *which*?
2 is the subject of the verb in the relative clause? Which is the object?
3 could be omitted?

Defining relative clauses

a *It's a show* ***that*** *is on every week.*
b *He's a singer* ***that*** *I can listen to all day long.*

Check page 144 for more information and practice.

13 **Combine the two sentences into one sentence with a relative clause. Omit the relative pronoun if possible.**

1 The play wasn't very good. I saw it last week.
The play *I saw last week wasn't* very good.
2 A Shakespeare production closed after only two weeks. It only sold 100 tickets.
The Shakespeare production ______ after only two weeks.
3 The book is the longest book he's ever read. He needed three months to finish it.
The book ______ he's ever read.
4 An actor has been given a pay raise. She demanded the same salary as her male colleagues.
An actor ______ a pay raise.
5 The character spoiled the story for me. She was played by Mara Wilson.
The character ______ the story for me.
6 You're talking about that documentary on New York, aren't you? We saw it together.
You're talking about ______ on New York, aren't you?

14 **Add the information in sentences 1–8 into the paragraph about body painters. Use a relative clause and *who* or *which*.**

1 Johannes Stötter uses human models to make art.
2 You cannot see the people because they are covered in paint.
3 The images have made him famous.
4 The painting became popular in 2013.
5 He made the video to show how the image was created.
6 Art cleverly tricks the eye in this way.
7 These artists use the human body as their canvas*.
8 The best international artists compete in bodypainting championships each year.

who uses human models to make art
Johannes Stötter is an Italian artist (1). He creates images of animals and plants with people (2). The images (3) are sculptures and they can take up to eight hours to complete. He painted a tropical frog (4), then a video (5) went viral. We seem to love any art (6). Johannes Stötter is one of a number of artists (7), but he is perhaps the best known. In fact, a few years ago, he won a few bodypainting championships (8).

canvas *cloth used to make paintings*

15 **Work in groups. Write one example of each of these things on a piece of paper. Don't show your classmates. Play the definitions game.**

an actor	an artist
an author	a book
a director	a movie or TV program
a musician or band	a painting
a play or musical	a song or album
a TV presenter	

A: *He was the artist who painted* Sunflowers *and who cut his ear off.*
B: *Van Gogh!*
A: *Correct!*

Angelfish by Johannes Stötter

9B Fast Art, Big Art

Reading Makes You Grow mural by Artez, in Argentina

MAKING A SPLASH

VOCABULARY BUILDING Expressions with *make*

1 **Look at the box and read the sample sentences. What do the phrases in bold mean?**

> Some common verbs in English don't mean very much on their own, but they mean different things depending on the expressions they are used in. *Make* is one example.
>
> *I never **make my bed** after I get up.*
>
> *If you don't **make a decision** soon, I'm leaving.*
>
> *So **30 times 17 makes**, umm, ... it **makes** 510, right?*
>
> *You're worried that you won't **make friends** with anyone at the new school, aren't you?*

2 **Match the expressions with *make* (1–8) with their meanings (a–h).**

1 Nobody goes into art to **make a good living**.
2 We wanted to **make the most of** our trip to Moscow by visiting as many museums and galleries as possible.
3 Older artists should **make way for** the younger generation.
4 A lot of his abstract work **doesn't make much sense** to me.
5 Her exhibition is going to **make quite a splash**.
6 I can't **make up my mind** whether I like this painting. I didn't think I liked it, but I keep coming back to it.
7 Can art **make a difference** in people's lives?
8 There's something powerful about her paintings. They **make a big impression** on me every time I see them.

a be memorable and affect someone
b give an opportunity to
c decide
d be noticed by a lot of people and be popular
e be difficult to understand
f earn enough money to live comfortably
g change things in an important way
h take advantage of something while it lasts

3 **In pairs, talk about four of the following.**

1 a time when it was hard to *make up your mind* about something
2 someone who has *made a big impression* on you
3 someone you admire who *makes a good living*
4 an opportunity that you didn't *make the most of*
5 an artist whose work doesn't *make sense* to you
6 a possession that has *made a big difference* to you

60 The art world is an exciting place for young artists these days. Old ways of making it professionally as an artist, such as art school and gallery exhibitions, are making way for new paths to success. Art is changing fast, with new ways to create, find success, and promote your work. Here are two young artists who are making a splash, each in their own way.

Artez is a Serbian street artist living in Belgrade, (1) ______________ . When he was a child, he practiced making his own tags, or names written in graffiti, in his notebooks at school. Since then, his graffiti has developed into public art on a large scale. Artez's style, which he describes as mixing photorealism* with illustration, is influenced by other artists such as the Maclaim crew, (2) ______________ . Now, even though he is only in his early thirties, Artez is gaining popularity abroad. Among other places, he has worked in India, Brazil, and Greece.

Sophie-chan has made a name as one of YouTube's leading manga* artists. Born in Iraq in 1990, in the middle of a war, Sophie had to change schools several times as her family moved around. It was difficult for her to make friends but she enjoyed drawing, (3) ______________ . Influenced by Japanese anime* cartoons on TV, she taught herself to draw her first manga drawings when she was thirteen. After seeing Marc Crilley, (4) ______________ , Sophie was inspired to upload her first painting video in 2008. Since then, she has produced many more, showing her art as well as offering tutorials and advice on how to draw.

Both artists make the most of social media to promote their work. Sophie's popularity on YouTube means that she makes money from it. Her channel is monetized, (5) ______________ . However, she doesn't earn a lot of money that way. After graduating, she worked as an engineer to save the money she needed to self-publish *The Ocean of Secrets*, her first book, (6) ______________ . Her online popularity means that she already has lots of followers who may buy the book.

Artez has active Facebook, Instagram, and Pinterest profiles, of course, but he is also part of a group of artists who support each other. He says that "healthy competition and an exchange of ideas can really motivate people to produce more, better, and faster. I was lucky to start my painting career on the streets of Belgrade and to become a part of such a lively community of artists!"

photorealism *a style of painting in which the paintings look like photographs*
manga *Japanese style of comic book*
anime *Japanese style of animated cartoons*

READING

4 **MY PERSPECTIVE**

Work in pairs. Look at the photo. How does reading make you grow? What have you read that has helped you grow?

5 Work in pairs. Which of these ways of becoming a professional artist are the most and least effective, in your opinion?

- start practicing at a young age
- study other artists' work
- work with other artists
- show videos of you doing your work
- upload examples of your work to social media
- study art at college
- choose a popular style of art that is easy to understand
- prepare for a different job in case you don't succeed as an artist

6 Read about two young artists, Artez and Sophie-chan. What do we learn about their childhoods, and how they influenced what they do? What kind of art do they do? How do they use social media to show their art?

7 Complete the article (numbers 1–6) with the relative clauses (a–f).

a where some of his murals can be seen
b which came out in 2015
c which kept her busy
d which means that she is paid a very small amount each time a viewer clicks on an ad shown on her videos
e who is one of the original YouTube manga artists
f who were some of the first people to create murals which almost look like photos

8 Work in pairs. How important have the ways of becoming a professional artist in Activity 5 been to Artez and Sophie-chan?

9 Work in groups. Discuss the questions.

1. Have you seen any good graffiti art or manga? Where?
2. Do you think graffiti and manga are really art forms? Why?
3. What other things that you enjoy watching / listening to, etc. do you consider art, (e.g., comedy, flash mobs, animation, rap, …)?

The Great Pyramid of Giza, Egypt, is one of the seven wonders of the Ancient World.

9C A Bit of Culture

1 Look at the photo. What would you be looking at: your phone or the pyramid?

2 Which of these aspects of culture do you enjoy? When do you watch, read, listen, or go to them? How much time each day do you spend on these things?

art (e.g., art websites, exhibitions)
music (e.g., classical, pop, live music, videos)
short films or animations
other people's social media sites (e.g., Instagram)
movies or plays at the theater
poems and short stories
talks (e.g., TED Talks)
TV or radio shows and podcasts
other forms of culture (what?)

GRAMMAR Defining and non-defining relative clauses

3 Look at the sentences in the Grammar box. Try reading them without the relative clauses in bold. Which relative clause contains information that completes the meaning of the sentence (defining relative clause)?

Defining and non-defining relative clauses

a *Artez's style,* ***which he describes as mixing photorealism with illustration,*** *is influenced by other artists.*
b *The Maclaim crew were some of the first people to create murals* ***which almost look like photos****.*
c *After seeing Marc Crilley,* ***who is one of the original YouTube manga artists,*** *Sophie was inspired to upload her first painting video in 2008.*
d *She was able to self-publish* The Ocean of Secrets, *her first book,* ***which came out in 2015****.*

Check page 144 for more information and practice.

4 Look at the sentences in the Grammar box again. Answer the questions.

1 Which relative pronoun can be replaced by *that*?
2 Can any of the relative pronouns be omitted?
3 What do you notice about the punctuation in these sentences?

5 Listen to part of a radio show. What is FOMO? Do you ever get it? 61

6 Complete the sentence beginnings (1–5) with the relative clauses (a–e). Add *which* or *who* if the clause is non-defining, and *that* if it is defining. Use commas where necessary. Then listen again to check. 61

1 Perhaps you stay up late just to play the video game
2 It's the last night they're showing *The Last Jedi*
3 It's the final episode of the show
4 You know that tomorrow you're going to find out what happens from your friends
5 And this creates a worry

a everyone is talking about.
b everyone's watching.
c won't go away.
d are watching it right now.
e you've always wanted to see.

7 Combine the sentences to make one sentence containing a non-defining relative clause.

1 FOMO is the secret disease that many people suffer from. It can affect anyone with access to the internet.

FOMO, which can affect anyone with access to the internet, is the secret disease many people suffer from.

2 When people start conversations with *Did you see… ?*, do you get an uncomfortable feeling in your stomach? This is a common phrase these days.
3 The people it affects run to their phone when they hear it "ping." They are worried that they might be missing something important.
4 Most notifications are really not worth looking at. They might be about music videos, movie trailers, funny cat videos, or profile photo updates.
5 Some young people spend up to eighteen hours a day reading or watching things. They check Facebook while answering texts and watching TV.
6 Studies have shown that we sleep less because of our devices. These include smartphones and tablets.

8 Work in pairs. Add at least three relative clauses to this paragraph to make it more informative.

There are many ways of fighting FOMO in your life. Sophie Kleeman*, who is a journalist,* has some advice for us about spending less time on our devices. First of all, phone settings can be changed to stop them from interrupting you. Phones can be a problem at night. Don't keep your phone in your bedroom even if it is on vibrate. Buy an alarm clock instead. Consider your social media and decide honestly whether you need 24-hour access to it. Could you just have it on your laptop? Another idea is to play Shame with friends. The first person to use his or her phone has to buy the coffee!

9 **PRONUNCIATION** Relative clauses

a Listen to the sentences. Do you hear a defining relative clause or a non-defining relative clause? Put commas in the sentences containing non-defining relative clauses. 62

1 She threw away the phone which didn't have a camera.
2 The men who didn't have tickets were told to leave the theater.
3 My sister who lives in Singapore is studying art.

b Listen to the same sentences being said a different way. How does the meaning change in each? 63

c Work in pairs. Practice saying the sentences in Activity 9a both ways.

10 **CHOOSE**

Choose one of the following activities.

1 Work in groups. Look at these different types of FOMO. Think of examples of each one in your lives and discuss which types are common among your friends. What can you do to fight FOMO?
- having to stay in while everyone else is having fun
- being too young to do something (e.g., watch horror movies)
- missing out on shared experiences

2 Work in pairs. Talk to your partner about a time when you have experienced FOMO. What advice can you offer each other?

3 Find out about a young artist from your country. Write a profile. Include information about the type of work they do, how they use social media, and how successful they are. Use relative clauses to make it informative.

At this movie premiere, most people experience the live moment with their phones. Some studies show, however, that the woman without the phone will probably have a better memory of it.

AUTHENTIC LISTENING SKILLS

Collaborative listening

One reason listening is difficult is because you won't understand everything that you hear. However, different people understand different parts of a message, so working together can increase your understanding.

1 Look at the Authentic Listening Skills box. Then listen to the news report and write down any words you hear. 64

2 Work in pairs. Compare what you wrote. Listen again and note anything you may have missed. 64

3 Work in pairs. Reconstruct the news report. Then listen again to check. 64

WATCH

4 Work in pairs. What kinds of reality TV are popular in your country? Which ones do you enjoy? Why? Are there any you don't like? Why?

My favorite reality TV show is Terrace House. *I think it's very popular in Japan. I like it because everyone is so polite!*

5 Watch Part 1 of the talk. Put these NRK TV programs in the order that they were broadcast. ▶ 9.1

a a program about a ship traveling along the coast
b a program about people knitting
c a program about a train trip

6 Watch Part 1 again. Use one or two words to complete the sentences. ▶ 9.1

1 There is no storyline, no script, no drama, no climax, and it's called ___________ .
2 On the surface, it sounds boring, because ___________ .
3 First a warning: viewers may find some of the images in the following report ___________ .

7 Work in pairs. Have you heard of or watched Slow TV? Is Slow TV something that you, your family, or friends might enjoy? Why?

8 Watch Part 2 of the talk. Match the two parts of the sentences. There are two endings (a–h) you do not need. ▶ 9.2

1 Thomas and his colleagues couldn't make a show about the war because
2 They decided on a show about a train trip because
3 The Bergen Railway trip was a good choice because
4 The show makers were surprised because
5 The show about the trip by ship was different because
6 They asked viewers questions because

a a lot of people watched it.
b it takes a long time.
c it was celebrating its 100th anniversary.
d the commissioning editor laughed at them.
e they didn't have enough time.
f they wanted help designing the show.
g they wanted to make a documentary.
h they would broadcast it live.

9 Watch Part 3 of the talk. Are these statements *true*, *false*, or *not given*? ▶ 9.3

1. Karl got in trouble with his teacher for being late to school.
2. The people waving were talking on the phone to people watching TV.
3. The queen was interviewed on the show.
4. When the queen appeared on the show, Twitter crashed.
5. The show holds a world record.
6. Thomas thinks that Slow TV was a fun idea but it isn't attractive anymore.
7. He thinks that good ideas for Slow TV shows are ideas that other people don't think are good.
8. Slow TV is becoming popular in other parts of the world.

10 **VOCABULARY IN CONTEXT**

a Watch the clips from the TED Talk. Choose the correct meaning of the words and phrases. ▶ 9.4

b Work in pairs. Tell your partner about each of the following:

- a TV show, game, or book that has *gripped* you recently, and why it is so good.
- an idea or plan you've *come up with* recently
- an event you went to where very few other people *showed up*
- the longest number of days *in a row* that you didn't go to school for some reason
- a difficult situation that you *handled* well
- a *buzzword* that's popular at the moment

CRITICAL THINKING Supporting your argument

Here are ways that speakers can support their argument.

a Ask the audience relevant questions or ask them to imagine themselves in a situation.
b Describe a series of events.
c Explain why their argument is true.
d Let the audience experience something so they can decide for themselves.
e Make comparisons.
f Provide statistics and other information.

11 Thomas argues that Slow TV provides surprisingly popular entertainment. Which of the techniques above does he use in his talk to support his argument?

12 What other ways does he use to persuade you that Slow TV can be entertaining?

CHALLENGE

NRK has made shows about trips, knitting, and bird watching. Thomas says, "we started looking for other things we could make Slow TV about." What Slow TV might be popular with your friends or people in your country?

In groups, choose the best idea and think about:

- why the idea is fun or engaging.
- who will watch it.
- how long it will run for.
- how the viewers will take part.

Present your Slow TV idea to the class. Decide what:

- would get the highest ratings.
- would be the most difficult to make.
- would be boring and addictive at the same time.

9E Well Worth Seeing

Useful language

Asking for recommendations

Is it worth watching / seeing / visiting / reading?

What did you think (about...)?

Is it any good?

Making recommendations

You have to go!

I'll send you the link.

You won't want to miss this.

It's worth watching.

I highly recommend it.

...is well worth seeing.

...is a must-see.

Showing reservation

It was OK / alright, I suppose.

I wouldn't bother if I were you.

I didn't think it was great.

You might like it if you have nothing else to do.

If you enjoyed..., you'll love...

It'll appeal to anyone who enjoys...

I don't normally like..., but...

I would recommend it to people who...

SPEAKING

1 Work in pairs. Whose recommendations do you trust most for things like books, restaurants, and tourist attractions? Put the following in order (1–5), where 1 is the most trustworthy. Do you use recommendations from anyone else?

- reviews in newspapers and magazines
- online comments by members of the public
- friends and family
- the tourist information office
- famous people

2 Listen to people talking about the same tourist attraction. What do they agree about? What do they disagree about? 65

3 Look at the Useful language box. Are the expressions more likely to be said by a friend (F), a TV presenter (TV), or both (B)?

4 Listen again. Which expressions in the Useful language box do you hear? 65

5 For each category below, write the names of one example that you would recommend and one that you wouldn't recommend.

a book	a movie	a theater production
a TV show	a work of art	an online video clip

6 Work in pairs. Look at your partner's list. Ask and answer questions about your recommendations and reservations.

WRITING An email describing a place and its culture

7 Work in pairs. What are some of the cultural attractions in your area, town, or city? Which would you recommend to a visitor? Why?

8 Read an email on page 153 from Macarena, who lives in Valparaíso in Chile. What things does she recommend to her friend Aki about her city?

9 Relative clauses are a good way of adding extra information. Read the email on page 153 again. Where could these relative clauses go in the email?

1 , which is why I think artists love the place so much
2 , which is where I'm going later with some friends
3 , which I got this morning
4 , which I'm not,

10 **WRITING SKILL** Paragraphing

a The email on page 153 contains five paragraphs. Read the Writing strategy box. What is the topic of each paragraph?

Paragraph 1 talks about the postcard that Aki sent.

b Choose one of the texts from the Writing Bank on pages 149–153. What is the topic of each paragraph? In pairs, discuss how the text has been organized.

11 Plan an email to a friend describing the place where you live. Include the usual sites, as well as the alternative cultural attractions. Use your ideas from Activity 7 to make notes and plan the paragraphs. Then write your email.

12 Read your classmates' emails. Are they well organized? Do you agree with their recommendations about the best attractions where you live?

Writing strategy

Paragraphing

- Paragraphs are groups of sentences which share a common topic. They help the reader follow the text. Start a new paragraph when you change topics.
- Before you start writing anything, make notes, then organize your notes into paragraphs.
- Finally, decide on the best order for the paragraphs.

Pyramid of the Feathered Serpent, from Teotihuacan, in the National Museum of Anthropology, Mexico City

10 Time

IN THIS UNIT, YOU...

- talk about how you spend your time.
- read about the clockmaker who changed the world.
- learn some time management tips for studying.
- watch a TED Talk about time management.
- write a pro and con essay.

Churchgate Railway Station, Mumbai, India

10A Spend Your Time Wisely

VOCABULARY Phrasal verbs about time

1 MY PERSPECTIVE

Work in pairs. Look at the photo and discuss the questions.

1 Do you think of yourself as a busy person? Do you relate more to the people in the photo who are rushing around or the people sitting down? Why?
2 How much time do you spend doing nothing much? Is this wasted time? Why?
3 When during the day are you normally busiest?

2 Read these common problems. Write 0–3 for each one (0 if you never experience the problem, and 3 if you experience it often). Work in pairs and compare your answers.

1 I always have to **wait around** for people to get ready to go out. They're so slow!
2 I have lots of things I want to do, but I never **get around to** doing any of them. I can't **fit** them **in** with all this school work.
3 I **hang out** with my friends most weekends, but we never do anything interesting together.
4 I was sick for a few days and I **fell behind** at school. It took forever to **catch up**.
5 I usually **put off** studying until the night before an exam, and sometimes I **run out of** time.
6 Teachers at my school sometimes **move** tests **up** without warning us.
7 We haven't taken a vacation this year because my dad can't **take** time **off** work.
8 I'm really **looking forward to** being on vacation. I'm desperate! I just need to **hold on** for a few more weeks.

3 Complete the sentences with the correct form of a phrasal verb in bold from Activity 2.

1 If they can't come to the party in May, let's ______________ it ______________ to April.
2 Haven't you done the dishes yet? When are you going to ______________ doing them?
3 We didn't finish the test—we ______________ time.
4 The last episode isn't until Friday. I can't ______________ that long! I want to know what happens!
5 I don't feel like ______________ for him all day while he decides.
6 There's nothing we want to see at the movies, so we could just ______________ at the café.

4 Put the words in the correct order to make questions. Then listen and check your answers. 66

1 do / like / hanging / out / who / with / you / ?
2 get / is / keep meaning / around / something / to / to / what / you / ?
3 are / doing / forward / on your next vacation / looking / to / what / you / ?
4 always / do / for as long as possible / off / put / what / you / ?
5 do / even when you are busy / fit / in / to / try / what / you / ?
6 ever / have / wait / do people / around / to / for you / ?
7 be / catch / hardest / if you fell behind / which subject / to / up / with / would / ?
8 do / if you could / off / right now / take / a week / what / would / you / ?

5 Work in pairs. Ask and answer the questions in Activity 4.

LISTENING

6 Work in groups. Make a list of things your older relatives might say about these things if they were asked the question, "What advice would you give young people?"

attitude toward life	dreams and ambitions
health	money and possessions
relationships	work and free time

Life is short, so don't keep putting off your dreams.

7 Listen to the advice of eight older people. How many of your ideas in Activity 6 did you hear? 67

8 Work in pairs. Can you remember the advice? Complete the sentences with no more than six words. Then listen again and check your answers. 67

Speaker 1	There's no point worrying about ________ yet.
Speaker 2	Don't accept anything without first ________ it.
Speaker 3	You're going to say: "I wish I had ________ myself."
Speaker 4	Don't wake up and realize you haven't ________ doing.
Speaker 5	Don't hold on to material ________, hold on to ________ instead.
Speaker 6	If only someone had told me earlier not to prioritize ________ friends.
Speaker 7	Brush ________.
Speaker 8	Basically, my advice is: ________.

9 **MY PERSPECTIVE**

Work in pairs. Which is the best piece of advice? Why?

GRAMMAR Third conditional

10 Look at the sentences in the Grammar box. Answer the questions (1–6).

Third conditional

a *If I had taken care of my teeth, I would have saved a lot of money.*
b *If someone had told me earlier not to prioritize work, I wouldn't have wasted so much time.*
c *I wish I had taken better care of myself in my youth.*
d *If only I hadn't worked so much.*

Check page 146 for more information and practice.

1. (Sentence a) Did she take care of her teeth? Did she save a lot of money?
2. (Sentences a and b) Can the speakers change these situations?
3. What form of the verb is used in the *if*-clause? What form of the verb is used in the result clause?
4. (Sentences c and d) You learned about *I wish* and *If only* on page 74. What time are they expressing in these sentences? What emotion is being expressed?
5. What structure is used with *I wish* and *If only* here?
6. (All sentences) Are the sentences describing real events or imaginary ones?

11 **Complete the secrets to a long life with the correct form of the verbs.**

Most hundred-year-olds have few regrets. If they didn't have such a positive view of life, they probably wouldn't have survived so long. Here are some of their secrets:

1 Jiroemon Kimura (Japan) lived all the way to 116. He said he __________ (not live) so long if he __________ (eat) big meals. He always had small portions.
2 Jeanne Louise Calment (France) is the only person to have lived to 122. She thought that if she __________ (worry) about her health, she __________ (die) much earlier.
3 Fred Hale (United States) believes he __________ (not surf) for the first time at 95 years old if he __________ (not eat) honey all his life.
4 Emma Morano (Italy) was the last person alive to be born in the 1800s. If she __________ (not live) as a single woman for most of her life, she __________ (be) a lot less healthy, she thought.
5 In a survey, a third of the hundred-year-olds questioned said they wished they __________ (spend) more time with loved ones.
6 A quarter of them said, "If only I __________ (save) more money when I was younger."

12 **Work in pairs. Read the story, then make as many sentences about it as possible using the third conditional.**

Sometimes sad events can lead to rewarding lives. Frida Kahlo was an artist who was famous for painting self-portraits. When she was six, she got polio. Her father also had a disability, and he paid a lot of attention to her and taught her about art.

She wanted to be a doctor, but she nearly died in an accident when she was eighteen. She spent months in bed painting.

Mexican painter Frida Kahlo (1910–1954)

Her family placed a mirror above her so she was able to paint herself. Frida never fully recovered from her injuries, but she became famous because of her self-portraits.

If sad things hadn't happened to Frida, ...

13 **Imagine it is the year 2090. Write three things about your long life that you have been happy about, and three things that you wish had been different. Then write a letter of advice to your younger self. Use the third conditional, including *If only* and *I wish*.**

Dear Me,

It's great to talk to you after all these years. Please don't worry—you have a great life. There are just a few things that I wish had been different. First, ...

10B The Man Who Mastered Time

VOCABULARY BUILDING Expressions with *time*

1 **Read about frequent words in English. Which of the expressions with *time* do you already use?**

> **The most frequent words in English**
>
> English has thousands of words, but some are much more frequent than others. In fact, the 700 most frequent words make up about 70 percent of all the English you hear and read. However, common words combine with others to create expressions with new meanings, so it's important to learn them. Here are some expressions with the word *time*, the 55th most common word:
>
> | | | |
> |---|---|---|
> | *3/4/5* **times** | *a full-***time** *job* | *a great* **time** |
> | *a long* **time** | *all the* **time** | *in my spare* **time** |
> | **on** *time* | *once upon a* **time** | *find the* **time** |

2 **Work in pairs. Find expressions with *time* in these sentences and check whether you know their meaning. Use a dictionary if necessary.**

1. His designs were years ahead of their time. Even now, some of them seem advanced.
2. I get strange messages from my brother from time to time. Does he send them to you sometimes, too?
3. I hope the plane takes off on time. I don't want to have to wait at the airport for hours.
4. If we don't leave now, we won't get there early enough. I want to get there in time for the start of the show.
5. In the past, life at sea was extremely dangerous. At one time, sailors would be lucky to live beyond forty years old.
6. While we waited, we passed the time playing cards.
7. It's my birthday in two days' time!
8. It's time to find out who this year's winner is!

3 **Work in pairs. Use expressions from Activity 2 to write five sentences that you think are true about your partner. Read your sentences to your partner. Were your sentences true?**

A *You don't like competitive sports, but you go running from time to time.*
B *That's not true! I play tennis—that's competitive.*

READING

4 **Look at the photo and read the encyclopedia entry and the biography quickly. What is the "Longitude Problem" and how did John Harrison solve it?**

5 **Read the article again. Are the statements *true*, *false*, or *not given*?**

1. Before 1700, sailors had no way of knowing where they were if they could not see land.
2. Clocks on land were more accurate than clocks on ships.
3. The disaster in 1707 encouraged the Longitude Prize to be set up.
4. People thought that a clock that was accurate enough to navigate on long sea trips would soon be built.
5. Harrison's clocks would be considered accurate today.
6. Harrison became angry with the Board.
7. Despite their cost, watches like Harrison's were soon seen as essential equipment for ships.
8. Harrison's work is appreciated more now than it was by the Board of Longitude.

6 **Find words and phrases in the article which mean the same as these expressions.**

1. many times (box)
2. at the same time (para 2)
3. before (para 2)
4. in no time (para 2)
5. stay accurate (para 2)
6. at the time (para 4)

CRITICAL THINKING Drawing conclusions

7 **Work in pairs. Read the Critical Thinking box. Then look at the statements in Activity 5 where the information was not given. Are they true or false? Why do you draw these conclusions?**

> We can use the information we read in texts to draw conclusions of our own. For example, from this sentence, what conclusions do you draw about the boy?
>
> *The boy kicked the dog.*
>
> You might conclude that the boy is cruel or violent, even though the text says nothing about his personality. Do you change your mind if you read *The boy kicked the dog by accident* or *The boy kicked the dog to protect his brother*?

8 **Discuss these questions about the Board of Longitude.**

1. What conclusions can you draw from the article about the Board of Longitude?
2. What information helped you draw these conclusions?
3. What information would you need to confirm your conclusions?
4. Did you draw any other conclusions from the article?

9 **Work in groups. Make a list of history's three greatest inventors. Find out more about each one and present them to the class. Explain why these people were the greatest. Take a class vote on the greatest of them all.**

A copy of John Harrison's Marine Timekeeper in the Royal Observatory, Greenwich, London

John Harrison: THE CLOCKMAKER WHO CHANGED THE WORLD

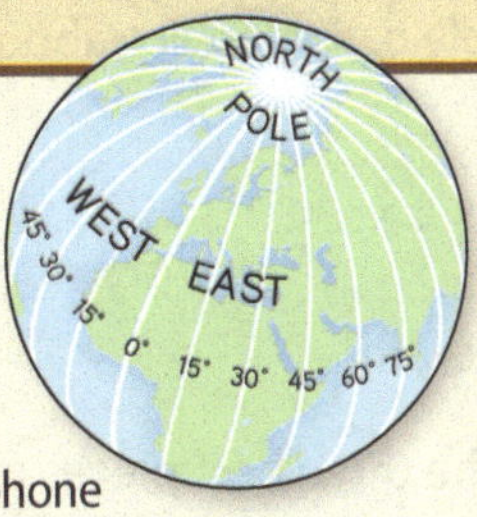

68 THE "LONGITUDE PROBLEM"

GPS technology allows you to know exactly where you are on Earth, to within a few meters. It is available to anyone with a smartphone or GPS watch. But at one time, it wasn't this easy. Before the eighteenth century, sailors could calculate how far north or south they were (their latitude) by measuring the height of the sun in the sky, but they couldn't know their position east or west (their longitude) accurately. Because the Earth rotates once every 24 hours, you had to know the exact time in order to navigate well. Good timekeeping on land was difficult, and almost impossible at sea. Time and again, ships got lost or crashed against the rocks, and thousands of sailors died each year.

In 1707, four ships were lost and 1,500 sailors died when ships from the British navy ran into rocks after getting lost in fog. Although this was a terrible tragedy, it was a common story in the eighteenth century because there was no way for ships to navigate accurately. In 1714, a prize of £20,000 (about $3.6 million today) was promised to anyone who could solve the "Longitude Problem." A group of experts, the Board of Longitude, was set up to judge proposals, which had to be accurate to within about 50 kilometers (or 31 miles). It included important politicians and scientists, who all believed the answer would be found in the stars.

Meanwhile, in the north of England, miles from the center of politics and science, the son of a carpenter was learning how to build clocks. By the time he was twenty, John Harrison had built his first pendulum* clock, and it wasn't long before he was building some of the most accurate clocks in the world. But Harrison knew that pendulums didn't work on a moving ship, and he wanted to win the Longitude Prize. Over the next 30 years, he invented mechanisms* that allowed clocks to keep the correct time, no matter how the sea was moving or how the temperature changed.

He presented a series of clocks and watches to the Board between 1735 and 1765. On three sea voyages they proved successful, but each time the Board ruled that the results could just have been good luck and refused to give him the prize. Harrison, now an old man, decided to speak to the king about the matter. Finally, in 1773, he was given a reward that he should have received a long time before. It wasn't the full prize, but it did mean he was rich for the last three years of his life.

In their day, Harrison's sea watches were way ahead of their time in terms of engineering and accuracy; it must have been like seeing a driverless car today. They were incredibly expensive to begin with, but very quickly it would have been unthinkable to go to sea without one. Explorers were able to map the world more accurately, and thousands of lives were saved. These days, Harrison is remembered as one of history's greatest inventors.

pendulum *a bar with a weight at one end that moves from side to side to keep a clock working*
mechanisms *parts of a machine*

10C Plenty of Time!

GRAMMAR Modals: past speculation, deduction, and regret

1 Work in pairs. Look at the photo and read the beginning of an article giving advice about exams. Discuss the questions.

1 What examples of people taking exams seriously are mentioned?
2 How serious are end-of-school exams in your country and your school?
3 Do you have a serious attitude toward exam preparation? What do you do?

It's that time of year when young people around the world are preparing for exams. If you think people where you live take it extremely seriously, consider South Korea, where college admission is so important that airplanes aren't allowed to take off during the country's main language listening test. Or Brazil, where as many as 8.6 million students take the Enem exam each year, competing for college placement. Or China, where questions from the Gaokao university admission exams are discussed in great detail on popular radio shows.

Sure, it's a stressful time, but there's a lot you can do to make the experience as stress-free as possible. Let's hear from the best people to offer advice—recent graduates who've been through it all before.

2 Listen to eight people giving advice about exams. Which speaker gives advice about: 69

a the time before an exam?
b the day of the exam?
c the time after the exam?

3 Listen again. Note the three best pieces of advice. 69

4 **MY PERSPECTIVE**

Work in pairs. Do you agree on which advice is the most useful? What advice would you add?

5 Look at the Grammar box. Which group of sentences (1 or 2) describes:

a real past situations that were possibly true?
b imaginary past situations that didn't happen?

Modals: past speculation, deduction, and regret

Group 1—speculation and regret

a *If I had passed, who knows? I* ***may not have chosen*** *this path.*
b *If I'd studied at the library, I* ***could have avoided*** *that.*
c *I* ***should have given*** *myself more time to review.*
d *I* ***shouldn't have listened*** *to my friends.*

Group 2—deduction

e *My friends* ***must have been*** *very stressed.*
f *My hair started to fall out, which* ***might have been*** *the stress.*
g *She* ***couldn't have prioritized*** *the questions correctly.*

Check page 146 for more information and practice.

6 Choose the correct options to complete the conversation. Then listen and check your answers. 70

A They (1) *can't / might / shouldn't* have put the grades on the website by now. They said they would be announced by the end of the day.
B It's only three o'clock. I'd be surprised if they were ready. Anyway, I don't want to know.
A Why not? You're smart. You (2) *can't / must / would* have done badly. If you did badly, then I (3) *can / must / should* have done even worse!
B I'm not so sure. You're good at geography. Oh look, here they are. I got a B.
A Oh, no! I'm sorry.
B No, it's fine. I knew I (4) *may / must / should* have studied more. Anyway, a B is fine. Look, you got an A. Good job!
A Wow! On a different day I (5) *might / should / wouldn't* have failed, because everything I reviewed the night before came up in the exam. I was just lucky.
B Luck has nothing to do with it. You (6) *could / must / would* have decided not to study at all, but you didn't.

7 **PRONUNCIATION** Weak forms: *have*

a Listen to the sentences at normal speed and slowed down. Is *have* pronounced the same way in both? In which sentence is *have* stressed? 71

1 I have to study tonight.
2 He couldn't have passed. He didn't study at all.

b Work in pairs. Practice the conversation in Activity 6 with the correct stress.

8 Work in pairs. Look at the situations (1–5). Discuss possible explanations for each of them.

1 Your cell phone bill is much higher than usual this month.

I shouldn't have talked to my friend in China for so long. I must not have noticed how long I was on the call.

2 When you arrive home, there are things all over the floor.
3 Your teacher came to your house to talk to your parents.
4 You texted a friend three times last night, but she didn't reply.
5 You waited for a bus for more than half an hour. Buses normally arrive every five minutes.

9 **CHOOSE**

Choose one of the following activities.

1 Write a situation similar to those in Activity 8. Read your situation to your classmates, who must come up with possible explanations.
2 Work in groups. Choose a photo from anywhere in this book. Make as many sentences as you can about it using *can't*, *could*, *may*, *might*, *must*, *should*, and *shouldn't have*.
3 Write about a time when you either passed or failed an exam. Write about the reasons for your success or failure, the consequences, and what you learned from the experience.

Students pose for photos with the expression "release your stress, let your dream fly" before college entrance exams in Hebei province, China.

10D Inside the Mind of a Master Procrastinator

"I think all of you are procrastinators."

TIM URBAN

Read about Tim Urban and get ready to watch his TED Talk. ▶ 10.0

AUTHENTIC LISTENING SKILLS

Guessing the meaning of new words

When we're listening, we often hear words and expressions with which we aren't familiar. However, we can often guess their meaning from the other words around them (their context), or what we already know about them. For example, you may not know the adjective *rewarding*, but if you recognize the verb *reward*, it may help you figure out its meaning.

1 **Look at the Authentic Listening Skills box. Read and listen to the first sentences of Tim's talk. Try to figure out the meaning of the words in bold.** 72

So in college, I was a government **major**, which means I had to write a lot of **papers**. Now, when a normal student writes a paper, they might **spread** the work **out** a little like this.

2 **Work in pairs. Read and listen to the next section of the talk. Discuss what these words and expressions might mean.** 73

my normal workflow	start off light	bump it up
kick it up into high gear	staircase	

But then came my 90-page senior thesis, a paper you're supposed to spend a year on. And I knew for a paper like that, my normal workflow was not an option… This is how the year would go. So I'd start off light, and I'd bump it up in the middle months, and then at the end, I would kick it up into high gear just like a little staircase. How hard could it be to walk up the stairs?

WATCH

3 **For each statement, which answer is most true for you?**

1 I often end up doing things days after I had meant to do them.
   a Like me **b** Sometimes like me **c** Not like me

2 If I don't do something right away, I forget to do it.
   a Like me **b** Sometimes like me **c** Not like me

3 I usually have to hurry to finish tasks on time.
   a Like me **b** Sometimes like me **c** Not like me

4 I get distracted and do fun things instead of work.
   a Like me **b** Sometimes like me **c** Not like me

5 I often say to myself, "I'll do it tomorrow."
   a Like me **b** Sometimes like me **c** Not like me

4 **Work in pairs. Compare your answers to Activity 3. Which of you is the bigger procrastinator?**

5 **Watch Part 1 of the talk. Complete what Tim says with one word in each blank.** ▶ 10.1

I thought that was the end of (1) __________ . But a week later I get a call, and it's the (2) __________ . And they say, "Is this Tim Urban?" And I say, "Yeah." And they say, "We need to talk about your (3) __________ ." And I say, "OK." And they say, "It's the (4) __________ one we've ever seen."

That did (5) __________ happen. It was a very, very (6) __________ thesis. I just wanted to enjoy that one moment when all of you thought, "This guy is (7) __________ !" No, no, it was very, very (8) __________ .

❻ Watch Part 2 of the talk. What three things does Tim say he does when he gets distracted? ▶ 10.2

1 He draws pictures on a piece of paper.
2 He keeps checking his emails.
3 He looks in the fridge.
4 He plays video games.
5 He reads interesting Wikipedia pages.
6 He watches videos on YouTube.

❼ Watch Part 3 of the talk. Mark these events (a–c) on the timeline. ▶ 10.3

a The TED organizers invite Tim to do a talk.
b Tim starts working on his TED talk.
c Tim's photo is put on the TED website.

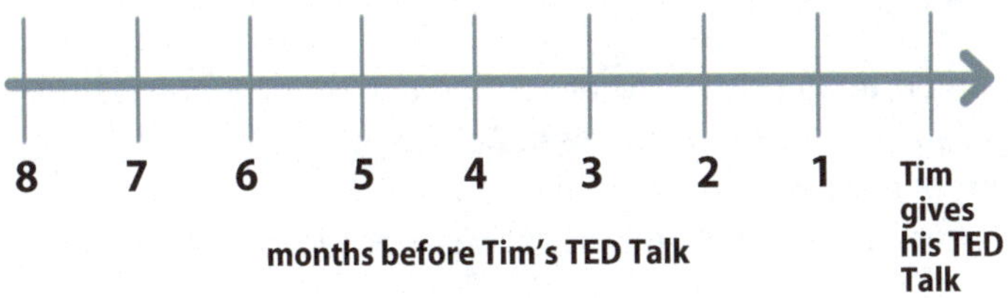

❽ Watch Part 4 of the talk. Which statement is <u>not</u> true according to Tim? ▶ 10.4

1 Self-starters are people who stop themselves from procrastinating.
2 It is difficult to stop procrastinating when there are no deadlines.
3 Procrastinating stops many people from achieving their dreams.

❾ **VOCABULARY IN CONTEXT**

a Watch the clips from the TED Talk. Choose the correct meaning of the words and phrases. ▶ 10.5

b Think of examples of the following things. Then compare your ideas with a partner.

- Things that people make a *big deal* about, but which aren't that important in your opinion.
- Things you've had *on your mind* recently.
- Reasons why people sometimes *stare*.
- Any *long-term* plans or goals you have.
- Things you might not be *aware* of if you are wearing headphones and listening to music in the street.

❿ Work in groups. Look at the different things that people do to stop procrastinating and getting distracted. Which tips would help you? Why? What are the advantages and disadvantages of each? Can you make any other suggestions?

- Break jobs into small steps. Give yourself mini-deadlines for each step. Check off the deadlines that you meet. Reward yourself with ten minutes to do fun things.
- Download an app on your computer that keeps you from visiting your favorite websites.
- Plan your next week by writing a list of things to do each day.
- Talk to friends. Help each other not procrastinate by asking what they want to achieve each week, and checking that they have done those things.

CHALLENGE

Work in pairs. Tim believes that "everyone is procrastinating on something in life." Tell your partner what *you* are procrastinating about and why.

10E Milestones

SPEAKING

Useful language

Explaining causes and reasons

That's why…
That's the reason…
The purpose of -ing is to…
The point of -ing something is to…
One of the main reasons is that / to…
Consequently,…
Therefore, …
…in order to…
…because of…
…so that…
…is caused by…

1 Work in pairs. Discuss how old you have to be to do these things in your country. What other legal age restrictions do you know about?

- vote
- graduate from school
- drive

2 Listen to Alper from Turkey and Jimena from Colombia. How old do you have to be in these countries to do the things in Activity 1? 74

3 Listen again. Answer the questions. 74

1 Why does Alper think the driving age should be higher?
2 Why does Jimena think a lower driving age is OK?
3 Why do they both believe the voting age should be lower?

4 Match 1–8 with a–h. Add one word to each item. Use the Useful language box to help you.

1 I sent him a text ____
2 Many birds in the northern hemisphere fly south in the winter ____
3 The city has a lot of roads for cyclists. That's ____
4 The only reason you should beep your car horn is ____
5 The number of seats in the theater has been reduced. ____ ,
6 The whole point of providing free college courses ____
7 Air pollution and traffic jams are caused ____
8 I went to school by car because ____

a the heavy rain.
b it's now harder to get tickets.
c the increase in privately owned cars.
d warn other users of the road that you are there.
e order to find food.
f that he would understand why I'm angry.
g to give people from poorer families access to education.
h there are so few road accidents.

5 Work in groups A and B. Imagine that the government in your country wants to change the legal age for one of the things in Activity 1.
Group A, make a list of reasons in favor of this proposal.
Group B, make a list of reasons why it might not be a good idea.

6 Work in pairs, one from group A and one from group B. Explain your side of the argument from Activity 5. Try to persuade your partner to agree with you.

WRITING A pro and con essay

7 Read the writing task below. How old do you think you will be when you leave home? Why?

In your English class, you have been discussing the pros and cons of different ages to leave home. For homework, your teacher has asked you to write an essay giving your reaction to the following statement: "Young people should leave home as soon as they finish school." Write your essay.

8 Work in pairs. Write three pros of (reasons for) leaving home when you finish school, and three cons (reasons against).

9 Read the pro and con essay on page 153. Which of the pros and cons you wrote in Activity 8 are mentioned? Is the writer's overall opinion for or against the statement?

10 **WRITING SKILL** Using discourse markers

a Read the essay on page 153 again. Find the words that help the reader follow the argument. Use the Useful language box to help you.

b Put the sentences in order (1–7). The first one has been done for you. How do the discourse markers help you?

- **a** Also, if your friends are going to college, you may want to share similar experiences with them.
- **b** Finally, if you start college sooner, you finish sooner, so you can start earning money.
- **c** First, you don't want to forget the things you learned in school.
- **d** On the other hand, the time before college is perfect for doing things that it might be harder to do later in life, such as traveling.
- **e** Overall, I think that you should only take time off before college if you have a clear idea of what you want to do in that time.
- **f** There are several reasons why it's a good idea to go straight from school to college, without taking time off in between. *1*
- **g** What's more, some schools prefer their students to have had some life experience before they start.

11 Write a pro and con essay. Choose one of these statements to write about. Use expressions from the Useful language box to make your arguments clear.

- A college education doesn't help prepare people for most jobs. Work experience is much more valuable.
- The legal age for driving is too low and should be raised.
- Young people do better by staying in their home town rather than moving to a new city.
- It is better to work on deadlines that other people set than to set them yourself.

12 Work in pairs with someone who has written about the same essay topic. Did you draw the same conclusions?

Useful language

Discourse markers

Sequencing arguments

First, Second, …

First of all, …

Finally, … / Lastly, …

Adding arguments for

Furthermore, …

What's more, …

Not only that, but…,

Introducing arguments against

On the other hand, …

However, …

Even so, …

Concluding

In conclusion, …

Overall, …

Personally, I believe that…

SUBJECT / OBJECT QUESTIONS

Wh- questions start with a question word (e.g., *What, Where, Who, When, How*). The question word sometimes asks about the subject and sometimes it asks about the object.

In **object questions**, the question word asks about the object of the verb. Use the auxiliary verb *do/does* in simple present and simple past questions (*am/were*, etc. in continuous tenses; *have/has*, etc. in perfect tenses). The auxiliary verb goes before the subject.

***Which movie** do you want to see? I want to see* **Jason Bourne**.
(*Which movie* asks about the object.)

***Who** have you spoken to? I've spoken to **Diane**.*
(*Who* asks about the object.)

Don't use a question word in *Yes/No* questions.

Did you call Diane? Yes, I did.

Some verbs have two objects (e.g., *tell, give, invite*). Questions can be asked about both objects.

Gurpreet gave Anita a present.

Who did Gurpreet give a present to? (Anita)

What did Gurpreet give Anita? (a present)

In **subject questions**, the question word asks about the subject. Don't use the auxiliary verb (*do/does*) in simple present and simple past questions.

***Who** likes this game? **I** like it.* (*Who* asks about the subject.)

***Which video** made you laugh the most? **The one with the cats** made me laugh the most.* (*Which video* asks about the subject.)

Not ~~***Who** does like the game?*~~ ~~***Which video** did make . . . ?*~~

In questions in other tenses, always use the auxiliary verb (e.g., *has, will, am*).

*Who **is** making all that noise?*

*Which movies **have** made the most money?*

▶ **Activities 1 and 2**

TALKING ABOUT THE PRESENT

To talk about the present, you can use the simple present, the present continuous, and the present perfect. (Some people think of the present perfect as a past tense, but it always has a connection to the present, so it is really a present tense.)

The simple present is used:

- to talk about things that are always or generally true (e.g., scientific facts).

*Some planets **have** many moons. Jupiter **has** at least 67!*

- to describe habits and routines (often with words like *sometimes* and *never*).

*I **don't** normally **go** out during the week, but sometimes I **go** to the movies on Saturdays.*

- with stative verbs (verbs of feeling, thinking, owning, and sensing) (e.g., *enjoy, think, belong, seem*).

*I **don't believe** that you stayed home all weekend.*

The present continuous is used:

- to talk about temporary actions happening at or around the present time, or at the time of speaking/writing.

*What's that man **doing**? He's **looking** for something.*

*I'm **reading** a really interesting book about technology right now.*

- to talk about changing situations.

*The world **is getting** warmer at a very fast rate.*

- with *always* to describe actions that happen often (and perhaps annoy the speaker).

*He's **always telling** lies about me. Don't listen to him!*

The present perfect is used:

- to describe actions that started in the past and continue in the present.

*Natsuki and I **have been** friends since we were young.*

To make negatives and questions in the simple present, use the auxiliary verb *do/does* + infinitive.

*She **doesn't** often **cry** in public.*

*Why **do** you **enjoy** making cakes and cookies?*

To make affirmatives, negatives, and questions in the present continuous, use the auxiliary verb *is/am/are* + *-ing*.

*He's **talking** to his friends online, so he **isn't listening** to me.*

*I'm **not studying** very hard right now.*

*Why **are** you always **stealing** my pens?*

To make affirmatives, negatives, and questions in the present perfect, use the auxiliary verb *have/has* + past participle.

*They've only **known** each other for two weeks.*

*She **hasn't been** very happy recently.*

*How long **have** you **lived** in Istanbul?*

▶ **Activities 3–7**

1 Are the questions correct? If not, correct the mistake.

1 Where does Henri work? (He works in Paris.)
2 What Ingrid does? (She's a pilot.)
3 Which bus does go downtown? (Bus number 12.)
4 Who saw the show yesterday? (We all saw it.)
5 What you were doing when the concert started? (We were stuck in traffic.)
6 Who loved Lina in the story? (She loved Antonio.)

2 Write subject and object questions about these sentences.

1 Tariq dropped his phone.
  a What did Tariq drop ?
  b Who dropped his phone ?
2 The children enjoy their math classes.
  a Who ______ ?
  b Which classes ______ ?
3 Evgeny watched three movies yesterday.
  a What ______ do yesterday?
  b How many ______ ?
4 Most of the class likes the new teacher.
  a Who ______ ? (subject)
  b Who ______ ? (object)
5 Karina has lost her purse.
  a What ______ ?
  b Who ______ ?
6 Kei told Naomi the secret.
  a What ______ Naomi?
  b Who ______ the secret to?

3 Choose the best option to complete the conversations.

1 A How often *do you go / are you going* camping?
  B Not that often, but we *plan / are planning* a trip soon.
2 A *Do you come? / Are you coming?* Hurry up!
  B Wait! *I need / I'm needing* to send my brother a text.
3 A I *normally take / have normally taken* the bus, but this week the bus drivers *don't work / aren't working*, so I *ride / I'm riding* my bike instead.
  B My mom *always takes / is always taking* me in the car.
4 A How long *are you having / have you had* a cell phone?
  B It's not mine. *I borrow / I'm borrowing* it from my sister.
5 A *You always play / You're always playing* computer games. You should go outside more!
  B *I'm finishing / I finish* my game now, and then I'll go out.
6 A Can you help me? *I'm looking / I've looked* for my hat. I *don't see / haven't seen* it since Saturday.
  B Sorry, *I don't know / I'm not knowing* where it is and *I'm doing / I've done* my homework right now. Can I help you look later?

4 Complete the sentences about changing situations with the correct form of these verbs.

become	eat	get	go up	use

1 Teenagers in many parts of the world ______ fatter because they ______ too much.
2 The temperature of the planet ______ year by year.
3 More and more people ______ text messaging as a way to communicate.
4 Riding a bike ______ popular in cities again because driving is slow and expensive.

5 Write questions with *How long*. Use the simple present or present perfect. Ask a classmate the questions.

1 know your best friend?
2 be your commute to school?
3 be at this school?
4 this lesson last?
5 be able to swim?
6 know how to speak English?
7 live in your house?

6 Match the two parts of the sentences.

1 I've enjoyed drawing and painting
2 I do some drawing or painting
3 I go to art class
4 I've been in the class
5 I'm painting a picture of a forest
6 In fact, I'm doing a lot of painting
7 But of course I'm not drawing anything

a for about two years. I've learned a lot since I started going.
b my whole life.
c almost every day, even if it's only a quick drawing.
d right now; I'm studying English!
e these days. More than ever!
f this week.
g twice a week.

7 Complete the conversation with the simple present, present continuous, and present perfect forms of the verbs.

A What jobs / your parents / do?
B Well, my mom is a doctor, but my dad / not / work / right now. He / study / to be a computer programmer.
A Oh, really? Why's that?
B He / be / a restaurant manager for most of his life, but he wants to do something different.
A And / he / like / computers?
B Oh, yes, he / always / play / with computers at home. My computer / never / work / because my dad / think / he can "improve" it!
A Oh, no! Well, I / hope / he learns how to fix your computer in this class!

ADJECTIVES ENDING IN *-ED* AND *-ING*

Many adjectives ending in *-ed* and *-ing* (participial adjectives) are formed from verbs. Many participial adjectives describe feelings.

The Aztec culture ***excites*** *a lot of visitors.* (verb)

We went on ***exciting*** *excursions from Mexico City.* (adjective)

I was ***excited*** *about visiting the Aztec pyramids.* (adjective)

Use *-ing* adjectives to describe what makes you feel an emotion (e.g., ***exciting excursions***; The excursions make us feel this way.)

Use *-ed* adjectives to describe how you feel (e.g., *I* ***was excited***; That's how I felt.)

▶ Activities 1 and 2

NARRATIVE FORMS

To tell stories or talk about actions in the past, use the simple past, past continuous, and past perfect.

Simple past

The simple past is used:

- to describe completed actions and situations in the past.

I ***bought*** *a ticket to Athens last week.*

- if actions happen one after another.

When the food ***arrived****, they* ***sat down*** *and* ***started*** *to eat.*

- to describe repeated past actions.

When I was younger, I ***walked*** *to school every day.*

The simple past is formed by adding *-ed* to the infinitive.

pack ⟶ *packed*
hope ⟶ *hoped* (add only *-d* if the infinitive ends in *e*)
stop ⟶ *stopped* (double the final consonant if the infinitive ends in a consonant + vowel + consonant)
study ⟶ *studied* (change the *y* to *i* if the infinitive ends in a consonant + *y*)

Many common verbs are irregular.

go ⟶ ***went*** *get* ⟶ ***got*** *catch* ⟶ ***caught***

For questions and negative forms in the simple past, use *did/didn't* with the infinitive.

Did *you* ***visit*** *the Guggenheim Museum when you were in New York?*

It's strange that we ***didn't meet*** *when we lived in Tokyo.*

The verb *be* is the only verb that doesn't use *did/didn't*.

Was *it a scary trip?* *I* ***wasn't*** *scared.*

For a list of irregular verbs, see page 148.

Past continuous

The past continuous is used:

- to give background information or to describe a situation when other things happen.

Some people ***were*** *already* ***dancing*** *when we arrived at the party.*

- to describe an incomplete action when another action happened.

The train ***left*** *while they* ***were buying*** *coffee.*

The actions are often connected with *when*, *while*, or *as*.

She was checking her bag ***when*** *she realized that her pen was missing.*

The past continuous is formed with *was/were* + present participle (*-ing* form).

While I ***was unpacking****, Joanna went to the reception to ask for a map.*

Past perfect

The past perfect is used to emphasize that one past action finished before another past action. The actions are often connected with *after*, *before*, and *already*.

She ***had*** *already* ***been*** *to Peru and didn't want to go back.*

The past perfect is formed with *had* + past participle. *Had* is often pronounced /d/ and written as a contraction, *'d*.

I didn't get to the concert on time because ***I'd missed*** *my train.*

used to

Use *used to* + infinitive to talk about situations, habits, and routines that were true in the past but are not true anymore. Don't use *used to* to talk about single actions.

They ***used to have*** *a house in Bucharest.* (situation)

She ***used to eat*** *meat.* (habit)

We ***used to see*** *them every Sunday.* (routine)

The simple past can be used to talk about these actions when the situation is clear:

They ***had*** *a house in Bucharest.* (It's clear that they don't have a house there now.)

~~*She ate meat.*~~ (It is not clear whether this happened once or many times, or whether she has stopped eating meat.)

Form negatives and questions using *did/didn't use to* + infinitive.

The voyage to America ***didn't use to be*** *as safe as it is today.*

Did *you* ***use to live*** *in an apartment?*

▶ Activities 3–6

1 Choose the correct option to complete the sentences.

1 If you get *bored / boring* reading on the train, try listening to audiobooks instead.
2 A *surprised / surprising* number of students spend more than two hours a day getting to and from school.
3 Were you *worried / worrying* about traveling alone on the train late at night?
4 Bolivia's cable cars look *frightened / frightening*, but many commuters say they feel more *relaxed / relaxing* after their trip.
5 The trip to the museum was *interested / interesting*, but I was very *tired / tiring* by the end of the day.
6 I understand when I'm in class, but when I'm doing my homework I get *confused / confusing*.
7 I didn't enjoy that at all! The taxi was driving too fast. It was *terrified / terrifying*!
8 Phew! Those stairs are *exhausted / exhausting*. They should put an elevator in your building.

2 Are the sentences correct? If not, correct the mistake.

1 Don't be worried. It's not an embarrassed photo of you at all. You look great!
2 Simon enjoyed watching horror movies, but he didn't like feeling frightening.
3 The activity is complicated and I'm not surprised that you feel confused.
4 Everyone told her the movie was great, but she was boring after the first ten minutes.
5 If you want to feel relaxing while you explore Canada's west coast, consider a cruise.
6 The news is shocking, isn't it?
7 Our vacation was fun, even though the weather was depressed.
8 You must be feeling disappointed with that result. What went wrong?

3 Match sentences 1–3 with a–c, and sentences 4–6 with d–f.

1 When the police **searched** the train, the man **got off**.
2 When the police **searched** the train, the man **was getting off**.
3 When the police **searched** the train, the man **had gotten off**.

a The man got off before the police started searching the train.
b The man got off at the same time as the police started searching the train.
c The man got off after the police started searching the train.

4 Everyone **had left** when she got home.
5 Everyone **left** when she got home.
6 Everyone **was leaving** when she got home.

d Everyone left after she got home.
e Everyone left before she got home.
f Everyone left at the same time as she got home.

4 Choose the correct option to complete the sentences. Sometimes both options are possible.

1 Where did you *go / use to go* last weekend?
2 When you were a child, *did you have / did you use to have* a bicycle?
3 I *talked / used to talk* to him after school every day.
4 We didn't *move / use to move* from Toronto to Vancouver until 2015.
5 As a family, we *didn't go / didn't use to go* to the movies unless it was somebody's birthday.
6 My father *smoked / used to smoke*.

5 Correct the mistake in each sentence.

1 Who was teaching you to ride a bike?
2 He ran out of money while he traveled in Germany.
3 Had you seen Gareth yesterday?
4 When I arrived in class, the exam already started.
5 Did you used to walk to school?
6 First I missed the bus, then I had lost my train ticket!

6 Complete the second sentence so that it means the same as the first sentence. Use between two and four words, including the word in bold.

1 John checked that no one was in the house, then he slowly opened the door. **until**
John didn't open the door ___________ that no one was in the house.
2 We spent every holiday with my grandparents when we were little, but we don't these days. **to**
We ___________ every holiday with my grandparents when we were little.
3 Everyone started to eat dinner before I got home. They still hadn't finished when I arrived. **eating**
When I got home, everyone ___________ dinner.
4 Marcos met a friend in Budapest before he went to Japan. **already**
When Marcos went to Japan he ___________ a friend in Budapest.
5 We got on the bus in the middle of an argument among all the passengers. **argue**
When we got on the bus, all the passengers ___________ .
6 She didn't bring her passport, so she couldn't get on the flight. **brought**
She couldn't get on the flight because she ___________ her passport.

SIMPLE PAST AND PRESENT PERFECT

The simple past is used for completed past actions in the past, often with expressions of completed time (*last week, yesterday*).

Australia ***beat*** *Fiji on Sunday in the World Cup.*

The present perfect is used to talk about:

- actions that started in the past and continue to the present.

Teams ***have played*** *modern ice hockey for almost 150 years.*
(This continues today.)

- actions in the past which are connected to a present situation.

He's ***been*** *sick this week, so he's not going to practice.*
(He still doesn't feel well.)

- past experiences when the exact time isn't stated.

*If they choose Lee, it's because he****'s played*** *more matches than Kal.*
(He played more matches at any point in the past until now.)

- recent actions.

*You haven't missed anything. They****'ve*** *just* ***started****.*
*The game****'s*** *already* ***finished****—you missed it!*
I ***haven't seen*** *her score yet, but she's looking very good.*

There are many cases where either the simple present or the present perfect can be used without much change in meaning.

The game just ***started****. (simple past)*
The game ***has*** *just* ***started****. (present perfect)*

The first example expresses that the start of the game is in the past; the second expresses that this is a recent event and connects it to the present. Both sentences are correct, with a slight difference in the intended meaning.

The present perfect is formed with *has/have* + past participle. *Has* and *have* are often contracted to *'s/'ve*.

*She****'s improved*** *her swimming style.*

Go has two past participle forms: *been* and *gone*. Use *been* to say someone went to a place and came back. Use *gone* to say that the person is still in that place.

He's ***been*** *to China.* (And now he's back home.)
He's ***gone*** *to China.* (He's still in China.)

For a list of irregular past participles, see page 148.

▶ **Activities 1 and 2**

PRESENT PERFECT AND PRESENT PERFECT CONTINUOUS

These tenses both describe actions that started or finished in the past but have a connection to the present. However, they emphasize different things.

Present perfect	Present perfect continuous
• emphasizes the fact that an action is finished. *William* ***has practiced*** *enough today. He's coming off the court.*	• emphasizes the fact that an action is unfinished. *Jo's* ***been practicing*** *all day. She won't stop until late.*
• emphasizes the present result of the action (i.e., *How many/much/often?*). *We****'ve played*** *five times. I****'ve won*** *two games and lost three.*	• emphasizes the action itself. *The girls* ***have been training*** *hard.*
• is used with stative verbs (e.g., *want, know, believe, be*). *I****'ve wanted*** *to try his racket ever since he bought it.*	• emphasizes the duration of an action. *They****'ve been playing*** *together for a couple of years.*

The present perfect continuous is formed with *has/have* + *been* + present participle.

A *Has Chloe* ***been practicing****?*
B *Yes, she* ***has****. She****'s been resting****, but will start again soon.*

Questions with *How long* are often formed with the present perfect continuous.

How long ***has*** *she* ***been competing*** *professionally?*

Time expressions

For and *since* are used with the present perfect and present perfect continuous to say how long an action has been going on.

They've been swimming ***for*** *an hour.* (*for* + period of time)
He's played golf ***since*** *the age of ten.* (*since* + point in time)

Use *ever* and *never* + the present perfect to say *at any/no time in the past.*

He's ***never*** *been snowboarding. Have you* ***ever*** *tried it?*

Use *already* and *just* + the present perfect to say that an action is complete.

We've ***already*** *played three games this morning.* (past action)
I've ***just*** *come back from work.* (I came back very recently.)

Yet is used in questions and negatives to ask if an action is complete, and to say it isn't.

Has the team won ***yet****?*
We haven't played any games ***yet****.*

▶ **Activities 3–6**

1 **Complete the paragraph with the simple past or present perfect form of the verbs.**

I (1) __________ (always love) the ocean, ever since I was a girl, so when a friend (2) __________ (invite) me to go sailing with her last summer, I was very excited. I (3) __________ (go) on boat trips many times in my life, but my first day sailing (4) __________ (be) very scary. There was a lot of wind and the boat almost (5) __________ (tip over)! However, I (6) __________ (not give up) that day, and now I love it. Since then, I (7) __________ (spend) almost every weekend at the sailing club or on the water. In fact, I (8) __________ (just buy) a small boat. I (9) __________ (not take) anyone sailing with me yet, but I (10) __________ (take) the boat out on my own on Wednesday for a short trip and it was great. I (11) __________ (not see) my friend for a while because she (12) __________ (go) to New Zealand to sail professionally!

2 **Correct the mistake in each sentence.**

1 We have had three games yesterday.
2 She hasn't tried yet rollerblading, but I'm sure she will.
3 The team competed in the tournament for more than 30 years. In fact, this year will be their 33rd year!
4 Oh, no! You hurt your arm. It looks really sore.
5 **A** Where's Tariq?
B He's been to the locker room to get ready.
6 José and I have played together since three years.
7 They hasn't won many matches so far this year.
8 I've met him since 2014.

3 **Choose the best option to complete the sentences.**

1 Two races have already *taken / been taking* place this morning, but it's *rained / been raining* since 2pm, so nothing is happening right now.
2 *I've hurt / I've been hurting* my leg, so I *haven't wanted / haven't been wanting* to compete in the last month.
3 Although she *has known / has been knowing* how to play chess since she was a little girl, she's only just *started / been starting* to play seriously.
4 **A** How far have you *swum / been swimming*?
B Well, *I've swum / I've been swimming* for 45 minutes, so about one mile, I think.
5 The coach *hasn't chosen / hasn't been choosing* me for the team yet, but *I've trained / I've been training* all year!
6 **A** How many times has your team *been winning / won* the cup?
B None, but they have a chance this year. They've *been playing / played* really well recently.
7 He's *been reading / read* books since he was five. He's *been finishing / finished* hundreds.

4 **Use the prompts to complete the conversations. Use the present perfect or present perfect continuous.**

1 **A** How long / you / play / hockey?
B Six years. In that time, I / play / for three different teams.
A And / your teams / win / any tournaments?
B We / not / win / any big trophies, but we won the local tournament last month.
2 **A** Where / you / be?
B I / work out / at the gym.
A You / not / take / a shower yet, that's for sure! You smell terrible!
B Give me a chance! I / only / be / home / five minutes.
3 **A** Who's that player with the ball? He / play / well so far.
B That's Gareth Bale. You must have heard of him! He / play / for Madrid all season.
A Of course I / hear / of him! But I didn't know what he looked like.

5 **Write *How long/many/much* questions in response to these comments. Use the simple past, present perfect, or present perfect continuous.**

1 I can't believe Serena Williams has won another Grand Slam!
______________? (Grand Slams / she / win)
2 The club is spending so much money on new players these days.
______________? (it / spend / so far)
3 Darya isn't doing tai chi anymore. She left the club a few weeks ago.
______________? (she / be / a member)
4 I met my oldest friend when we played volleyball on vacation together.
______________? (you / know / each other)
5 I'm not enjoying riding my bike anymore. I'm thinking about selling it.
______________? (you / bike)
6 This new tennis racket was expensive.
______________? (it / cost)

6 **Put the words in parentheses in the correct place in the sentences.**

1 Have you run a marathon? (ever)
2 He bought some new sneakers. (just)
3 They've won before. (never)
4 Has she played for the team? (yet)
5 We've met a famous person. (never)
6 I haven't had time to wash my football cleats. They're very dirty! (yet)
7 I've done some exercise today. (already)
8 Did you arrive? Get your swimsuit on! (just)

FUTURE PLANS, INTENTIONS, AND ARRANGEMENTS

Present continuous and *going to*

Both the present continuous and *going to* can be used to talk about future plans. They often have the same meaning.

***Are you having** lunch with your uncle tomorrow?*

***I'm going to have** lunch with my uncle tomorrow.*

The present continuous is more commonly used to talk about things the speaker has already decided to do and made arrangements for, involving other people.

***We're eating** at Coco's. The table is booked for 7pm.*

Going to is more commonly used to talk about plans and intentions the speaker definitely plans to do, but which are not firm arrangements yet.

***I'm not going to have** the soup. I don't like spicy food.*

Going to is used to talk about intentions when there is no clear time given. The present continuous cannot be used here.

***I'm going to read** that book.* (= I plan to read it in the future.)

~~I'm reading that book.~~ (= I'm reading it at the moment.)

will

Will is used:

- to talk about decisions made at the moment of speaking. These are often offers to help or promises.

*You're going to the supermarket? **I'll give** you a ride.*

*I **won't say** anything about it to him, I promise.*

- when you haven't made any plans, but you are thinking about hopes, expectations, beliefs, and plans. *Will* is often used with words and expressions like *I think*, *I'm sure*, *probably*, *possibly*, *maybe*, or *perhaps*.

*I haven't decided who I'll invite. **I'll probably ask** Sanjay.*

may/might

Another way to talk about plans and intentions that aren't firm decisions yet is to use *may* or *might*.

*She **may** ask Sanjay.* (= It's possible that she will ask him.)

*I **might** stay in tonight. It depends on what's on TV.*
(= It's possible that I will stay in.)

Use *may* and *might* with *possibly*. Use *will* with *probably*.

Simple present

The simple present is used:

- for events in the future which are on timetables or schedules.

*The restaurant **opens** at six o'clock.*

- after time expressions with *when*, *until*, *after*, *as soon as*, *if*, and *unless*. *Will* is used in the main clause.

***When** you **speak** to Hanif next week, will you say hi for me?*

▶ Activities 1–4

MAKING PREDICTIONS

Will or *going to* is often used to make predictions.

will

Will is used for future events that are certain to happen.

*Dinner **will be** ready in ten minutes.*

Will is often used with *think*, *expect*, *imagine*, and *know*, and expressions like *I'm sure*. *Will* is usually contracted to *'ll*.

*I **imagine** he**'ll want** a big dinner. He didn't eat lunch.*

If the sentence is negative, *not* usually goes with the first verb.

*I **don't think** she'll eat it.* (Not ~~*I think she won't eat it.*~~)

going to

Going to is often used when there is a clear reason in the present for the prediction.

*This food is very hot. You**'re going to burn** your mouth. Be careful!*

may/might

May or *might* can be used if the speaker is less certain that a prediction is true.

*It **might** rain. If it does, we can eat indoors.*

Future continuous and future perfect

The future continuous is used to talk about an action that the speaker knows or thinks will be in progress at a certain point in the future. The future continuous is formed with *will* + *be* + *-ing*.

***Will** restaurants **be serving** insects as sweet or savory dishes?*

The future perfect is used to talk about an action that the speaker knows or thinks will be finished before a given time in the future. The future perfect is formed with *will* + *have* + past participle.

*I **won't have finished** this work before 10pm.*

▶ Activities 5 and 6

1 Choose the best option to complete the sentences.

1 I haven't written much of the essay yet, but I'm *working / going to work* on it soon.
2 What time *does the plane / is the plane going to* take off?
3 Those bags look heavy. *I'm going to / I'll* help you carry them to the car.
4 *I'll / I'm going to* make a sandwich. Do you want one?
5 What *will you / are you going to* wear to the party?
6 I'll have a pizza. What *might you / are you going to* have?
7 *I spend / I'm spending* a few days with a friend after I *visit / will visit* my grandparents.
8 I don't know what to do. I have to study, but I *might / will* go to the park instead.

2 Complete the sentences using the pairs of verbs in the correct form.

call + give	find out + text	get + arrive
get + not be	understand + talk	

1 I imagine the audience __________ very excited when he __________ at the stadium in an hour.
2 Until Dad __________ home with the groceries, there __________ any lunch.
3 He __________ the situation better after you __________ to him.
4 When you __________ what's happening, __________ you __________ me? You can't call me at work.
5 I __________ you as soon as they __________ me the results.

3 Complete the offers and decisions using the correct form of these verbs.

be	call	~~carry~~	cook	help	make

1 **A** These grocery bags are heavy.
B I *'ll carry* them for you.
2 **A** Could you help me clean the kitchen in about an hour?
B I'm sorry, I can't. I __________ Beril with her computer then.
3 **A** Make sure you get to the restaurant on time.
B I __________ late, I promise.
4 **A** Where's Agata? She said she'd be here ten minutes ago.
B I __________ her.
5 **A** I'm not going to have time to cook dinner today.
B You told me that yesterday. I told you, I __________. I bought some fish this morning.
6 **A** This coffee tastes horrible!
B Oh, no! I put salt in it, not sugar! Sorry! I __________ some more.

4 Use the prompts to write the questions or answers.

1 Q: __________? (what / do / weekend)
A: I'm getting my hair cut and going to a party.
2 Q: Can you let me know what the doctor says?
A: OK. __________. (I / text / you / after / speak / to her)
3 Q: __________? (you / see / anyone / this evening)
A: Yes, Judit is meeting me after basketball.
4 Q: Could you try not to wake Olivia? She's sleeping.
A: __________. (I / not / make / a sound)
5 Q: So, __________? (you / think / you / go back / to that restaurant)
A: I don't know. The food wasn't that good, but the atmosphere was great.
6 Q: Could you please ask Seong-ja if she's coming on the trip?
A: Sorry, __________ (I / not / see / her) until Tuesday, when we're having coffee.

5 Complete the sentences with the future continuous or future perfect form of the verbs.

1 Good evening, everybody. We __________ (eat) in about twenty minutes, so you have time to get a drink.
2 This time next week, I __________ (receive) my culinary diploma. I'm excited, but sad the program is ending.
3 Marc will stay in your bedroom. But don't worry—he __________ (not stay) long. Just a few days.
4 By the time you get this note, I __________ (go), so if you need anything from the store, call me.
5 At the speed he's running, he __________ (not cross) the finish line before it gets dark!
6 We've decided to go to the burger place this evening. __________ (you join) us?

6 Complete the conversation with the best form of the verbs.

A I'm taking my brother to the park. Do you want to come?
B What are you going to do there?
A I'm not sure. I imagine Victor (1) __________ (want) to go rollerblading.
B In that case, I (2) __________ (definitely come). (3) __________ (you leave) in the next five minutes?
A Victor has to get ready and put his rollerblades on. I think we (4) __________ (be) ready in about ten minutes.
B Oh! I just remembered. Carrie's going to call me, so I (5) __________ (not be) able to come with you.
A Should we just meet at the park?
B Good idea. I (6) __________ (see) you at the park gate. Tell Victor that when he sees me, I (7) __________ (wear) my rollerblades, too.

VERB + *-ING* OR INFINITIVE WITH *TO*

forget + *-ing* is used to talk about memories
I'll never ***forget receiving*** *my first job offer. I was so excited!*

forget + infinitive with *to* indicates things you need to do
Don't ***forget to send*** *me a text when you arrive.*

go on + *-ing* talks about an action that is in progress
They ***went on talking*** *after the meeting had finished.*

go on + infinitive with *to* talks about doing one thing after doing something else
After college, she ***went on to become*** *a lawyer.*

mean + *-ing* talks about the consequence of an action
I can't be late again! It would ***mean losing*** *my job!*

mean + infinitive with *to* talks about intentions or plans
Sorry, I ***meant to call*** *you earlier.*

regret + *-ing* talks about things you are sorry you did
I ***regret not taking*** *that job. I hate this job!*

regret + infinitive with *to* introduces something bad
I ***regret to say*** *that you didn't get the job.*

remember + *-ing* talks about memories
I clearly ***remember leaving*** *the letter on your desk.*

remember + infinitive with *to* talks about things you need to do
Did you ***remember to buy*** *some stamps?*

stop + *-ing* talks about an action ending
The camera ***stopped working*** *after I dropped it.*

stop + infinitive with *to* gives the reason for ending an action
They ***stopped to look*** *at the view.*

try + *-ing* talks about ways of solving problems, or experiments
Isn't it working? Have you ***tried restarting*** *it?*

try + infinitive with *to* talks about things that are difficult to do
She ***tried to fix it****, but it was impossible.*

▶ Activity 1

PRESENT AND PAST MODALS

must/shouldn't

In terms of meaning, *have to* and *must* are usually interchangeable to express obligation. However, *have to* is much more common in American English (which makes *must* sound a bit stronger). Use *have to* or *must* + infinitive for obligations. Use *have to* in questions.

I ***must call*** *my brother to congratulate him on his new job.*

Do *you* ***have to do*** *that now?*

In the past, use *had to*, not *must*.
I ***had to walk*** *to work because the buses weren't running.*

Use *can't* + infinitive to talk about things that are prohibited. You can also use *not allowed to*.
You ***can't ask*** *questions until the end of the presentation.*

Use *couldn't* or *wasn't/weren't allowed to* for prohibition in the past.
I ***couldn't wear*** *jeans yesterday because I had an interview.*
I ***wasn't allowed to*** *touch my sister's computer.*

Use *don't/didn't have to, don't/didn't need to* to say that something is <u>not</u> obligatory or necessary. Do not use *must*.
I ***didn't have to wear*** *a uniform in my last job.*
You ***don't need to worry*** *about it. Everything will be fine.*

Use *must* to express deductions (things that you think are true based on evidence you have).
She ***must be*** *the boss. She's wearing a suit.*

can/can't/could

Use *can/can't* or *be able to* to say whether something is possible, or someone is able to do something.
Robots ***can serve*** *food, but they* ***can't eat****.*

Use *can/can't* or *be allowed to* to talk about permission.
They ***can*** *start and finish work when they want.*
Were *you* ***allowed to take*** *three weeks off?*

Use *could* or *was/were able to* for possibility or ability in the past. Use *could* for general ability. For a single event, use *was/were able to / managed to*.
My computer stopped working, but I ***was able to save*** *my work. I* ***couldn't*** *finish the document though.*

Can't (but not *can*) is also used to talk about deductions.
It ***can't be*** *lunchtime already. I've only just had breakfast.*

should/shouldn't

Should and *shouldn't* are used to talk about advice.
Should *I wear a suit to the interview?*

Ought to is also used for advice. It is less common, and sounds more formal, in American English.
You ***ought to*** *see a career counselor.*

▶ Activities 2–5

1 Complete the sentences with the pairs of verbs. Change the form of the verb where necessary.

forget + arrive	forget + pay	go on + chat
go on + win	mean + hurt	mean + miss
regret + do	regret + inform	remember + put
remember + set	stop + do	stop + look
try + open	~~try + talk~~	

1 I know she's angry, but you haven't even *tried talking* to her yet. I'm sure she'd listen.
2 He __________ the door, but the key got stuck in the lock.
3 I __________ my cell phone charger in my bag, but it isn't there now.
4 Can you __________ your alarm for 7:30 tomorrow morning, please?
5 The team started doing poorly, but they __________ the game.
6 It was late, but they __________ into the night.
7 Can you __________ that? It's really annoying!
8 I __________ in the window of the new store on Main Street.
9 We __________ you that we are unable to accept your application.
10 It was a stupid thing to do, but I don't __________ it because it was so much fun.
11 Oh, no! I think I __________ for my drink! I'll have to go back to the café right away.
12 I'll never __________ on the island. It was so beautiful!
13 I could go back home to get an umbrella, but that would __________ my train.
14 I didn't __________ you. It was an accident.

2 Choose the correct option to complete the sentences.

1 Do I *must* / *have to* answer this email?
2 Employees in most companies *are allowed to* / *don't need to* choose when to take vacation.
3 I didn't get the job, but I *could* / *managed to* find a better one.
4 I have a good typing speed now, but I *couldn't* / *shouldn't* type very well when I started.
5 My boss says I *should* / *have to* go to the conference.
6 Receptionists *can't often* / *don't often have to* work after the office closes.
7 The old stars of silent movies *didn't need to* / *shouldn't* have good voices.
8 We *can't* / *aren't allowed to* talk to our colleagues. The boss thinks we're wasting time!

3 Complete the sentences with *must* or *can't*.

1 **A** It's eight o'clock. Is Paco still at work?
B Yes. He __________ love his job!
2 **A** Oh, no! The printer's broken again!
B It __________ be. It was working ten minutes ago.
3 **A** Oh, that's your phone.
B It __________ be Shona—she said she would call.
4 **A** You know that Kristina's leaving?
B Really? That __________ be true. She told me she likes her job.

4 Complete the second sentence so that it means the same as the first sentence. Use a form of *can*, *have to*, or *must*.

1 A few years ago, wearing a suit was obligatory in the office.
A few years ago, you __________ in the office.
2 I really think it is important for me to eat less sugar.
I really __________ less sugar.
3 They weren't allowed to take breaks during work hours.
They __________ during work hours.
4 Is it obligatory to wear a helmet when you ride a bicycle in your country?
__________ when you ride a bicycle in your country?
5 It isn't possible to use the printer because there isn't any paper.
You __________ because there isn't any paper.
6 It wasn't necessary for him to buy a new phone.
He __________ a new phone.
7 Smoking was permitted in the building until last year.
You __________ in the building until last year.
8 The manager says that it is necessary to arrive at the store half an hour before it opens.
We __________ at the store half an hour before it opens.
9 Eating and drinking are prohibited in the library.
You __________ in the library.

5 Correct the mistake in each sentence.

1 When I was younger, I didn't have to touch my parents' computer.
2 When do we must tell the teacher if we can't go on the school trip?
3 We shouldn't complete the project until next week, so we've got lots of time.
4 When you finish your lunch you must not to do the dishes. I'll do them later.
5 Working with criminals must not be an easy job for police officers.

ZERO AND FIRST CONDITIONAL

Conditional sentences have a main clause and an *if*-clause. An *if*-clause describes a condition; the main clause describes the result of the condition.

If the same result always happens, the result clause is in the present (zero conditional). If the result is a possible future situation, the result clause is in a future form (first conditional).

In zero and first conditional sentences, the *if*-clause is in the present tense.

The *if*-clause can go before or after the result clause. Use a comma to separate the clauses in sentences that start with the *if*-clause.

*You will feel some pain **if** you don't take these pills.*

***If** you don't take these pills, you will feel some pain.*

Zero conditional

Zero conditional sentences describe situations that are generally or always true. The result clause can be in the simple present, with an imperative or a modal.

*If you heat ice, it **melts**.* (simple present)

*If you have a headache, **take** an aspirin.* (imperative)

*You **should see** a doctor if a headache doesn't go away.* (modal)

First conditional

First conditional sentences describe possible future situations. The result clause is usually formed with *will/won't*.

*The toothache **won't stop** if you don't take the pills.*

Other modals or an imperative can replace *will*.

*If you go to the pharmacy, **pick up** my prescription, please.*

*He **may hurt** his feet if he keeps walking in those boots.*
(= It's possible that he will hurt his feet.)

*If your eyes hurt, you **should check** whether you need glasses.*
(= It will be a good idea to check.)

*I **can help** you get home if you're tired after the race.*
(= I will be able to help you.)

unless

Unless means *if… not*. It can replace *if* in some conditional sentences.

*The pain will go away **unless** you forget to take your pills.*

*The pain will go away **if** you **don't** forget to take your pills.*

▶ Activities 1 and 2

SECOND CONDITIONAL

The second conditional describes situations that the speaker can imagine, but are not real now and not likely to happen in the future.

I would be very bored if I didn't have my phone with me.
(I have my phone with me now, so I'm not bored.)

The second conditional is formed with *would* + infinitive in the result clause and the simple past in the *if*-clause.

*She **would help** if she **knew** what to do.*

The *if*-clause can go before the main clause, but a comma is used to separate the clauses.

***If** she **knew** what to do, she **would help**.*

Would is often contracted to *'d*.

*I**'d** help you if I could.*

Was or *were* can be used with *I*, *he*, *she*, and *it*. *Were* is more formal. The phrase *If I were you* is often used to give advice.

*If she **was/were** here, I'm sure she'd agree.*

*I'd see a doctor if I **were** you.*

Would can be replaced with *could* to mean *would be able to*.

*I **could** come to the first aid class with you if I had some time.*

Would can be replaced with *might* to mean *possibly would*.

*He **might** feel better if he took some time off.*

I wish and *If only*

When you want a present situation to be different, you can use the second conditional.

*If there **was** an elevator, wheelchair users **would have** access.*

Use *I wish* and *If only* to emphasize this feeling. *If only* and *I wish* are followed by verbs in the past form.

***I wish** there **was** an elevator—then wheelchair users would have access.*

***If only** the restaurant **had** an elevator!*

First or second conditional?

If the situation is a real possibility, use the first conditional with *will* in the result clause and the simple present in the *if*-clause.

*I**'ll go** if I **can**.* (It's possible that I can go.)

*I**'d go** if I **could**.* (It's impossible or very unlikely that I can go.)

▶ Activities 3–5

1 **Complete the paragraph with the correct form of the verbs. Use the simple present, *will*, *can*, *should*, or *may*.**

If you (1) __________ (wake up) with a sore throat, it may be the beginning of an infection. Salt water is a good way to stop the pain, but you (2) __________ (drink) it, just hold it in your mouth. Take acetaminophen if it (3) __________ (continue) to be sore. Be careful—you (4) __________ (pass) your infection on to other people if you share drinks. And if you cough, you (5) __________ (cover) your mouth to protect other people. Wash your hands regularly. You (6) __________ (pass) on infections if you don't. Unless you (7) __________ (have) a fever, however, you (8) __________ (go) outside, but keep warm. Normally, a sore throat (9) __________ (get) better in a few days unless you (10) __________ (take care) of it.

2 **Correct the mistake in each sentence.**

1 If he'll feel sick, I'll make him some green tea.
2 The pain's gone now. I won't take another pill if it comes back.
3 This website says it should be very difficult for a broken bone to heal if it's in the foot.
4 Unless the doctor is happy with your progress, you can go home tomorrow.
5 I call the school and tell them you are sick if your stomachache gets worse.
6 Normally, the teachers let the children play outside unless it will rain.
7 Many people think that you should get a cold if you go out in wet weather.
8 If you're feeling sick, you will see a doctor.

3 **Choose the correct form to make sentences in the second conditional. In which sentence are both answers correct?**

1 If I could have any tattoo, I *chose / would choose* a tiger.
2 I wouldn't get a tattoo if you *paid / would pay* me. I don't like them.
3 If I *was / were* rich, I'd ask the dentist to fix my teeth so that they were perfect.
4 I *couldn't / wouldn't* afford that much work on my teeth unless I won the lottery.
5 I wish my feet *weren't / wouldn't be* so big.
6 If I *had / have* more time, I'd learn to dance.
7 I'd love to go shopping. If only I *didn't / wouldn't* have that doctor's appointment!
8 If I became an actor or writer, I *might / would* change my name, but I'm not sure.

4 **Complete the sentences about the imaginary situations.**

1 The teacher is angry with him because he doesn't help his classmates.
If he *helped his classmates*, the teacher *wouldn't be angry with him*.
2 I can't go out with you this evening because I have a lot to do.
I __________ with you this evening if I __________ a lot to do.
3 She has to take care of her brother because their parents both work.
She __________ her brother if __________.
4 I'm afraid our printer's broken, so you can't print the photo here.
If only our printer __________—then you __________ the photo here.
5 It's such a shame that they can't come to visit us anymore.
I __________ still come to visit us!
6 The library's closed, so I have to study at home.
If the library __________, I __________.
7 A car is parked in front of our car, so Mom can't drive to work.
Mom would __________ if __________ in front of our car.
8 It's so sad that Patricio doesn't live here anymore.
If only __________.

5 **Are the situations a real future possibility, an imagined present situation, or an unlikely future situation? Choose the correct options to complete the sentences.**

1 He'll probably visit tomorrow. If I *saw / see* him, *I'd / I'll* let you know.
2 What *will / would* you buy if you *win / won* a million dollars?
3 We can't help you, I'm afraid. If we *had / have* a car, *we'd / we'll* give you a ride to the station.
4 What *will / would* you do to celebrate if you *pass / passed* your tests? I'm going to buy a new pair of shoes!
5 It's a shame about the weather. If it *isn't / wasn't* raining, *I'll / I'd* take the dog for a walk.
6 I can't believe you left your passport at home! We *will / would* be in Singapore now if you *aren't / weren't* so forgetful.
7 I know you can't go to the movies tonight, but what *will / would* you see if you *can / could*?
8 I'm not sure if your magazine is in my bag. *I'd / I'll* bring it to school on Monday if it *is / was*.

PASSIVE VOICE

Sentences in English can be active or passive. A sentence is active when the subject of the verb is the person or thing doing the action. This person or thing is called the agent.

***They sold** the last copy of the game yesterday.* (*They* is the agent because they did the selling of the game. *They* is also the subject of the verb *sold*.)

A sentence is passive when the object of the verb becomes the subject.

***The last copy of the game** was sold yesterday.*

The passive is used when the agent:

- is unknown or unimportant.

*Most athletic shoes **are made** in China or other Asian countries.* (It is not known specifically who makes them, and any information about which shoe companies make athletic shoes isn't as important as where they are made.)

- is people in general.

*Athletic shoes **can be bought** cheaply because factories in these countries keep their costs down.* (Anyone with enough money can buy athletic shoes.)

- is obvious or already mentioned.

*One of the largest athletic shoe companies is Yue Yuen. At their factories in China, sneakers **are manufactured** ~~by Yue Yuen~~ for many famous brands.*

- is important new information in the sentence, so the agent is included at the end.

*David Beckham **was paid** $3.3 million for an advertising campaign **by Adidas**.* (Notice that *by* is used to introduce the agent.)

The passive voice is formed with the verb *be* + past participle. The auxiliary verb shows the tense of the passive verb phrase.

*Most clothes **are sewn** using sewing machines these days.* (simple present)

*This jacket **was made** in Turkey.* (simple past)

*Sorry, but all the small sizes **have been sold**.* (present perfect)

*The shoes **had been damaged** before the clothes arrived at the store.* (past perfect)

*We often shop during the January sales, when items **can be bought** at cheaper prices.* (modal)

▶ Activities 1–3

HAVE / GET SOMETHING DONE

To explain that you are asking someone else to do something for you, without saying who, use *have / get* + something + past participle.

*I **had my watch repaired** recently.*

*She **got some flowers delivered** to her grandmother.*

Have and *get* mean the same thing here, but *get* is usually less formal.

*They **had** their house valued at $250,000.*

*Where do you **get** your hair cut?*

The structure is called "causative" because you cause it to happen. Often you cause it to happen because you pay for the service, but this is not always the case.

*I **had my friend arrive** early so she could help me with the preparations.*

Have can also be used for an action you didn't cause to happen.

*She **had her wallet stolen**. There was a lot of money in it.*

*Have you **had your email hacked**? I've just received a strange email from you.*

▶ Activities 4 and 5

1 In which sentence (a or b) would you leave out the agent?

1 **a** The shoplifter was arrested by policemen after she stole a coat.
b The woman was caught stealing clothes by 62-year-old store detective, Maureen Backwell.

2 **a** All of the cookies we made have been bought by people.
b I didn't bake them. They were baked by my sister.

3 **a** The school bought the computers. However, they weren't bought by the school for the students.
b The computers were donated by the school to a charity.

2 Choose the correct option to complete the sentences.

1 We understand better now how the environment *affects* / *is affected by* the products that we buy.
2 In the past, most products, such as food, *are* / *were* produced locally, often just a few miles away.
3 Nowadays, products *are* / *had* transported over long distances, often from other countries.
4 Take the milk you had for breakfast. It *may be* / *may have been* driven the length of the country to get to your town.
5 What's more, it's possible that the carton that the milk comes in had been *made* / *making* even farther away, on the other side of the world.
6 The environment *is* / *was* constantly damaged by pollution from all the transportation required to get our daily milk on the table.
7 We must also think about what happens to the carton after it *has been* / *was* thrown away.
8 If the carton *hadn't been* / *isn't* recycled, it will be buried or burned, which releases greenhouse gases.

3 Read the sentences about "supermarket science." Complete the second sentence so that it means the same as the first. Use no more than three words.

1 Supermarket designers have designed every part of this store to make you spend more money.
Every part of this supermarket __________ to make you spend more money.
2 They have put products that they want us to buy on shelves at eye level so we can see them easily.
Products that they want us to buy __________ on shelves at eye level so we can see them easily.
3 It was the same when we were children. They encouraged us to choose the expensive children's food in the same way.
It was the same when we were children. __________ to choose the expensive children's food in the same way.
4 These days, they keep items like milk at the back of the store so that you have to walk through the whole store to find them.
These days, items like milk __________ at the back of the store so that you have to walk through the whole store to find them.
5 Store owners had encouraged customers to spend more than they planned long before doing so became a "science."
Customers __________ to spend more than they planned long before doing so became a "science."
6 For example, someone designed the shopping cart in 1938 to make customers buy more.
For example, the shopping cart __________ in 1938 to make customers buy more.
7 Store owners also placed the fruit, vegetables, and fresh bread at the front of the store to make customers want to come in.
The fruit, vegetables, and fresh bread __________ at the front of the store to make customers want to come in.
8 They even trick our ears! They play slow music to keep people from rushing, so they spend more money.
They even trick our ears! Slow music __________ to keep people from rushing, so they spend more money.

4 Put the words and phrases in the correct order. You will need to change the form of the verbs.

1 after / by a cleaning company / clean / have / the house / the party / we
2 before / fix / get / happens / please / the fire alarm / something terrible
3 change / from companies / have / he / he received / his phone number / so many unwanted calls / that
4 a new pair / buying / have / I / instead of / my old sneakers / repair
5 can / clean / get / I / suit / this / where / ?
6 all the walls / before they moved in / have / paint / they
7 your car / every year / have / test / should / you
8 before you send it / check / for errors / get / your college application

5 Use an expression with *have* or *get* to replace the words in italics so the sentence means the same.

1 He left the car at the garage ~~for the mechanics to change the oil~~. *to get the oil changed*
2 The man took his suit to the dry cleaner's *so they could clean it*.
3 She went to the florist's and *told the lady there to send some flowers* to her mother.
4 Once a month, my grandfather *goes to the barber shop, where a man cuts his hair*.
5 Before we could go on vacation, I had to *pay a photographer to take a photo* for my passport.
6 They were so tired in the evening that they *called a restaurant to deliver some Chinese food* to the house.

REPORTED SPEECH

Reported statements and questions

To report statements and questions, use a reporting verb, like *tell*, *say*, or *ask*. The reporting verb can be followed by the direct speech in quotations (" "), or by a *that*-clause. It is usually not necessary to include *that*.

"I've been here before." → ***She said,*** *"I've been here before."*

"I've been here before." → *She said* (**that**) *she'd been there before.*

say, tell, and *ask*

The most common reporting verbs are *say*, *tell*, and *ask*. *Ask* always reports a question or request; *say* and *tell* report statements. *Tell* and *ask* need a direct object, but *say* doesn't.

"The weather has been good." → *He* ***said*** *that the weather had been good.* OR *He* ***told us*** *that the weather had been good.*

"Where do you live?" → *He* ***asked the man*** *where he lived.*

Several changes are made to a sentence when it is reported.

Tense changes

The verb tense usually changes to a past tense.

- The simple present changes to the simple past.

"I ***speak*** *French."* → *She said she* ***spoke*** *French.*

- The simple past changes to the past perfect.

"We ***didn't do*** *it."* → *They said they* ***hadn't done*** *it.*

- The present perfect changes to the past perfect.

*"****Have*** *you eaten?"* → *He asked me if I* ***had eaten***.

- The present continuous changes to the past continuous.

*"I'****m seeing*** *the mechanic tomorrow."* →
She explained that she ***was seeing*** *the mechanic the next day.*

- The past perfect stays the same.

*"They'****d*** *already* ***read*** *that book."* →
*I told him that they'****d*** *already* ***read*** *that book.*

- *Will* and *shall* change to *would*.

"I ***won't*** *call you until tomorrow."* →
He said that he ***wouldn't*** *call me until the next day.*

- *Must* changes to *had to*.

"I ***must*** *call my sister!"* →
She remembered that she ***had to*** *call her sister.*

- *Can* changes to *could*.

*"****Can*** *I drive?"* → *He asked me if he* ***could*** *drive.*

Changes in questions

In reported questions, the subject comes before the auxiliary verb.

"Where ***have you*** *been?"* → *She asked me where* ***I had*** *been.*

To report *yes/no* questions, use *if / whether* with no question mark.

"Do you own a phone?" → *He asked me* ***if*** *I owned a phone.*

"Is this your first time in Seoul?" →
They asked me ***whether*** *it was my first time in Seoul.*

Other changes

Pronouns, time expressions, and other reference words (*you*, *my*, *now*, *this*, etc.) often change.

*"****We*** *love* ***you****."* → ***They*** *said that* ***they*** *loved* ***her***.

"We're going shopping later ***today****."* →
They told her they were going shopping later ***that day***.

"We lived ***here*** *many years ago, in* ***this*** *house."* →
She said that they had lived ***there*** *many years ago, in* ***that*** *house.*

Reporting verbs with *that*

Add, admit, complain, claim, explain, and *reply* (followed by *that*) are common reporting verbs.

They ***complained that*** *they didn't have time.*

▶ **Activities 1–4**

Verb patterns with reporting verbs

Reporting verbs indicate the function of the direct speech they report (asking a question, telling someone to do something, suggesting something, etc.)

"What did you see?" →
The policeman ***asked*** *Jenny to tell him what she had seen.*

"You need to clean your bedroom." → *My dad* ***told*** *me to clean my bedroom.*

"Yes, OK, I'll come with you." → *I* ***agreed*** *to go with him.*

"Why don't you get a cleaner?" → *She* ***suggested*** *getting a cleaner.*

Verbs followed by *to* + infinitive

agree, claim, offer, promise

She ***promised to give*** *the book back.*

Verbs followed by someone + *to* + infinitive

ask, invite, remind, tell

They ***invited me to join*** *them on the walk.*

Verbs followed by the *-ing* form

admit, recommend, suggest

I had to ***admit being*** *a little frightened.*

Note: *admit* can also be followed by *to* + *-ing*.

▶ **Activities 5 and 6**

1 Complete the reported speech with the correct form of *say*, *tell*, or *ask*.

1 Did you __________ that you wanted a cheese sandwich?
2 I __________ you the hotel didn't have a swimming pool.
3 They __________ that they didn't want to see the movie because it started too late.
4 He __________ me what the time was because he didn't have a watch.
5 Can I __________ you where you bought that dress? It's beautiful.
6 It wasn't easy to __________ the audience that the show had been canceled.

2 Complete the reported speech sentences.

1 "I go there every Saturday." ⟶ She said that she __________ there every Saturday.
2 "I didn't enjoy that meal at all." ⟶ He told me that he __________ the meal at all.
3 "They're starting at the new school in two weeks." ⟶ He said they __________ at the new school in two weeks.
4 "We'll find out the winner next week." ⟶ He said that they __________ the winner the following week.
5 "I can't see the whiteboard." ⟶ He told the teacher that he __________ the whiteboard.
6 "I visited the museum after I'd studied Egyptian history." ⟶ He told me he __________ the museum after he __________ Egyptian history.
7 "It's alright, everyone. I've found my phone." ⟶ She said that she __________ her phone.
8 "While you're here, you must visit the castle." ⟶ I told them that while they __________ there, they __________ the castle.

3 Complete the second sentence so that it means the same as the first.

1 "I've been in Antarctica with my team for six months."
She told the reporter that __________ .
2 "I'm studying small fish that live here."
She explained __________ .
3 "I arrived last November, at the beginning of summer."
She said __________ .
4 "The temperature is -25° today."
She told him that the temperature __________ .
5 "I don't want to leave this magical place."
She said that __________ .
6 "But I can't stay. I must catch the plane to New Zealand tomorrow."
But she explained that __________ .

4 Report the questions. Use *He asked her*.

1 "What kind of camera do you use for your videos?"
2 "How many videos have you posted on YouTube?"
3 "Are you happy with the number of people who watch your videos?"
4 "Do you post videos every day?"
5 "Have you ever made a video that people didn't like?"
6 "Will you ever stop posting on YouTube?"

5 Complete the reported speech using these verbs in the correct form, and three more words.

add	admit	ask	claim
complain	explain	reply	tell

1 Jerry: "Oh, no! This is terrible. We've run out of chocolate."
Jerry __________ run out of chocolate.
2 Jerry: "Paulo, did you eat it?"
He __________ had eaten it.
3 Paulo: "No, it wasn't me."
Paulo __________ been him.
4 Paulo: "And anyway, I'm not eating chocolate right now."
He __________ eating chocolate at that time.
5 Paulo: "You see, I'm on a diet."
He __________ on a diet.
6 Jerry: "But I saw you eating chocolate this morning!"
Jerry __________ seen him eating chocolate that morning.
7 Paulo: "OK, it was me. I ate it."
Finally, Paulo __________ eaten it.
8 Jerry: "Well, you need to buy some more next time you're at the store."
Jerry __________ some more.

6 Match the two parts of the sentences.

1 The doctor recommends
2 He suggested
3 He's invited
4 I told
5 One student admitted
6 She asked me
7 She offered to
8 Thanks for reminding

a give me a ride.
b me to buy Michaela a present.
c me to have dinner at his house.
d playing a game while we waited.
e staying in bed for a few days.
f to buy some bread when I went shopping.
g cheating on an exam.
h you to stay in the classroom while I was gone.

DEFINING RELATIVE CLAUSES

Relative clauses give more information about a noun. They have a similar function to an adjective or prepositional phrase.

*the **late** show* (an adjective)

*the show **at ten o'clock*** (a prepositional phrase)

*the show **that's after this one*** (a relative clause)

Defining relative clauses complete the meaning of the main clause. Without them, sentences don't communicate their full meaning. Defining relative clauses often help to identify, define, or classify the subject or object of the main clause.

"That's the show."

"Which one?"

*"The show **I was telling you about**."* (This information is essential because it tells us which show.)

Relative pronouns

Use the relative pronouns *who*, *which*, and *that* to introduce relative clauses. Use *who* to introduce people and *which* to introduce things or ideas.

*It wasn't Mike Leigh **who** directed the movie. It was Ken Loach.*

*The movie **which** I enjoyed most last year was* Rogue One.

In defining relative clauses, *who* and *which* can be replaced with *that*.

*It wasn't Mike Leigh **that** directed the movie...*

*The movie **that** I enjoyed the most...*

The relative pronoun can be the subject or the object of the relative clause. If the relative pronoun is the subject, you must use the pronoun, and the verb in the relative clause agrees with the subject.

*This is the channel **which** only shows reality TV shows.*

If the relative pronoun is the object, you don't have to use the pronoun.

That's the show ~~that~~ I was telling you about.

If the relative pronoun represents a person and is the object of the relative clause, you can use *whom* instead of *who*. However, most people don't use *whom* because it sounds very formal.

*He's the man **whom** I spoke to at the theater.* (formal)

A relative pronoun replaces the subject or object in the relative clause, so it's not included twice.

*The viewers **who** ~~**they**~~ completed the survey were all men.*

*The viewers **who** the producers interviewed ~~**them**~~ all said they enjoyed the second season.*

▶ Activities 1–3

DEFINING AND NON-DEFINING RELATIVE CLAUSES

In defining relative clauses, the information in the relative clause completes the meaning of the sentence because it helps to define a noun in the main clause. The following sentence is not clear without the relative clause, because it is not known which movie it is talking about.

*The movie **I'm going to see** is called* The Bachelors.

However, relative clauses are often used to give extra information that is not necessary for the sentence to be clear.

Gravity, ***which won seven Oscars**, was directed by Alfonso Cuarón.*

In this sentence, the information *won seven Oscars* is not essential for the main clause to be complete on its own.

Gravity *was directed by Alfonso Cuarón.*

The relative clause here is non-defining, meaning it doesn't define a noun from the main clause. Non-defining clauses give extra information that is not necessary for the sentence to be clear.

With non-defining relative clauses:

- don't replace *who* or *which* with *that*.

*The painting, ~~**that**~~ **which** is worth over $10 million, has been removed for cleaning.*

- you cannot omit the relative pronoun, even if it is the object of the relative clause.

*The main character, **who** I thought was terrific, is played by Olivia Coleman.*

In written English, non-defining relative clauses are separated from main clauses by commas (see examples above).
In spoken English, the speaker usually pauses before and after the relative clause.

▶ Activities 4–7

1 Complete the sentences with *who* or *which*. If the relative pronoun is not necessary, leave a blank.

1 It was my dad __________ bought the tickets.
2 Isn't that the same actor __________ you saw last week in that play about the war?
3 Is it right that Hollywood produces the movies __________ make the most money around the world?
4 There aren't many movie sequels __________ I enjoy.
5 The last portrait __________ she painted was in 1932.
6 *Supersize Me* was the first documentary __________ talked about the dangers of fast food.
7 The first thing __________ we have to do is advertise.

2 Join the two sentences using a relative clause.

1 My sister is the one. She told me about the exhibition.
My sister is the one who told me about the exhibition.
2 This is the book. I read it when I was on vacation.
____
3 This is the song. It won the award for best R&B song.
____
4 That's the architect. He went on to design the new library.
____
5 She's the dancer. I spoke to her after the performance.
____

3 Write one sentence using the information. Use a defining relative clause.

1 All the galleries / they're taking part in this year's art festival / they can be found on the website.
All the galleries that are taking part in this year's art festival can be found on the website.
2 Every picture is made of old glass / the artists found it in trash cans and recycling centers.
3 Older shows / they were made before 2005 / they won't be available online until 2019.
4 Please show tickets / they were bought online / show them at the main theater box office.
5 Viewers / they want to vote for the best singer / they need to call this number.

4 Join these sentences using a non-defining relative clause.

1 I was born in 2001. The movie *Shrek* came out in 2001.
2 My favorite author is Marguerite Abouet. She wrote the *AYA* graphic novels.
3 The only musical I've ever seen is *Les Misérables*. It's been playing in the city for years.
4 *She's Just A Shadow* stars Tao Okamoto. She is one of several new successful Japanese actors.
5 Look at his Facebook page. It has a photo of his new baby.

5 Add commas to these sentences where necessary.

1 A silent disco is an event where the music comes from headphones instead of loud speakers.
2 To anyone who is not wearing headphones, it looks as if a crowd of people is dancing in silence.
3 The music which is played by a DJ is broadcast by radio to the dancers' headphones.
4 Often two or three DJs work at the same time which means that dancers can choose the type of music they want to dance to.
5 Silent discos are sometimes organized by nightclub owners who are not allowed to play loud music late at night.

6 Delete *who* or *which* where possible. Replace *who* or *which* with *that* where possible.

1 Her poetry, which is suitable for radio, is meant to be read out loud.
2 Her self-portraits, which were all she painted, were always colorful.
3 Beyoncé is a singer who I really want to see live before she retires.
4 People who want to listen to the podcast can subscribe to the newsletter.
5 The ballet which will be performed next is the annual production of *The Nutcracker*.
6 The director, who spent ten years as a mountaineer, also wrote the script.
7 The member of the band who I thought really made the show special was the drummer.
8 This play is set in a city which is based on the writer's hometown.

7 Correct the mistake in each sentence.

1 There are many theaters in the city only show popular musicals.
2 She's the opera singer which is singing at the Opera House tonight.
3 The woman who she is speaking at the moment is the writer Han Kang.
4 The tickets, that I bought outside the venue, were twice as expensive as the ones I bought online.
5 The sketch I'm drawing it is part of my art project.
6 The *Sculptures in the Park* exhibition which is part of the summer festival goes on until September 15th.
7 She starred in the *Alien* series, that were some of the first science fiction movies to have a female main character.
8 Her fourth novel, was published last year, has earned her many fans around the world.

THIRD CONDITIONAL

The third conditional is used to talk about an imaginary past that is different from what really happened. It lets the speaker talk about the possible consequences of these imagined events.

If humans had lived at the same time as dinosaurs, the dinosaurs would have died out more quickly. (Humans didn't live at the same time as dinosaurs. The dinosaurs didn't die out more quickly.)

The third conditional is often used to express regret or sadness that the past was not different.

If I had understood the importance of an education, I wouldn't have left school when I was fifteen.

Like all conditionals, third conditional sentences have two clauses: an *if*-clause (the condition) and a main clause (the result). The verb in the result clause is usually formed with *would/wouldn't have* + past participle, and the *if*-clause is formed with *had/hadn't* + past participle.

*We **would have caught** the train if you **hadn't arrived** so late.*

The *if*-clause can go at the beginning of the sentence or the end. When the *if*-clause starts the sentence, a comma separates the clauses.

*She would have missed the meeting **if** she hadn't driven fast.*

***If** she hadn't driven fast**,** she would have missed the meeting.*

Both *had* and *would* can be contracted to *'d*. To determine whether *'d* is *had* or *would*, look at the word after it. If it is a verb in the infinitive, the contraction is *would*; if it is a past participle, the contraction is *had*.

*I**'d have** made some cookies if I**'d known** you were coming.*
(I **would** have… if I **had** known)

If only and *I wish*

If only and *I wish* are structures which share similar form and meaning to the third conditional. They express the condition, but not the result.

***If only** I had remembered my camera.* (If I had remembered my camera, I could take a picture of this wonderful view now.)
***I wish** you had been there with me.* (If you had been there, I wouldn't have felt scared.)

If only and *I wish* can be used to express a desire for things to be different in the past.

***If only** the trip **wasn't** so long. We would be there by now.* (Second conditional. They are still traveling. It is talking about the present.)

***If only** the trip **hadn't been** so long. We would have had more time there.* (Third conditional. They stopped traveling before now. It is talking about the past.)

▶ Activities 1–4

MODALS: PAST SPECULATION, DEDUCTION, AND REGRET

Could, may, might, would, wouldn't + have done can be used to talk about the consequences of imaginary past events (to speculate about the past). Sentences that speculate describe events which couldn't possibly be true because they didn't happen.

*You didn't wear your helmet? You **could have had** an accident!*

Third conditional

In third conditional sentences, *might, may,* and *could* can replace *would*.

*If the alarm had worked, I **may have woken** up on time.*

Regret

Could, might, may, should, and *shouldn't + have done* can be used to speculate about events that the speaker wishes were different in the past (i.e., to express regret).

*You can't come? I've already bought the tickets! I **could have saved** $50!*
*If only someone had warned us about the weather. We **might not have gotten** so wet.*
*I knew it was his birthday and I forgot to tell you. I **should have let** you know. I'm sorry.*

Thinking about possible pasts

Must, might, may, could, and *can't + have done* can be used to talk about past events that could possibly be true (to make deductions). *Must* is used if you are sure that something is true. *Can't* is used if you are sure it is not true. *Might, may,* or *could* is used if it is possible that something is true.

A *Haile isn't here. He **must have gone** out.*
B *Or he **may have decided** to go take a nap upstairs.*
A *No, he **can't have done** that. Look, his coat isn't here. He **might have gone** shopping. The fridge is empty.*
B *Or he **could have gone** to visit Mohammed. I know he was planning to go over to his house.*

▶ Activities 5 and 6

1 Choose the correct option to complete the sentences.

1 If *I'd gone / I went* to college, I wouldn't have started a successful business when I was twenty.
2 I wouldn't *learn / have learned* so much when I was young if I hadn't listened to older people.
3 I wish I *had taken / took* good care of myself when I was 20.
4 *If / If only* I had traveled more when I was young.
5 I *would / wouldn't* have been able to buy such a big house if I *didn't work / hadn't worked* hard as a young man.
6 If I *had eaten / ate* less, I wouldn't have gotten sick.
7 I wish *I'd spent / I spent* more time with my mom last summer.
8 If *I'd / I would have* known the test was going to be so easy, I *would / wouldn't* have spent all weekend studying!

2 Which sentences in Activity 1 express regret?

3 Read the article and complete sentences 1–6 with the correct form (positive or negative) of the verbs.

Before the 19th century, every town in the US kept its own time. This was not a problem until the railroads were built, because people traveled slowly and couldn't communicate quickly. In a large country like the US, there were more than 300 local times for train companies to choose from, which was confusing for passengers. The American railroad companies reduced the number of time zones to four in 1883, even though other countries' railroads had been using standard time for more than 30 years.

During the two World Wars, a system of "daylight saving" was introduced to save energy in winter. However, there was no national law, so individual states and cities could choose whether or not to put their clocks back an hour. In some areas, it was not unusual to have to change your watch several times during a short trip. Bus drivers working on a route in West Virginia and Ohio had to change their watches seven times over just 35 miles! Finally, in 1966, the Uniform Time Act solved the problem.

1 If towns ___________ (be able) to communicate quickly, they ___________ (keep) the same time.
2 Time differences ___________ (be) a problem if people ___________ (travel) faster.
3 If there ___________ (be) fewer time zones, passengers ___________ (get) confused.
4 The US ___________ (solve) the problem much earlier if they ___________ (follow) other countries.
5 Bus drivers in West Virginia and Ohio probably wished there ___________ (be) a national law!
6 If the government ___________ (pass) the Uniform Time Act in 1966, it's possible they ___________ (continue) to live with this situation for many years.

4 Use the word in bold to complete the second sentence so it means the same as the first sentence.

1 Do you ever regret not going to college? **wish**
Do ___________ to college?
2 I feel sick now because I ate that burger. **only**
If ___________. I feel sick!
3 I bought an expensive jacket, so I didn't have enough money for a pair of jeans. **hadn't**
If ___________ for a pair of jeans.
4 He needed to go back to the store because he left his wallet there. **remembered**
He ___________ to pick up his wallet.
5 The trip was so slow! I should have taken the train. **quicker**
The trip ___________ the train.

5 Complete the sentences using *must*, *might*, *should*, *shouldn't*, or *can't*.

1 There was a knock at the door. It ___________ have been Ana, and I didn't want to speak to her.
2 If I had studied Chinese when I was at school, I ___________ have understood what he was saying.
3 Izuo said he would definitely be here by 3:00. It's 3:30, so he ___________ have been delayed.
4 She didn't say hello. She ___________ have seen me.
5 Weren't you cold at the game? I was freezing! I ___________ have brought a sweater.
6 The mountaineers ___________ have survived, but sadly, the rock fell when they were under it.
7 You ___________ have left your purse in the car, because it's not there now. I've looked.
8 I ___________ have told him my password, because now he keeps changing my profile picture.

6 Correct the mistakes in the dialogs.

1 **A** That's your brother over there.
B No, that must not be him. He's at home because he has a cold.
2 **A** Are you happy with third place in the race?
B Not really. I could had done much better if I'd had more sleep last night.
3 **A** Are you going for a run today?
B No, I don't have time. I must have gone yesterday when I had more time.
4 **A** You can have told me you'd gone to the mall. I'd have come too.
B I did tell you. Didn't you get my text?
5 **A** She was really angry with me. I didn't do anything wrong.
B Well, you might have done something to make her upset.

IRREGULAR VERBS

INFINITIVE	SIMPLE PAST	PAST PARTICIPLE
beat	beat	beaten
become	became	become
bend	bent	bent
bet	bet	bet
bite	bit	bitten
blow	blew	blown
break	broke	broken
bring	brought	brought
broadcast	broadcast	broadcast
build	built	built
burn	burned/burnt	burned/burnt
burst	burst	burst
cost	cost	cost
cut	cut	cut
deal	dealt	dealt
dig	dug	dug
dream	dreamed/dreamt	dreamed/dreamt
fall	fell	fallen
feed	fed	fed
fight	fought	fought
forget	forgot	forgotten
forgive	forgave	forgiven
freeze	froze	frozen
hide	hid	hidden
hit	hit	hit
hold	held	held
hurt	hurt	hurt
keep	kept	kept
kneel	kneeled/knelt	kneeled/knelt
lay	laid	laid
lead	led	led
lend	lent	lent
let	let	let
lie	lay	lain
light	lit	lit
lose	lost	lost
mean	meant	meant
misunderstand	misunderstood	misunderstood
must	had to	had to
ring	rang	rung

INFINITIVE	SIMPLE PAST	PAST PARTICIPLE
rise	rose	risen
sell	sold	sold
set	set	set
shake	shook	shaken
shine	shone	shone
shoot	shot	shot
shrink	shrank	shrunk
shut	shut	shut
sink	sank	sunk
slide	slid	slid
spend	spent	spent
split	split	split
spread	spread	spread
stand	stood	stood
steal	stole	stolen
stick	stuck	stuck
strike	struck	struck
swear	swore	sworn
tear	tore	torn
throw	threw	thrown
upset	upset	upset
wake	woke	woken
win	won	won

UNIT 1 A review

In the first paragraph, explain the basic storyline and introduce the main characters.

Try to include at least two or three reasons for reading the book or watching the movie. You should also include points against it. If you are recommending it, make sure there are more positive points than negative ones.

Breathe is Sarah Crossan's second novel, written in 2012. The main characters are three teenagers with different abilities. It is set in a terrible future, a world with very little oxygen, so most of the animals and humans are dead. The survivors live in cities protected by roofs. The three friends have to leave the safety of their city to find a mysterious place called The Grove. What I really loved was the plot, which is full of action and mystery. It is an exciting book, and I couldn't put it down.

Another thing that I really liked was the way the story is told by the three main characters. This means you get to see the same events in different ways. Alina is strong and angry, Bea is smart but also the bravest, and Quinn is smart and funny. They all have qualities that you can understand.

One thing that lets the book down is the sudden change in Alina's personality. Half way through the novel, she becomes kinder and more loving, but I didn't understand why.

I would really recommend *Breathe*. It reminds us that a lot of the things that we need—trees, water, air—may not be here forever. We need to protect our planet. But what makes it really worth reading is its vision of the future.

Include any basic information about the book or movie, such as the title, author or director, and date of publication or release.

Make sure you express your personal reaction to the book or movie.

In your final paragraph, give a clear recommendation, either positive or negative.

UNIT 2 A story

Set the scene in the first paragraph, with background information such as when and where the story takes place.

Use adverbs to comment on the story.

Use longer sentences to describe or explain the situation.

Three years ago, I went to Thailand. I wanted to visit a beautiful island. My cousin had just returned from an island called Koh Tao, and told me I could catch a bus and a boat there.

Unfortunately, no one spoke English at the bus stop, and the destinations were written in Thai, so I didn't understand anything. Eventually, an old man pointed to a bus that was just about to leave. I got on the bus.

During the long trip, I looked out of the window. I was just falling asleep when the driver shouted "Koh Tao!" I got out and looked around. I couldn't see water, just a quiet road. A man on a motorcycle came over. "Koh Tao?," I asked. He just pointed to his bike. I didn't have any choice. I got on the bike.

He drove fast. When he stopped, I saw a boat. A sign said "Koh Tao ferry." After so many hours feeling completely lost, I ended up just where I needed to be!

Use narrative tenses (simple past, past continuous, past perfect) to show how the different actions relate to each other.

Use shorter sentences to describe the action and move the story along.

If the story needs to start or end with a given sentence, it should fit logically with the rest of the story.

UNIT 3 An opinion essay

In an opinion essay, make sure you state your opinion clearly in the first paragraph.

Don't forget to include one or two points against your opinion. They show that you have considered both sides of the argument, so they make your argument stronger.

State your opinion again in the final paragraph, but say it in a different way from the way you said it in the first paragraph.

The amount of time that children spend playing sports at school has decreased in many countries. These days, students are spending more time in the classroom working on subjects like math and English. Of course, these subjects are important, but I do not think it is a good idea to take time away from sports.

Sports have many benefits. First, many of us enjoy playing them. Personally, the day when we play sports is the day I enjoy most. Some students do not enjoy academic subjects, but they like sports and PE class, and this may encourage them to enjoy school more. Second, there is no question that young people are spending too much time in front of screens. People aren't doing enough exercise in their free time, so schools should help. Finally, sports are good for the brain as well as the body, in my opinion. If I have just done exercise, I have more energy for learning.

However, it's true that children have a lot to study these days, so if they're spending time at school playing sports, they have to do more work at home. Also, there are other important subjects such as art and music. Should we give them time, too?

Overall, I would say that sports are as important as any other school subject. In fact, schools should prepare students for healthy lives as well as future jobs. I strongly believe that making sports a required subject would help achieve this goal.

In the second paragraph, write at least three points that support your opinion.

Use connectors like *First*, *Also*, and *Finally* to structure your argument.

Using questions can make a point more interesting or powerful.

UNIT 4 A social media update

You can leave out the subject (***We** finally reached*) in some sentences in informal social media posts. This makes it sound as if you are writing it during the trip, like a diary entry or a postcard.

Exclamations (*What a…!*, *It's so…!*) help the reader understand the writer's emotions.

Finally reached Leh last night after three incredible days in Delhi! We rushed around the Red Fort (not much time, and it's huge!), then wandered through the streets of the old city. What a beautiful place! It was boiling though, so we're all happy to feel the fresher weather of the Himalayas. The train to Leh crawled along, but at least we were able to rest. Delhi is exhausting!

My host family are super friendly and welcoming. Last night, they cooked a vegetable curry with delicious little dumplings called *momos*. Over the next week, we'll be learning how to make a few tasty local dishes.
We'll have to buy the ingredients ourselves from local markets. But tomorrow we're hoping to go hiking in the hills if the weather's good. And I'm also planning to interview some of the people in town for my culture project. I think there will be plenty of time for that—we're here for two weeks.
Next week there's the Ladakh Festival. I'm looking forward to it!

Use descriptive vocabulary to make the writing more interesting.

Emotionally powerful words make the writing more interesting, too.

Talk about recent events.

Also talk about future plans and hopes.

UNIT 5 A cover letter

1-3-5 Kamiosaki
Shinagawa-ku, Tokyo 141-0021
Japan

Re: Application for summer work May 25, 2018

To Whom It May Concern:

I am writing to apply for the job advertised on summerwork.com. I believe I am a good candidate for the job.

While I have not worked as a caregiver before, I have a lot of experience helping my father, who uses a wheelchair, get in and out of the car. What is more, I am not a bad cook and would be happy to clean the house.

I am a friendly person who gets along well with people. I am hard-working and enthusiastic, and I am sure that I would bring these qualities to the job. I would say I am a fast learner.

I finish school on June 22, and would be able to start then. I can continue until September 5.

I look forward to hearing from you soon.

Sincerely,
Aya Fujito

Begin formal letters with *To Whom It May Concern* or *Dear Sir or Madam* if you don't know the name of the person, and *Dear Mr./Mrs. Smith* if you know the name.

Always begin formal letters by giving your reason for writing.

Do not use contractions in formal letters: *I am*, not *I'm*.

Don't forget to include practical information about your availability, etc.

This phrase is used to ask for a reply in formal letters.

Keep paragraphs short. Include a paragraph describing any relevant experience, skills, or qualifications you may have. Use a separate paragraph for personal qualities.

End formal letters with a polite and professional salutation, like *Yours Sincerely*, *Sincerely yours*, or *Best regards*.

UNIT 6 An informal email describing people

From: aditi@yahoo.in
To: mauricio@terra.com.br
Subject: Extraordinary talents

Hi Mauricio,

Thanks for your email. It was great to hear about Brazil. Recife sounds like a great place—very different from Mumbai. And thanks for your invitation—if only I could afford it, I'd say yes, for sure.

You asked me for some help with your presentation about people with extraordinary lives here in India. I have an interesting one for you! Her name's Sudha Chandran. She's a famous actress and dancer.

She started dancing when she was three. At sixteen she lost her right foot. Everyone thought it was sad that she wouldn't achieve her dream of becoming a professional dancer, but she is a determined person, and she learned to dance with a new artificial foot. The traditional *bharathanatyam* dance is really hard, but she's still one of the best. She's an inspiration—she proves that we can't let barriers keep us from achieving what we want.

Anyway, I hope this helps. If you need any more information, just ask. 😄

All the best, and write soon! Oh, and I'm attaching a photo of Sudha for you.
Aditi

Your subject should summarize the most important reason for writing.

Hi and *Hello* ___ , are suitable ways of starting informal emails. (*Dear* ___ is for more formal emails and letters.)

Contractions make emails more informal and friendly. So do punctuation marks like exclamation marks (!), emojis (😄), and dashes (—).

Other ways of ending informal emails include: *Love*, *Lots of love*, and *Regards*.

Use short forms of words (e.g., *Thanks* for *Thank you*). Abbreviations such as *BTW* (*by the way*) and *LOL* (*laugh out loud*) are also acceptable in informal emails.

Mention any documents, photos, or links that you are sending with the email.

UNIT 7 An announcement

Include a clear heading to help the reader identify the item easily.

You can use a question to attract the reader.

Include key words in your description.

State clearly the type of person who might want the item.

Squier Affinity Telecaster
Selling price: $100

Payment: PayPal / cash on collection
Seller rated: 96%

Looking for an inexpensive guitar with a great rock and blues sound? Classic-looking electric guitar with "Telecaster"-shaped body. Same yellow wood finish as the original 1950s Tele. Would suit a beginner or intermediate guitarist.

My first guitar. Had it for five years. Used, but in good condition with only a few scratches and marks on the body. Just bought a new guitar, which is why I'm selling this one.

Guitar currently sells for about $200 new. Cost of delivery depends on where you are, or free local pick up in Kingston area. Shipping within three days of receipt of payment.

Be precise in your headings.

Describe your item in as much detail as possible. Be accurate.

Women's bright red special occasion dress
Condition: good, second-hand

Start bid: $40
Bidding closes: Thursday 03/05/18, 22:00 EST

Beautiful dress; perfect for a party. It has a lovely full skirt, a black flower pattern, and long sleeves. Hasn't been worn very often, and has recently been professionally cleaned, so in very good condition.

Global shipment (seller is in Jamaica), payment by bank transfer. Bidding closes soon.

UNIT 8 A complaint email

Look at the writing tips on page 151 about beginning and ending formal letters.

Explain clearly why you are complaining.

Use formal linkers to connect your points.

State exactly what you want the company to do.

Include any documents or evidence that support your complaint with your email.

To Whom It May Concern:

I am writing to complain about the poor customer service I received from you recently.

Last week, I was given a $10 gift card for Strand Records, so on April 23 I visited your website and bought an album online (order # YH6398X). Unfortunately, the website did not accept the code, and consequently I had to pay with a credit card.

When I listened to the album, I realized that the wrong tracks had been downloaded. The artist was correct, but it was an old album that I already have. I called your helpline, but despite your company's good reputation for customer service, the man I spoke to was not very helpful. He suggested entering the code again, but when I explained that I had already done this, he said it was company policy not to give new codes. He also suggested I was trying to get a free album, which was very rude.

My experience with Strand Records has not been satisfactory so far. That said, I am sure that you can correct the situation. I would like a refund for the money I spent on the album, and a new code so that I can use my gift card. Also, after my experience with your helpline, I expect an apology for the trouble you caused me.

I am attaching copies of the receipt for the old album and of the gift card that didn't work.

I look forward to hearing from you soon.

Sincerely,
Park Seo-yeon

Strand Records: $10 gift card
Free shipping on any order.
Enter this code at checkout: **T65WPGY9**

UNIT 9 An email describing a place and its culture

Look at the writing tips on page 151 about beginning and ending informal emails.

In the first paragraph, respond to any recent communication you have received from the person you are writing to.

Order your main points about the place logically. Include at least three or four pieces of information.

Use connectors to join ideas.

Use the last paragraph to look ahead to future communication (*Write back soon!*) or a meeting.

Hi Aki,

Thanks for your postcard. What a surprise! I never get postcards! Nara looks like a fun city. And it was great hearing your news. I'm glad everything is going well for you. I'm sorry this isn't a postcard, but you wanted me to tell you about Valparaiso, and I can tell you more in an email. ;-)

I guess what the city is most famous for is the museum dedicated to Pablo Neruda, who was a famous Chilean poet. The museum is OK, but unless you're a poetry fan I wouldn't bother paying to go in. The views over the city are fantastic though (and free!).

What I really love about the city is its location. It's so mountainous, and next to the ocean, so I'd recommend spending a lot of time just exploring. I love taking the *ascensores*, which are like very small trains on the steep hills. It's also well known for the paintings that decorate the streets and buildings. There's color everywhere!

And finally, you can't come to Valparaiso without spending a day at the beach. Our fishing harbor, La Caleta Portales, is a wonderful place to relax, but also to watch the fishermen and market traders.

Anyway, I hope you get to visit me here one day so you can see it for yourself. Even better, though, would be if I could come and see you in Japan!

Best wishes,
Macarena

UNIT 10 A pro and con essay

The first paragraph introduces the topic. You can describe the current situation, say why the topic is relevant or important now, explain that it is a topic that people disagree about, and compare the past and present situation.

The second paragraph presents arguments in favor of the statement (the pros). Include two or three arguments.

Use connecting words to structure your argument (e.g., *First of all*, *What's more*, *Not only that, but*).

Start the third paragraph with a discourse marker that introduces arguments against the statement (the cons).

The third paragraph gives the cons of the statement. Include two or three cons.

Conclude with your own opinion about the statement.

"Young people should leave home as soon as they finish school." Discuss.

The age that young people leave home depends on many things, such as the age at which they finish school or college, get married, or get a job. But for young people, is it better to stay at home with your family as long as possible, or should you leave home as soon as you finish school?

There are several reasons why leaving home when you finish school might be a good idea. First, it's important to learn life skills, such as how to make money and manage it, when you are young. It's also important to start being responsible for yourself as soon as possible. The more responsibility you have, the more freedom you have. Of course, if you go to college in a different city, you will need to move.

However, living away from your family means paying for your own accommodations and food, which could be expensive. What's more, there are many boring things that you have to start doing, like cooking and cleaning. Not only that, but it might be lonely living away from family.

Personally, I don't believe that you should leave home right after school, because it's so expensive. Even so, moving away from your parents is usually the best way to grow up. Consequently, if you can't afford to move out immediately, you should start thinking about doing it soon.

UNIT 1

ability (n)	/ə'bɪlɪti/
action (n)	/'ækʃən/
affection (n)	/ə'fɛkʃən/
argument (n)	/'ɑrgjəmənt/
attack (n/v)	/ə'tæk/
automatically (adv)	/ˌɔtə'mætɪkli/
brave (adj)	/breɪv/
breathe (v)	/brið/
chance (n)	/tʃæns/
character (n)	/'kærɪktər/
characteristic (n)	/ˌkærɪktə'rɪstɪk/
come down (phr v)	/ˌkʌm 'daʊn/
come out (phr v)	/ˌkʌm 'aʊt/
comedy (n)	/'kɒmɪdi/
common (adj)	/'kɒmən/
communicate (v)	/kə'mjunɪˌkeɪt/
confused (adj)	/kən'fjuzd/
confusion (n)	/kən'fjuʒən/
connect (v)	/kə'nɛkt/
conservation (n)	/ˌkɒnsər'veɪʃən/
control (n)	/kən'troʊl/
curiosity (n)	/ˌkjʊri'ɒsɪti/
cut down (phr v)	/'kʌt 'daʊn/
definitely (adv)	/'dɛfənɪtli/
delighted (adj)	/dɪ'laɪtɪd/
depressed (adj)	/dɪ'prɛst/
depression (n)	/dɪ'prɛʃən/
disappointed (adj)	/ˌdɪsə'pɔɪntɪd/
disappointment (n)	/ˌdɪsə'pɔɪntmənt/
effect (n)	/ɪ'fɛkt/
embarrassed (adj)	/ɛm'bærəst/
embarrassing (adj)	/ɛm'bærəsɪŋ/
embarrassment (n)	/ɛm'bærəsmənt/
emotion (n)	/ɪ'moʊʃən/
end up (phr v)	/'ɛnd 'ʌp/
enjoyment (n)	/ɛn'dʒɔɪmənt/
estimate (v)	/'ɛstəˌmeɪt/
event (n)	/ɪ'vɛnt/
excitement (n)	/ɪk'saɪtmənt/
exhausted (adj)	/ɪg'zɔstɪd/
exhaustion (n)	/ɪg'zɔstʃən/
exist (v)	/ɪg'zɪst/
expect (v)	/ɪk'spɛkt/
expedition (n)	/ˌɛkspə'dɪʃən/
experience (n)	/ɪk'spɪəriəns/
express (v)	/ɪk'sprɛs/
friendliness (n)	/'frɛndlinɪs/
gender (n)	/'dʒɛndər/
get out of (phr v)	/ˌgɛt 'aʊt əv/
get to do something (phr)	/'gɛt tə 'du ˌsʌmθɪŋ/
happiness (n)	/'hæpinɪs/
hide (v)	/haɪd/
homesick (adj)	/'hoʊmˌsɪk/
host (n)	/hoʊst/
human (adj/n)	/'hjumən/
hurt (v)	/hɜrt/
increase (v)	/ɪn'kris/
joy (n)	/dʒɔɪ/
loneliness (n)	/'loʊnlinɪs/
lonely (adj)	/'loʊnli/
memorable (adj)	/'mɛmərəbəl/
muscle (n)	/'mʌsəl/
mysterious (adj)	/mɪ'stɪəriəs/
mystery (n)	/'mɪstəri/
nearby (adj)	/'nɪər'baɪ/
nervous (adj)	/'nɜrvəs/
nervousness (n)	/'nɜrvəsnɪs/
novel (n)	/'nɒvəl/
operator (n)	/'ɒpəˌreɪtər/
oxygen (n)	/'ɒksɪdʒən/
personality (n)	/ˌpɜrsə'nælɪti/
photograph (v)	/'foʊtəˌgræf/
planet (n)	/'plænɪt/
plot (n)	/plɒt/
positive (adj)	/'pɒzɪtɪv/
powerful (adj)	/'paʊərfəl/
protect (v)	/prə'tɛkt/
protected (adj)	/prə'tɛktɪd/
publish (v)	/'pʌblɪʃ/
quality (n)	/'kwɒlɪti/
rainforest (n)	/'reɪnˌfɔrɪst/
reader (n)	/'ridər/
recognize (v)	/'rɛkəgˌnaɪz/
recommend (v)	/ˌrɛkə'mɛnd/
regularly (adv)	/'rɛgjələrli/
relationship (n)	/rɪ'leɪʃənˌʃɪp/
relaxed (adj)	/rɪ'lækst/
remind (v)	/rɪ'maɪnd/
research (n)	/'risɜrtʃ/
respond (v)	/rɪ'spɒnd/
sadness (n)	/'sædnɪs/
safety (n)	/'seɪfti/
scared (adj)	/skɛərd/
scientist (n)	/'saɪəntɪst/
seriously (adv)	/'sɪəriəsli/
service (n)	/'sɜrvɪs/
situation (n)	/ˌsɪtʃu'eɪʃən/
skill (n)	/skɪl/
smart (adj)	/smɑrt/
smile (n/v)	/smaɪl/
social (adj)	/'soʊʃəl/
speed (n)	/spid/
stressed (adj)	strɛst/
sudden (adj)	/'sʌdən/
suggest (v)	/sə'dʒɛst/
survivor (n)	/sər'vaɪvər/
teenage (adj)	/'tinˌeɪdʒ/
vision (n)	/'vɪʒən/
voice (n)	/vɔɪs/
warn (v)	/wɔrn/
whether (conj)	/'hwɛðər/
worth (adj)	/wɜrθ/
wrinkle (n)	/'rɪŋkəl/

UNIT 2

a handful of (n)	/ə 'hændfʊl əv/
abandon (v)	/ə'bændən/
amusement park (n)	/ə'mjuzmənt ˌpɑrk/
avid (adj)	/'ævɪd/
backpack (v)	/'bækˌpæk/
be supposed to (phr)	/ˌbi sə'poʊzd tə/
blog (n)	/blɒg/
cable (n)	/'keɪbəl/
choice (n)	/tʃɔɪs/
commute (v)	/kə'mjut/
completely (adv)	/kəm'plitli/
consider (v)	/kən'sɪdər/
construction site (n)	/kən'strʌkʃən ˌsaɪt/
cruise (n)	/kruz/
destination (n)	/ˌdɛstə'neɪʃən/
don't get me wrong (phr)	/'doʊnt ˌgɛt mi 'rɔŋ/
energetic (adj)	/ˌɛnər'dʒɛtɪk/
eventually (adv)	/ɪ'vɛntʃuəli/
excursion (n)	/ɪk'skɜrʒən/
exhausting (adj)	/ɪg'zɔstɪŋ/
ferry (n)	/'fɛri/
frightened (adj)	/'fraɪtənd/
frozen (adj)	/'froʊzən/
get to (phr v)	/'gɛt tu/
get to know (phr)	/'gɛt tə 'noʊ/
get up (phr v)	/'gɛt 'ʌp/
ghost (n)	/goʊst/
go down (phr v)	/'goʊ 'daʊn/
go up (phr v)	/ˌgəʊ 'ʌp/
ground (n)	/graʊnd/
height (n)	/haɪt/
icy (adj)	/'aɪsi/
identify (v)	/aɪ'dɛntəˌfaɪ/
industrial (adj)	/ɪn'dʌstriəl/
injury (n)	/'ɪndʒəri/
look around (phr v)	/'lʊk ə'raʊnd/
look up (phr v)	/'lʊk 'ʌp/
manage (v)	/'mænɪdʒ/
normally (adv)	/'nɔrməli/
option (n)	/'ɒpʃən/
plan (v)	/plæn/
public transportation (n)	/'pʌblɪk ˌtrænspər'teɪʃən/
region (n)	/'ridʒən/
resident (n)	/'rɛzɪdənt/
risk (n)	/rɪsk/
rooftop (n)	/'rufˌtɒp/
rope (n)	/roʊp/
route (n)	/rut/
shy (adj)	/ʃaɪ/
sight (n)	/saɪt/
skyscraper (n)	/'skaɪˌskreɪpər/
slide (n)	/slaɪd/
standard (adj)	/'stændərd/
story (n)	/'stɔri/
subway (n)	/'sʌbˌweɪ/
subway station (n)	/'sʌbweɪ ˌsteɪʃən/
surrounded by (trees) (phr)	/sə'raʊndɪd ˌbaɪ ('triz)/
taste (n)	/teɪst/
team up with (phr v)	/'tim 'ʌp ˌwɪð/
terrifying (adj)	/'tɛrəˌfaɪɪŋ/
tower (n)	/'taʊər/
train track (n)	/'treɪn ˌtræk/
tunnel (n)	/'tʌnəl/
typical (adj)	/'tɪpɪkəl/
urban exploration (n)	/'ɜrbən ˌɛksplə'reɪʃən/
viewpoint (n)	/'vjuˌpɔɪnt/
voyage (n)	/'vɔɪɪdʒ/
willing (adj)	/'wɪlɪŋ/

UNIT 3

academic (adj)	/ˌækəˈdɛmɪk/
achieve something (phr)	/əˈtʃiv ˌsʌmθɪŋ/
alternative (adj)	/ɔlˈtɜrnətɪv/
although (conj)	/ɔlˈðoʊ/
among (prep)	/əˈmʌŋ/
amount (n)	/əˈmaʊnt/
architect (n)	/ˈɑrkɪˌtɛkt/
athlete (n)	/ˈæθlit/
attitude (n)	/ˈætɪˌtud/
aware (adj)	/əˈwɛər/
barely (adv)	/ˈbɛərli/
beat someone (phr)	/ˈbit ˌsʌmwʌn/
behavior (n)	/bɪˈheɪvjər/
benefit (n)	/ˈbɛnəfɪt/
bounce (v)	/baʊns/
break a record (phr)	/ˈbreɪk ə ˈrɛkərd/
celebrate (v)	/ˈsɛləˌbreɪt/
celebration (n)	/ˌsɛləˈbreɪʃən/
compare (v)	/kəmˈpɛər/
compete (v)	/kəmˈpit/
competitor (n)	/kəmˈpɛtɪtər/
costume (n)	/ˈkɒstum/
court (n)	/kɔrt/
culture (n)	/ˈkʌltʃər/
dangerously (adv)	/ˈdeɪndʒərəsli/
decrease (v)	/dɪˈkris/
destroy (v)	/dɪˈstrɔɪ/
difficulty (n)	/ˈdɪfɪˌkʌlti/
discourage (v)	/dɪsˈkʌrɪdʒ/
diving (n)	/ˈdaɪvɪŋ/
do something (phr)	/ˈdu ˌsʌmθɪŋ/
do your best (phr)	/ˈdu jər ˈbɛst/
dramatically (adv)	/drəˈmætɪkli/
effective (adj)	/ɪˈfɛktɪv/
encourage someone to do something (phr)	/ɪnˈkɜrɪdʒ ˌsʌmwʌn tə ˈdu ˌsʌmθɪŋ/
energy (n)	/ˈɛnərdʒi/
estimated (adj)	/ˈɛstəˌmeɪtɪd/
feel proud (phr)	/ˈfil ˈpraʊd/
field (n)	/fild/
fresh water (n)	/ˈfrɛʃ ˈwɔtər/
give someone a sense of (phr)	/ˈgɪv ˌsʌmwʌn ə ˈsɛns əv/
give up (phr v)	/ˈgɪv ˈʌp/
go on (phr v)	/ˈgoʊ ˈɒn/
gym (n)	/dʒɪm/
gymnastics (n)	/dʒɪmˈnæstɪks/
habitat (n)	/ˈhæbɪˌtæt/
hero (n)	/ˈhɪəroʊ/
hunt (v)	/hʌnt/
hunting (n)	/ˈhʌntɪŋ/
I believe in you (phr)	/ˌaɪ bɪˈliv ɪn ˈju/
impossible (adj)	/ɪmˈpɒsəbəl/
incredibly (adv)	/ɪnˈkrɛdəbli/
influence (v)	/ˈɪnfluəns/
join in (phr v)	/ˈdʒɔɪn ˈɪn/
karate (n)	/kəˈrɑti/
keep up (phr v)	/ˈkip ˈʌp/
killing (n)	/ˈkɪlɪŋ/
knock out (phr v)	/ˈnɒk ˈaʊt/
limit (n)	/ˈlɪmɪt/
loss (n)	/lɔs/
majority (n)	/məˈdʒɔrɪti/
make sense (phr)	/ˈmeɪk ˈsɛns/
mandatory (adj)	/ˈmændəˌtɔri/
marathon (n)	/ˈmærəˌθɒn/
measure (v)	/ˈmɛʒər/
opponent (n)	/əˈpoʊnənt/
overall (adv)	/ˈoʊvərˈɔl/
percent (n)	/pərˈsɛnt/
personally (adv)	/ˈpɜrsənəli/
physical (adj)	/ˈfɪzɪkəl/
play an important role (phr)	/ˈpleɪ ən ɪmˈpɔrtənt ˈroʊl/
population (n)	/ˌpɒpjəˈleɪʃən/
preparation (n)	/ˌprɛpəˈreɪʃən/
professional (adj)	/prəˈfɛʃənəl/
push one's limits (phr)	/ˈpʊʃ ˌwʌnz ˈlɪmɪts/
raise money (phr)	/ˈreɪz ˈmʌni/
recover (v)	/rɪˈkʌvər/
reduce (v)	/rɪˈdus/
referee (n)	/ˌrɛfəˈri/
reflect (v)	/rɪˈflɛkt/
replace (v)	/rɪˈpleɪs/
represent someone (phr)	/ˌrɛprɪˈzɛnt ˌsʌmwʌn/
rink (n)	/rɪŋk/
salary (n)	/ˈsæləri/
score a goal (phr)	/ˈskɔr ə ˈgoʊl/
score points (phr)	/ˈskɔr ˈpɔɪnts/
shadow (n)	/ˈʃædoʊ/
shortly (adv)	/ˈʃɔrtli/
similar (adj)	/ˈsɪmələr/
solve (v)	/sɒlv/
spectator (n)	/ˈspɛkteɪtər/
sprint (n)	/sprɪnt/
stay healthy (phr)	/ˈsteɪ ˈhɛlθi/
strength (n)	/strɛŋθ/
strongly (adv)	/ˈstrɔŋli/
survey (n)	/ˈsɜrveɪ/
swollen (adj)	/ˈswoʊlən/
take on (phr v)	/ˈteɪk ˈɒn/
take part (phr v)	/ˈteɪk ˈpɑrt/
take up (phr v)	/ˈteɪk ˈʌp/
talented (adj)	/ˈtæləntɪd/
though (adv)	/ðoʊ/
threat (n)	/θrɛt/
track (n)	/træk/
trade (n)	/treɪd/
tradition (n)	/trəˈdɪʃən/
traditional (adj)	/trəˈdɪʃənəl/
train for an event (phr)	/ˈtreɪn fər ən ɪˈvɛnt/
train hard (phr)	/ˈtreɪn ˈhɑrd/
trophy (n)	/ˈtroʊfi/
warm up (phr v)	/ˈwɔrm ˈʌp/
weapon (n)	/ˈwɛpən/
work out (phr v)	/ˈwɜrk ˈaʊt/

UNIT 4

aim (v)	/eɪm/
basic (adj)	/ˈbeɪsɪk/
coconut (n)	/ˈkoʊkəˌnʌt/
combined (adj)	/kəmˈbaɪnd/
concentrate (v)	/ˈkɒnsənˌtreɪt/
contain (v)	/kənˈteɪn/
crawl (v)	/krɔl/
damage (n)	/ˈdæmɪdʒ/
deal (n)	/dil/
deep-fried (adj)	/ˈdipˈfraɪd/
delicious (adj)	/dɪˈlɪʃəs/
diet (n)	/ˈdaɪət/
disgusting (adj)	/dɪsˈgʌstɪŋ/
distinguish (v)	/dɪˈstɪŋgwɪʃ/
doubt (n)	/daʊt/
eastern (adj)	/ˈistərn/
environment (n)	/ɛnˈvaɪrənmənt/
explore (v)	/ɪkˈsplɔr/
farming (n)	/ˈfɑrmɪŋ/
festival (n)	/ˈfɛstəvəl/
flour (n)	/flaʊər/
good-looking (adj)	/ˈgʊd ˈlʊkɪŋ/
government (n)	/ˈgʌvərnmənt/
grill (n)	/grɪl/
guess (v)	/gɛs/
hike (v)	/haɪk/
homemade (adj)	/ˈhoʊmˈmeɪd/
honest (adj)	/ˈɒnɪst
hope to (v)	/ˈhoʊp tə/
huge (adj)	/hjudʒ/
illustrate (v)	/ˈɪləˌstreɪt/
in conflict with (phr)	/ˌɪn ˈkɒnflɪkt ˌwɪð/
incredible (adj)	/ɪnˈkrɛdəbəl/
ingredient (n)	/ɪnˈgridiənt/
interview (v)	/ˈɪntərˌvju/
introduce (v)	/ˌɪntrəˈdus/
junk food (n)	/ˈdʒʌŋk ˌfud/
local (adj)	/ˈloʊkəl/
long term (n)	/ˈlɔŋ ˈtɜrm/
look forward to (phr v)	/ˈlʊk ˈfɔrwərd tu/
meat-eater (n)	/ˈmitˌitər/
modern-looking (adj)	/ˈmɒdərnˌlʊkɪŋ/
move out (phr v)	/ˈmuv ˈaʊt/
nation (n)	/ˈneɪʃən/
natural (adj)	/ˈnætʃərəl/
old-fashioned (adj)	/ˈoʊldˈfæʃənd/
plenty (pron)	/ˈplɛnti/
prawn (n)	/prɔn/
process (n)	/ˈprɒsɛs/
processed (adj)	/ˈprɒsɛst/
raw (adj)	/rɔ/
reach (v)	/ritʃ/
recently (adv)	/ˈrisəntli/
recipe (n)	/ˈrɛsəpi/
rice-filled (adj)	/ˈraɪsˌfɪld/
rise (v)	/raɪz/
roll (n)	/roʊl/
rush (v)	/rʌʃ/
secret (n)	/ˈsikrɪt/
spicy (adj)	/ˈspaɪsi/
stall (n)	/stɔl/
steamed (adj)	/stimd/
stick with (phr v)	/ˈstɪk ˌwɪð/
style (n)	/staɪl/
sweet-tasting (adj)	/ˈswitˌteɪstɪŋ/
tasty (adj)	/ˈteɪsti/
think of (phr v)	/ˈθɪŋk əv/
undercooked (adj)	/ˌʌndərˈkʊkt/
unhealthy (adj)	/ʌnˈhɛlθi/
vegetarian (n)	/ˌvɛdʒɪˈtɛəriən/
vinegar (n)	/ˈvɪnɪgər/
vitamin (n)	/ˈvaɪtəmɪn/
wander (v)	/ˈwɒndər/
waste (v)	/weɪst/

wealthy (adj)	/ˈwɛlθi/
weight (n)	/weɪt/
welcoming (adj)	/ˈwɛlkəmɪŋ/
well-balanced (adj)	/ˈwɛlˈbælənst/
well-known (adj)	/ˈwɛlˈnoʊn/
wheat (n)	/hwit/

UNIT 5

act (v)	/ækt/
admit (v)	/ədˈmɪt/
advertise (v)	/ˈædvərˌtaɪz/
agency (n)	/ˈeɪdʒənsi/
application (n)	/ˌæplɪˈkeɪʃən/
apply (v)	/əˈplaɪ/
appreciate (v)	/əˈpriʃiˌeɪt/
appreciated (adj)	/əˈpriʃiˌeɪtɪd/
arrest (v)	/əˈrɛst/
assignment (n)	/əˈsaɪnmənt/
basically (adv)	/ˈbeɪsɪkli/
be allowed to (phr)	/ˈbi əˈlaʊd tu/
be responsible for (phr)	/ˈbi rɪˈspɒnsəbəl fɔr/
billion (n)	/ˈbɪljən/
break the law (phr)	/ˈbreɪk ðə ˈlɔ/
calm (adj)	/kɑm/
candidate (n)	/ˈkændɪˌdeɪt/
career prospects (phr)	/kəˈrɪər ˌprɒspɛkts/
catering (n)	/ˈkeɪtərɪŋ/
cause (v)	/kɔz/
challenging (adj)	/ˈtʃælɪndʒɪŋ/
come to (phr v)	/ˈkʌm tu/
committed (adj)	/kəˈmɪtɪd/
competitive (adj)	/kəmˈpɛtətɪv/
condition (n)	/kənˈdɪʃən/
continue (v)	/kənˈtɪnju/
control (n/v)	/kənˈtroʊl/
count on (phr v)	/ˈkaʊnt ˌɒn/
create (v)	/kriˈeɪt/
creative (adj)	/kriˈeɪtɪv/
crime (n)	/kraɪm/
criminal (n)	/ˈkrɪmɪnəl/
deal with (phr v)	/ˈdil ˌwɪð/
demanding (adj)	/dɪˈmændɪŋ/
employed (adj)	/ɛmˈplɔɪd/
employee (n)	/ɛmˈplɔɪi/
employer (n)	/ɛmˈplɔɪər/
enthusiastic (adj)	/ɪnˌθuziˈæstɪk/
faithfully (adv)	/ˈfeɪθfəli/
fault (n)	/fɔlt/
fighting (n)	/ˈfaɪtɪŋ/
flexible (adj)	/ˈflɛksəbəl/
full-time job (phr)	/ˈfʊlˌtaɪm ˈdʒɒb/
give away (phr v)	/ˈgɪv əˈweɪ/
glance (v)	/glæns/
go back (phr v)	/ˈgoʊ ˈbæk/
grateful (adj)	/ˈgreɪtfəl/
hear from (phr v)	/ˈhɪər frəm/
image (n)	/ˈɪmɪdʒ/
in charge of (phr)	/ˌɪn ˈtʃɑrdʒ əv/
in the industry (phr)	/ˈɪn ði ˈɪndəstri/
intensive (adj)	/ɪnˈtɛnsɪv/
involve (v)	/ɪnˈvɒlv/
learner (n)	/ˈlɜrnər/
madam (n)	/ˈmædəm/
management (n)	/ˈmænɪdʒmənt/
mean to (phr v)	/ˈmin tu/
media (n)	/ˈmidiə/
observe (v)	/əbˈzɜrv/
officer (n)	/ˈɔfɪsər/
out of work (phr)	/ˈaʊt əv ˈwɜrk/
own (v)	/oʊn/
particularly (adv)	/pərˈtɪkjələrli/
part-time work (phr)	/ˈpɑrtˌtaɪm ˈwɜrk/
personal (adj)	/ˈpɜrsənəl/
physically (adv)	/ˈfɪzɪkli/
piece of cake (phr)	/ˈpis əv ˈkeɪk/
prevent (v)	/prɪˈvɛnt/
productive (adj)	/prəˈdʌktɪv/
professional (n)	/prəˈfɛʃənəl/
public (adj)	/ˈpʌblɪk/
regret (v)	/rɪˈgrɛt/
result (n)	/rɪˈzʌlt/
scene (n)	/sin/
security (n)	/sɪˈkjʊrɪti/
sir (n)	/sɜr/
spot (v)	/spɒt/
stressful (adj)	/ˈstrɛsfəl/
system (n)	/ˈsɪstəm/
temporary (adj)	/ˈtɛmpəˌrɛri/
total (n)	/ˈtoʊtəl/
tough (adj)	/tʌf/
treat (v)	/trit/
trouble (n)	/ˈtrʌbəl/
trust (v)	/trʌst/
turn out (phr v)	/ˈtɜrn ˈaʊt/
valuable (adj)	/ˈvæljuəbəl/
welcomed (adj)	/ˈwɛlkəmd/
well-paid (adj)	/ˈwɛl ˈpeɪd/
wheelchair (n)	/ˈhwilˌtʃɛər/
wonder (v)	/ˈwʌndər/
work in (phr v)	/ˈwɜrk ˌɪn/
work on (phr v)	/ˈwɜrk ˌɒn/

UNIT 6

access (v)	/ˈæksɛs/
adapted (adj)	/əˈdæptɪd/
advantage (n)	/ədˈvæntɪdʒ/
allow (v)	/əˈlaʊ/
artificial (adj)	/ˌɑrtəˈfɪʃəl/
attach (v)	/əˈtætʃ/
bacteria (n)	/bækˈtɪəriə/
beat (v)	/bit/
blood vessel (n)	/ˈblʌd ˌvɛsəl/
bone (n)	/boʊn/
bring up (phr v)	/ˈbrɪŋ ˈʌp/
calculation (n)	/ˌkælkjəˈleɪʃən/
calculator (n)	/ˈkælkjəˌleɪtər/
cell (n)	/sɛl/
claim (v)	/kleɪm/
colorful (adj)	/ˈkʌlərfəl/
concept (n)	/ˈkɒnsɛpt/
determined (adj)	/dɪˈtɜrmɪnd/
digestive system (n)	/dɪˈdʒɛstɪv ˌsɪstəm/
directly (adv)	/dɪˈrɛktli/
disability (n)	/ˌdɪsəˈbɪlɪti/
earth (n)	/ɜrθ/
electronic (adj)	/ɪlɛkˈtrɒnɪk/
enable (v)	/ɛnˈeɪbəl/
entirely (adv)	/ɪnˈtaɪərli/
evolution (n)	/ˌɛvəˈluʃən/
expert (n)	/ˈɛkspɜrt/
extend (v)	/ɪkˈstɛnd/
extension (n)	/ɪkˈstɛnʃən/
extraordinary (adj)	/ɪkˈstrɔrdəˌnɛri/
feeling (n)	/ˈfilɪŋ/
gap (n)	/gæp/
get into (phr v)	/ˈgɛt ˈɪntu/
hand in (phr v)	/ˈhænd ˈɪn/
impressive (adj)	/ɪmˈprɛsɪv/
inspiration (n)	/ˌɪnspəˈreɪʃən/
instance (n)	/ˈɪnstəns/
lifetime (n)	/ˈlaɪfˌtaɪm/
light up (phr v)	/ˈlaɪt ˈʌp/
look as if (phr)	/ˈlʊk əz ˌɪf/
lung (n)	/lʌŋ/
material (n)	/məˈtɪəriəl/
medical (adj)	/ˈmɛdɪkəl/
movement (n)	/ˈmuvmənt/
nut (n)	/nʌt/
obviously (adv)	/ˈɒbviəsli/
operation (n)	/ˌɒpəˈreɪʃən/
outcome (n)	/ˈaʊtˌkʌm/
particular (adj)	/pərˈtɪkjələr/
presentation (n)	/ˌprɛzənˈteɪʃən/
proud (adj)	/praʊd/
purpose (n)	/ˈpɜrpəs/
range (n)	/reɪndʒ/
rock (n)	/rɒk/
science fiction (n)	/ˈsaɪəns ˈfɪkʃən/
seem (v)	/sim/
sense (n)	/sɛns/
shape (n)	/ʃeɪp/
skeleton (n)	/ˈskɛlɪtən/
skin (n)	/skɪn/
sound like (phr v)	/ˈsaʊnd ˌlaɪk/
sum (n)	/sʌm/
support (v)	/səˈpɔrt/
switch (v)	/swɪtʃ/
talent (n)	/ˈtælənt/
technology (n)	/tɛkˈnɒlədʒi/
tongue (n)	/tʌŋ/
tremendous (adj)	/trəˈmɛndəs/
unless (conj)	/ʌnˈlɛs/

UNIT 7

a good deal (phr)	/ə ˈgʊd ˈdil/
absolutely (adv)	/ˌæbsəˈlutli/
afford to do something (phr)	/əˈfɔrd tə ˈdu ˌsʌmθɪŋ/
apart from (phr)	/əˈpɑrt frʌm/
bank account (n)	/ˈbæŋk əˌkaʊnt/
bargain (n)	/ˈbɑrgɪn/
be in debt (phr)	/ˈbi ɪn ˈdɛt/
beyond (prep)	/biˈɒnd/
brand (n)	/brænd/
break down (phr v)	/ˈbreɪk ˈdaʊn/
browse (v)	/braʊz/
bug (n)	/bʌg/
busily (adv)	/ˈbɪzəli/
classic (adj)	/ˈklæsɪk/
collection (n)	/kəˈlɛkʃən/
currently (adv)	/ˈkʌrəntli/
cycle (v)	/ˈsaɪkəl/

delivery (n)	/dɪˈlɪvəri/
depend on (phr v)	/dɪˈpɛnd ˌɒn/
do without (phr v)	/ˈdu wɪðˈaʊt/
donate to charity (phr)	/ˈdoʊneɪt tə ˈtʃærɪti/
drown (v)	/draʊn/
eagerly (adv)	/ˈigərli/
efficiency (n)	/ɪˈfɪʃənsi/
equipment (n)	/ɪˈkwɪpmənt/
essential (adj)	/əˈsɛnʃəl/
exception (n)	/ɪkˈsɛpʃən/
experiment (n)	/ɪkˈspɛrəmənt/
fix (v)	/fɪks/
get a refund (phr)	/ˈgɛt ə ˈrifʌnd/
get rid of (phr)	/ˌgɛt ˈrɪd əv/
global (adj)	/ˈgloʊbəl/
guitarist (n)	/gɪˈtɑrɪst/
habit (n)	/ˈhæbɪt/
healthily (adv)	/ˈhɛlθɪli/
hold on (phr v)	/ˈhoʊld ˈɒn/
hole (n)	/hoʊl/
household (adj)	/ˈhaʊsˌhoʊld/
importantly (adv)	/ɪmˈpɔrtəntli/
independently (adv)	/ˌɪndɪˈpɛndəntli/
inexpensive (adj)	/ˌɪnɪkˈspɛnsɪv/
intermediate (adj)	/ˌɪntərˈmidiɪt/
item (n)	/ˈaɪtəm/
knitting (n)	/ˈnɪtɪŋ/
lady (n)	/ˈleɪdi/
lifestyle (n)	/ˈlaɪfˌstaɪl/
live for (phr v)	/ˈlɪv ˌfɔr/
logo (n)	/ˈloʊgoʊ/
naked (adj)	/ˈneɪkɪd/
object (n)	/ˈɒbdʒɛkt/
occasion (n)	/əˈkeɪʒən/
occasionally (adv)	/əˈkeɪʒənəli/
original (adj)	/əˈrɪdʒənəl/
pay back (phr v)	/ˈpeɪ ˈbæk/
pay more for (phr)	/ˈpeɪ ˈmɔr fɔr/
pay off one's debts (phr)	/ˈpeɪ ˈɔf wʌnz ˈdɛts/
payment (n)	/ˈpeɪmənt/
possession (n)	/pəˈzɛʃən/
pour (v)	/pɔr/
precious (adj)	/ˈprɛʃəs/
professionally (adv)	/prəˈfɛʃənəli/
progress (n)	/ˈprɒgrɛs/
put up (phr v)	/ˈpʊt ˈʌp/
rather than (phr)	/ˈræðər ðən/
reaction (n)	/riˈækʃən/
realistically (adv)	/ˌrɪəˈlɪstɪkli/
ridiculous (adj)	/rɪˈdɪkjələs/
rock (adj)	/rɒk/
roommate (n)	/ˈrumˌmeɪt/
rubbish (n)	/ˈrʌbɪʃ/
sale (n)	/seɪl/
scratch (n)	/skrætʃ/
seller (n)	/ˈsɛlər/
set up (phr v)	/ˈsɛt ˈʌp/
shop around (phr v)	/ˈʃɒp əˈraʊnd/
similarly (adv)	/ˈsɪmələrli/
sleeve (n)	/sliv/
spread (v)	/sprɛd/
squeeze (v)	/skwiz/
stuff (n)	/stʌf/
suburbs (n)	/ˈsʌbɜrbz/
supporter (n)	/səˈpɔrtər/
take back (phr v)	/ˈteɪk ˈbæk/
temporarily (adv)	/ˌtɛmpəˈrɛrəli/
thoughtful (adj)	/ˈθɔtfəl/
throw away (phr v)	/ˈθroʊ əˈweɪ/
toothpaste (n)	/ˈtuθˌpeɪst/
transfer (n)	/ˈtrænsfər/
transparent (adj)	/trænsˈpærənt/
transport (v)	/trænsˈpɔrt/
uncomfortable (adj)	/ʌnˈkʌmftəbəl/
unfamiliar (adj)	/ˌʌnfəˈmɪljər/
unnecessary (adj)	/ʌnˈnɛsəˌsɛri/
within (prep)	/wɪðˈɪn/

UNIT 8

accept (v)	/ækˈsɛpt/
annoyed (adj)	/əˈnɔɪd/
apology (n)	/əˈpɒlədʒi/
argue (v)	/ˈɑrgju/
avoid (v)	/əˈvɔɪd/
background (n)	/ˈbækˌgraʊnd/
border (n)	/ˈbɔrdər/
certain (adj)	/ˈsɜrtən/
code (n)	/koʊd/
comment (n)	/ˈkɒmɛnt/
communication (n)	/kəˌmjunɪˈkeɪʃən/
compared to (phr)	/kəmˈpɛərd tu/
complain (v)	/kəmˈpleɪn/
connect with (phr v)	/kəˈnɛkt ˌwɪð/
consequently (adv)	/ˈkɒnsɪˌkwɛntli/
couple (n)	/ˈkʌpəl/
customer service (n)	/ˈkʌstəmər ˈsɜrvɪs/
debate (n)	/dɪˈbeɪt/
demonstrate (v)	/ˈdɛmənˌstreɪt/
despite (prep)	/dɪˈspaɪt/
develop (v)	/dɪˈvɛləp/
direct (adj)	/dɪˈrɛkt/
discover (v)	/dɪˈskʌvər/
discussion (n)	/dɪˈskʌʃən/
documentary (n)	/ˌdɒkjəˈmɛntəri/
don't care about (phr)	/ˈdoʊnt ˈkɛər əˌbaʊt/
due to (prep)	/ˈdu tu/
emotional (adj)	/ɪˈmoʊʃənəl/
error (n)	/ˈɛrər/
examine (v)	/ɪgˈzæmɪn/
face to face (adv)	/ˈfeɪs tə ˈfeɪs/
face-to-face (adj)	/ˈfeɪstəˈfeɪs/
fluent (adj)	/ˈfluənt/
friendship (n)	/ˈfrɛndʃɪp/
general (adj)	/ˈdʒɛnərəl/
get distracted (phr)	/ˈgɛt dɪˈstræktɪd/
get my message out (phr)	/ˈgɛt maɪ ˈmɛsɪdʒ ˌaʊt/
get together (phr v)	/ˈgɛt təˈgɛðər/
good listener (n)	/ˈgʊd ˈlɪsənər/
have a point to make (phr)	/ˈhæv ə ˈpɔɪnt tə ˌmeɪk/
helpful (adj)	/ˈhɛlpfəl/
hit (n)	/hɪt/
impatient (adj)	/ɪmˈpeɪʃənt/
impersonal (adj)	/ɪmˈpɜrsənəl/
impolite (adj)	/ˌɪmpəˈlaɪt/
incorrect (adj)	/ˌɪnkəˈrɛkt/
increasingly (adv)	/ɪnˈkrisɪŋli/
indirect (adj)	/ˌɪndɪˈrɛkt/
individual (adj)	/ˌɪndɪˈvɪdʒuəl/
informal (adj)	/ɪnˈfɔrməl/
interact (v)	/ˌɪntərˈækt/
interactive (adj)	/ˌɪntərˈæktɪv/
interpersonal skills (n)	/ˌɪntərˈpɜrsənəl ˈskɪlz/
irregular (adj)	/ɪˈrɛgjələr/
irrelevant (adj)	/ɪˈrɛləvənt/
irresponsible (adj)	/ˌɪrɪˈspɒnsəbəl/
kid (n)	/kɪd/
link (n)	/lɪŋk/
major (adj)	/ˈmeɪdʒər/
make connections (phr)	/ˈmeɪk kəˈnɛkʃənz/
make my living (phr)	/ˈmeɪk maɪ ˈlɪvɪŋ/
mission (n)	/ˈmɪʃən/
misunderstanding (n)	/ˌmɪsʌndərˈstændɪŋ/
nevertheless (adv)	/ˌnɛvərðəˈlɛs/
nod (v)	/nɒd/
online forum (n)	/ˈɒnlaɪn ˈfɔrəm/
passionately (adv)	/ˈpæʃənɪtli/
pay attention (phr)	/ˈpeɪ əˈtɛnʃən/
policy (n)	/ˈpɒləsi/
post on social media (phr)	/ˈpoʊst ɒn ˈsoʊʃəl ˈmidiə/
press (v)	/prɛs/
promise (v)	/ˈprɒmɪs/
refund (n)	/ˈrifʌnd/
reputation (n)	/ˌrɛpjəˈteɪʃən/
respond to texts (phr)	/rɪˈspɒnd tə ˈtɛksts/
rude (adj)	/rud/
satisfactory (adj)	/ˌsætɪsˈfæktəri/
send texts (phr)	/ˈsɛnd ˈtɛksts/
session (n)	/ˈsɛʃən/
share photos (phr)	/ˈʃɛər ˈfoʊtoʊz/
simply (adv)	/ˈsɪmpli/
task (n)	/tæsk/
tone (n)	/toʊn/
unaware (adj)	/ˌʌnəˈwɛər/
untrue (adj)	/ʌnˈtru/
unusual (adj)	/ʌnˈjuʒuəl/
update (n)	/ˈʌpˌdeɪt/
urgent (adj)	/ˈɜrdʒənt/
version (n)	/ˈvɜrʒən/
widely (adv)	/ˈwaɪdli/

UNIT 9

abroad (adv)	/əˈbrɔd/
acting (n)	/ˈæktɪŋ/
active (adj)	/ˈæktɪv/
alive (adj)	/əˈlaɪv/
animated (adj)	/ˈænɪˌmeɪtɪd/
appeal (v)	/əˈpil/
attraction (n)	/əˈtrækʃən/
audience (n)	/ˈɔdiəns/
beautifully (adv)	/ˈbjutəfəli/
broadcast (n/v)	/ˈbrɔdˌkæst/
buzzword (n)	/ˈbʌzˌwɜrd/
career (n)	/kəˈrɪər/
central (adj)	/ˈsɛntrəl/
charge (v)	/tʃɑrdʒ/
community (n)	/kəˈmjunɪti/
crew (n)	/kru/
decorate (v)	/ˈdɛkəˌreɪt/
design (n)	/dɪˈzaɪn/
edit (v)	/ˈɛdɪt/
editing (n)	/ˈɛdɪtɪŋ/

episode (n)	/ˈɛpɪˌsoʊd/
exchange (n)	/ɪksˈtʃeɪndʒ/
exhibit (n)	/ɪgˈzɪbɪt/
fascinating (adj)	/ˈfæsəˌneɪtɪŋ/
fisherman (n)	/ˈfɪʃərmən/
gain (v)	/geɪn/
gallery (n)	/ˈgæləri/
genuinely (adv)	/ˈdʒɛnjuɪnli/
graduate (v)	/ˈgrædʒuˌeɪt/
gripped (adj)	/grɪpt/
handle (v)	/ˈhændəl/
harbor (n)	/ˈhɑrbər/
highly (adv)	/ˈhaɪli/
hire (v)	/ˈhaɪər/
in a row (phr)	/ˈɪn ə ˈroʊ/
inspire (v)	/ɪnˈspaɪər/
invisible (adj)	/ɪnˈvɪzəbəl/
knee (n)	/ni/
leading (adj)	/ˈlidɪŋ/
listener (n)	/ˈlɪsənər/
lively (adj)	/ˈlaɪvli/
look like (phr v)	/ˈlʊk ˌlaɪk/
lyrics (n)	/ˈlɪrɪks/
make a big impression (phr)	/ˈmeɪk ə ˈbɪg ɪmˈprɛʃən/
make a decision (phr)	/ˈmeɪk ə dɪˈsɪʒən/
make a difference (phr)	/ˈmeɪk ə ˈdɪfrəns/
make a good living (phr)	/ˈmeɪk ə ˈgʊd ˈlɪvɪŋ/
make friends (phr)	/ˈmeɪk ˈfrɛndz/
make one's bed (phr)	/ˈmeɪk wʌnz ˈbɛd/
make quite a splash (phr)	/ˈmeɪk ˌkwaɪt ə ˈsplæʃ/
make the most of (phr)	/ˈmeɪk ðə ˈmoʊst əv/
make up one's mind (phr)	/ˈmeɪk ˌʌp wʌnz ˈmaɪnd/
make way for (phr)	/ˈmeɪk ˈweɪ fɔr/
mural (n)	/ˈmjʊrəl/
ocean (n)	/ˈoʊʃən/
outdoor (adj)	/ˈaʊtˌdɔr/
performance (n)	/pərˈfɔrməns/
poet (n)	/ˈpoʊɪt/
poetry (n)	/ˈpoʊɪtri/
portrait (n)	/ˈpɔrtrɪt/
position (n)	/pəˈzɪʃən/
produce (v)	/prəˈdus/
production (n)	/prəˈdʌkʃən/
profile (n)	/ˈproʊfaɪl/
promote (v)	/prəˈmoʊt/
rainy (adj)	/ˈreɪni/
refer to (phr v)	/rɪˈfɜr tu/
relax (v)	/rɪˈlæks/
scale (n)	/skeɪl/
script (n)	/skrɪpt/
sculpture (n)	/ˈskʌlptʃər/
setting (n)	/ˈsɛtɪŋ/
show up (phr v)	/ˈʃoʊ ˈʌp/
spirit (n)	/ˈspɪrɪt/
statue (n)	/ˈstætʃu/
steep (adj)	/stip/
stranger (n)	/ˈstreɪndʒər/
studio (n)	/ˈstudiˌoʊ/
success (n)	/səkˈsɛs/
theme (n)	/θim/
tip (n)	/tɪp/
upload (v)	/ˈʌpˌloʊd/
venue (n)	/ˈvɛnju/
verse (n)	/vɜrs/
viewer (n)	/ˈvjuər/

UNIT 10

accommodation (n)	/əˌkɒməˈdeɪʃən/
accuracy (n)	/ˈækjərəsi/
accurate (adj)	/ˈækjərɪt/
accurately (adv)	/ˈækjərɪtli/
ahead (adv)	/əˈhɛd/
ahead of its time (phr)	/əˈhɛd əv ɪts ˈtaɪm/
at one time (phr)	/æt ˈwʌn ˈtaɪm/
awful (adj)	/ˈɔfəl/
be time to (phr)	/ˌbi ˈtaɪm tu/
because of (phr)	/bɪˈkɔz əv/
begin with (phr v)	/bɪˈgɪn ˌwɪð/
big deal (interj)	/ˈbɪg ˈdil/
bring forward (phr v)	/ˈbrɪŋ ˈfɔrwərd/
calculate (v)	/ˈkælkjəˌleɪt/
catch up (phr v)	/ˈkætʃ ˈʌp/
crash into (phr v)	/ˈkræʃ ˈɪntu/
debt (n)	/dɛt/
decision (n)	/dɪˈsɪʒən/
dental (adj)	/ˈdɛntəl/
deserve (v)	/dɪˈzɜrv/
election (n)	/ɪˈlɛkʃən/
engineering (n)	/ˌɛndʒɪˈnɪərɪŋ/
exact (adj)	/ɪgˈzækt/
expense (n)	/ɪkˈspɛns/
fall behind (phr v)	/ˈfɔl bɪˈhaɪnd/
fit in (phr v)	/ˈfɪt ˈɪn/
freedom (n)	/ˈfridəm/
from time to time (phr)	/frəm ˈtaɪm tə ˈtaɪm/
get around to (phr v)	/ˈgɛt əˈraʊnd tu/
hang out (phr v)	/ˈhæŋ ˈaʊt/
in time for (phr)	/ɪn ˈtaɪm fɔr/
in two days' time (phr)	/ɪn ˈtu ˌdeɪz ˈtaɪm/
insurance (n)	/ɪnˈʃʊərəns/
invent (v)	/ɪnˈvɛnt/
inventor (n)	/ɪnˈvɛntər/
judge (v)	/dʒʌdʒ/
knowledge (n)	/ˈnɒlɪdʒ/
land (n)	/lænd/
long-term (adj)	/ˈlɒŋˌtɜrm/
lose one's mind (phr)	/ˈluz wʌnz ˈmaɪnd/
meaningful (adj)	/ˈminɪŋfəl/
meanwhile (adv)	/ˈminˌhwaɪl/
mile (n)	/maɪl/
navy (n)	/ˈneɪvi/
on one's mind (phr)	/ˈɒn wʌnz ˈmaɪnd/
on time (phr)	/ˈɒn ˈtaɪm/
otherwise (adv)	/ˈʌðərˌwaɪz/
owe (v)	/oʊ/
partly (adv)	/ˈpɑrtli/
pass the time (phr)	/ˈpæs ðə ˈtaɪm/
politician (n)	/ˌpɒlɪˈtɪʃən/
politics (n)	/ˈpɒlɪtɪks/
present (v)	/prɪˈzɛnt/
proposal (n)	/prəˈpoʊzəl/
put off (phr v)	/ˈpʊt ˈɔf/
question (v)	/ˈkwɛstʃən/
refuse (v)	/rɪˈfjuz/
respect (v)	/rɪˈspɛkt/
responsibility (n)	/rɪˌspɒnsəˈbɪlɪti/
responsible (adj)	/rɪˈspɒnsəbəl/
reward (n)	/rɪˈwɔrd/
rule (v)	/rul/
run out of (phr v)	/ˈrʌn ˈaʊt əv/
sailor (n)	/ˈseɪlər/
series (n)	/ˈsɪəriz/
stare (v)	/stɛər/
stay aware (phr)	/ˈsteɪ əˈwɛər/
successful (adj)	/səkˈsɛsfəl/
tend (v)	/tɛnd/
therefore (adv)	/ˈðɛərˌfɔr/
tragedy (n)	/ˈtrædʒɪdi/
truth (n)	/truθ/
vote (v/n)	/voʊt/
voting (n)	/ˈvoʊtɪŋ/
wait around (phr v)	/ˈweɪt əˈraʊnd/
youth (n)	/juθ/